Here She Is

Here She Is

THE **COMPLICATED** **REIGN** OF THE **BEAUTY PAGEANT** IN **AMERICA**

HILARY LEVEY FRIEDMAN

BEACON PRESS
BOSTON

BEACON PRESS
Boston, Massachusetts
www.beacon.org

Beacon Press books
are published under the auspices of
the Unitarian Universalist Association of Congregations.

23 22 21 20   8 7 6 5 4 3 2 1

This book is printed on acid-free paper that meets the uncoated paper
ANSI/NISO specifications for permanence as revised in 1992.

Text design and composition by Kim Arney

Library of Congress Cataloging-in-Publication Data

Names: Friedman, Hilary Levey, author.
Title: Here she is : the complicated reign of the beauty
pageant in America / Hilary Levey Friedman.
Description: Boston : Beacon Press, [2020] | Includes
bibliographical references and index.
Identifiers: LCCN 2020002552 (print) | LCCN 2020002553 (ebook) |
ISBN 9780807083284 (hardcover) | ISBN 9780807083642 (ebook)
Subjects: LCSH: Miss America Pageant. | Beauty contests—United States. |
Feminine beauty (Aesthetics)—United States. | Feminism—United States.
Classification: LCC HQ1220.U5 F75 2020 (print) | LCC HQ1220.U5 (ebook) |
DDC 791.6/60973—dc23
LC record available at https://lccn.loc.gov/2020002552
LC ebook record available at https://lccn.loc.gov/2020002553

For Pamela Anne Eldred,
Miss America 1970—but just "Mom" to me—without whom
none of any of this would have been possible.

CONTENTS

Beauty and Brains

CAN'T REMEMBER EVER NOT knowing what a beauty pageant was.

In my childhood home I saw crowns on bookshelves instead of books.

I innately understood that you earned a crown by winning a beauty pageant.

To win a pageant you had to be beautiful and thin. You also had to be a good public speaker and a good performer, which in my mind meant singing or dancing.

Oh, and never go to the grocery store without a full face of makeup on or your hair perfectly coiffed.

In other words, you should look and be like my mother, Miss America 1970, Pamela Eldred.

I am the only child of a divorced former beauty queen. My parents split when I was three, so from a very young age I spent weekends at fashion shows, dance competitions, modeling classes, and, yes, beauty pageants.

But I was never the one onstage. Mom was in the spotlight and I was in the shadows. I sat in the audience or backstage, reading a book as I observed all the onstage and offstage shenanigans while Mom worked as a judge, emcee, or instructor.

One weekend, when I was about nine, we went to a child beauty pageant. Kid pageants were not Mom's usual side hustle (she was a cosmetologist who did facials and electrolysis during the week, and she wrote a fashion and beauty column for a local newspaper), but she was asked to judge, and a check was a check. Mom did not like child pageants, thinking the girls were too young to compete based on how they looked, but I was *fascinated*. Here were girls, younger than I was, competing for a crown. I remember they appeared onstage modeling beautiful, heavily rhinestoned dresses, with their hair in elaborate updos and their lips brightly colored. After doing their beauty walks, the contestants had to answer a question posed by the emcee. Some of the competitors' responses were not exactly eloquent. After I saw who won I thought, "Huh, maybe I could do this." I asked Mom if I could try competing in one of these kid pageants sometime.

Mom replied with the best advice she has ever given me: "If you compete in a pageant and you win, even if you deserve it, people will say you only won because of me. And, even if you deserve to win, you might lose because of me. Better that you find your own path."

While this was in fact fantastic guidance, part of me knows that we both understood that I simply was not "pageant material." Like most nine-year-olds in the 1980s, I was in desperate need of orthodontia, and perhaps some better corrective eyewear. But I would have been able to overcome those (temporary) impediments had I been physically beautiful—which I'm not.

I am not digging for compliments; I'm matter-of-fact about my appearance. At the highest level of pageantry there is a minimum bar of physical attractiveness required to win. I think of this in the same way that there is a minimum height bar to play basketball professionally or a minimum bar of flexibility and strength to be an Olympic gymnast—and, yes, a minimum amount of intelligence needed to be a college professor.

Plus, I know firsthand what beautiful looks like. When Mom was Miss America, legendary sports writer Frank Deford described her as "a little doll, with a face left over from Valentine's Day, and a body made out of Steuben glass."[1] I often tell people that I'm not being self-deprecating when I say that Mom and I look nothing alike. She has blonde hair, mine is brown. She has green eyes and, again, mine are brown. Our facial shapes are different as well, though I did inherit her hourglass figure, albeit with a more zaftig flair.

Hard as it is for me to admit, when I tell people I look nothing like my mom, what I'm actually doing is apologizing. I'm apologizing for the question I think I see in the eyes of some: "How is *she* the daughter of a

Miss America?!" I'm trying to head off the thought in someone's mind that "the good looks sure skipped a generation."

Needless to say, growing up the daughter of a Miss America has not always been easy.

But it would have been worse if I hadn't followed the advice Mom gave me after we went to that child beauty pageant: to find my own path. Early on, it was clear that school was my thing and it was where I excelled (my parents had a particularly bad and dramatic divorce and doing well in school was also my way of trying to show people that the craziness hadn't impacted me, but that's a story for another time). Being a smart bookworm became my identity.

In my mind, a dichotomy developed—Mom was the beauty and I was the brains.

Still, sequins and rhinestones were in my DNA. While I knew I'd never compete in a beauty pageant, I loved them. I adored the ritual and the excitement. *Especially* Miss America.

Each year the Miss America Pageant sent all former Miss Americas the competition magazine. Every August I couldn't wait for the heavy, large envelope to arrive in my mailbox in West Bloomfield, Michigan, from Atlantic City, New Jersey. As soon as I got that package, I would rip it open and start reading the seventy-five-page-ish "book." I studied the year's contestants, focusing on each of their talents, ambitions, and majors, along with where they went to college. By reading that program book I learned about colleges and universities across the country, ones I may never have heard of otherwise. Then I would rate all the state queens based on their personal information and photos, predicting the Top 10 and who would win the crown.

When the Pageant (Miss America is always referred to with a capital *P* in my mind) aired live on NBC, the second Saturday after Labor Day, I would sit in front of the family television with Mom and my maternal grandparents, whom we lived with. In the same room where Mom's pageant crowns sat on the bookshelf, we gathered, shouting out our favorites and who we thought would join Mom in the Miss America "sisterhood."

In September 1987 I squealed and screamed when Miss Michigan, Kaye Lani Rae Rafko, became Miss America 1988. It was the first victory for my home state since Mom had won almost twenty years before. As Rafko took her victory walk down the long runway in Convention Hall to the iconic song "There She Is," I turned to Mom with bright eyes and exclaimed, "Now I can meet a *real* Miss America!" (She's never let me live that one down . . .)

Thus began my prolonged campaign to see Miss America crowned in person. I lobbied, I cajoled, and I begged until Mom gave in. It took two years, but in September 1989 I got to attend my first Miss America Pageant. It was Mom's first time going back to Atlantic City in over a decade.

My first time at Miss America was both disappointing and impressive. When I walked in Convention Hall, I was shocked and dismayed that it did not really look like the extravagant place I had seen on television. In fact it was kind of dumpy, with concrete floors and holes in the ceiling.

But the contestants and current Miss America wowed me. That year Gretchen Carlson was giving up her crown as Miss America 1989. Carlson was a student at Stanford University, which even fourth grade me knew was a big deal, and an exceptional violinist. I remember watching with my mouth hanging open as she played during the preliminary competitions. (These were held over three nights when all fifty-one contestants competed in evening gown, swimsuit, and talent in order to decide on the Top 10 for the final televised pageant.) Carlson showed me that a Miss America didn't have to only dance or sing to be talented.

The Miss America I saw crowned the final night, Miss Missouri, Debbye Turner, reinforced that. Her talent was marimba playing—at one point using four mallets—and it was extraordinary. That she did it while wearing a red, fully sequined jumpsuit only made it more impressive in my eyes. Turner was in her final year of veterinary school at the University of Missouri when she won, which I also thought was very cool. Turner's first runner-up, Virginia Cha, who played the piano, had recently graduated from Princeton University, which I knew was Ivy League, although I didn't quite understand what that meant.

That year was the first to include a new competition segment known as "platform," the most significant expansion of the Miss America competition since talent became a mandatory category back in 1938. Each contestant had to identify a social cause about which she felt strongly and which she would advocate for throughout her year as Miss America. Turner's platform was "Motivating Youth to Excellence," and her interest in role models and mentorship took her to the White House and beyond during her year as Miss America.

Going to my first Miss America Pageant helped expand my thoughts on what a Miss America could do, and what she might look like (Turner was African American and Cha Korean American). Honestly, I admired these women for putting themselves out there in such a public way, seemingly able to be beautiful, smart, talented, and thin all at once. For them, beauty and brains were not mutually exclusive.

A few months after we returned home from the Miss America 1990 pageant, Mom got a letter in the mail that the following year's Pageant, the seventieth anniversary, was going to be special. Bert Parks, who had emceed the Pageant for nearly twenty-five years, was returning. Parks hosted his first Miss America Pageant in 1955, its second year on television. In 1979 he was controversially fired for being too old, and Miss America fans felt they had never been able to say a proper good-bye. With a round anniversary coming up, and Parks's health in decline, the Pageant decided it was time to welcome him back. To mark the occasion they wanted as many of "Bert's Miss Americas" as possible to attend. The plan was that he would introduce them during the telecast and serenade them one last time with "There She Is."

Now, I had a thing for Bert Parks. I had watched him announce Mom as Miss America dozens of times on a well-worn VHS tape. To me, he was the one who made wishes come true, a fairy godfather. I simply *had* to go back and meet him. Mom was super resistant to attending the Pageant because being on national television meant buying an expensive gown. But again, I lobbied, cajoled, and begged. In September 1990 we made our way back to Atlantic City carrying the long, red, sequined dress she had saved up to purchase. About thirty other Miss Americas joined Mom there, with the eldest being Miss America 1933. Parks had presided over about half of their crownings.[2]

My second visit to Miss America was a much more elaborate affair. There were various events for "the formers" that week, which Mom and I both attended. When Mom would introduce me at these events, invariably someone would ask me, "Oh, do you want to be Miss America too?" The first time someone asked I remember feeling slightly flattered. The question had not even come up the previous year. But as people kept asking me the same question, I started to get annoyed. It felt a bit condescending and made me think that unless I followed Mom's path, I wasn't doing something worthwhile.

On our third day in Atlantic City I got to meet *the* Bert Parks. I shook his hand and proudly introduced myself.

And then Parks, of all people, asked, "So are you going to be Miss America someday like your mom?"

I paused for a moment before retorting, "No, I'm going to be the first female president."

Parks's response was to roar with laughter and pat me on the head.

The ten-year-old budding feminist in me was less than thrilled with the interaction.

The next day Parks's return to the Miss America stage did not go exactly as planned either. When he was introducing the former Miss Americas on live TV, two of his cue cards got stuck together. All the Miss Americas from the 1970s were skipped, as he jumped from Miss America 1969, Judi Ford, to Miss America 1980, Cheryl Prewitt.[3] Do you remember who Miss America 1970 was? Yes, that's right: my mom.

I took this on-air flub inordinately hard, sobbing as soon as Mom came back to her seat. I cried so hard that Mom picked me up to sit on her hip, like when I was a smaller child. As she settled me, I heard a sickening tearing sound as all the beading on that side of her dress fell off—which only made me weep more. This trip was a bust. First, Bert Parks had assumed I wanted to be a mini–Miss America and laughed at me, and then not only had he messed up but he had done it *on my mom.*

Eighteen months later, Parks passed away.[4] Twenty-nine years elapsed before Mom would attend Miss America again, in December 2019, to celebrate the fiftieth anniversary of her crowning. And I am almost certainly not going to be America's first female president—I mean, at this point it *should not* take that long, though it hasn't happened yet. But as I reflect on that trip back when I was in fifth grade, I can see that pageantry, politics, and feminism have always been intertwined for me.

Beauty pageants trace the arc of American feminism. Pageants may appear to be an unexpected instrument for this, due to feminist critiques of them. In reality, the history of pageants mirrors the many monumental changes related to a woman's place in society, while still showing how far we have to go in our expectations of and for women and girls.

Over the years, as both a sociologist and the daughter of a Miss America, I have come to see Miss America as possibly the best example of the difficult and complicated nature of American womanhood. At the one-hundredth anniversary of Miss America the contestants walk in six-inch heels, speak knowledgeably about foreign policy, entertain in the talent competition, advocate for a social issue (now known as a "social impact initiative"), and compete with a smile while wearing a full set of false eyelashes—all while earning various advanced degrees. But the expectations of these pageant contestants are only slightly more extreme than expectations heaped on young women today: compete in the classroom, but do it with a smile; dominate on the sports field or stage, but do it while looking effortlessly beautiful; be socially conscious on social media, but do it while modeling all the right angles on Instagram.

Since it began in 1921 Miss America has been the gold standard pageant, the dominant competition against which other pageants define themselves, either in opposition or conformity. Its first runner-up is Miss USA, which started as a spinoff in 1952. (I often sum up the difference between Miss America and Miss USA as the three *T*'s: talent, tuition, and tits. Miss America has the first two and Miss USA has the last.) Second runner-up is Distinguished Young Woman, which originally started as America's Junior Miss in 1958 and helped inspire the creation of Miss America's Outstanding Teen in 2005. Both teen pageants have a fitness competition in place of swimsuit.

But each year there are literally thousands of smaller pageants—held in rural communities, on college campuses, at regional festivals and fairs—that tens of thousands desperately want to win. There are pageants for Native American girls, married women, teenagers in wheelchairs, drag queens, petite females, and much more. Miss America is a major focus, but it is far from the only pageant that matters—in general and in this book.

While there is a diversity of pageants, there is little diversity within pageants. Most pageants favor women who display thin, fit, and able bodies, light skin, and long hair. The assumption is that most pageant contestants are heterosexual, Christian, and middle class. Though all the crowns from the various pageants sparkle, there will always be some tarnish on them because of groups who are excluded when a representative of a particular community is selected as the pageant winner.

Yet, winning means something. Many dismiss beauty pageant contestants, until someone they know wins. A title gets a young woman invited to speak at conferences, attend dinners with community leaders, and advocate for an issue that is meaningful to her. When a lot of people find out my mother is a former Miss America they are often impressed and fascinated in spite of themselves. Only ninety-two women have ever worn the Miss America crown and only sixty-eight have earned the title of Miss USA.

It's a common statement in pageant circles that "you're more likely to have a son win the Super Bowl than a daughter become Miss America." While this is clearly a numbers game (a football roster has around fifty players and there is only one Miss America per year), the sentiment remains. Winning a crown is an accomplishment that almost always reflects years of investment in practicing a talent, in working hard in school, or in perfecting the body—sometimes in ways that punish and damage the body and mind in ways similar to NFL players.

I have never competed in a beauty pageant, but I can tell you their complicated story.

The Feminist Arc of Pageantry

O N SEPTEMBER 10, 2017, my former student Cara Mund became Miss America 2018.

I was in Atlantic City that Sunday night when the crown was placed on Cara's head. My voice was hoarse for days after, thanks to hours of screaming, but that couldn't dull my contact high from seeing someone close to me achieve her childhood dream. It was a full circle moment for me, growing up the daughter of a Miss America (who was the first ballet dancer to win) and then watching a young dancer I knew transform into a Miss America.

Cara and I met in the fall of 2015 when she enrolled in an upper-level undergraduate seminar I was teaching at Brown University called "Beauty Pageants in American Society." At the end of the semester I became Cara's thesis advisor; a thesis is not required to graduate from Brown, but it is necessary if you want to graduate with academic honors. Following her graduation from Brown, with honors, Cara headed home to compete in the Miss North Dakota 2016 pageant.

When Cara told me about her plans, I said that there was no way I was going to miss seeing her compete. In June 2016 I made the journey to Williston, North Dakota, where she was named first runner-up. While the result fell short of Cara's goal, it was clear to me that she had what it took to win. Cara—a petite brunette with piercing blue eyes—commanded the stage, exuding charisma and winning the interview, talent, and platform phases of the competition.

All except for one: swimsuit.

Over the next year Cara dedicated herself to becoming Miss North Dakota 2017. It was her last year of age eligibility to compete in the Miss America program and she was all in. Cara went on a strict diet and she worked out for hours each day. That June her hard work paid off as she was crowned Miss North Dakota. She even won the swimsuit competition.

Three months later, when the Miss America crown was placed on her head, Cara became the first-ever winner from North Dakota and the first-ever Ivy League graduate. It seemed like a happily-ever-after ending to a fairy-tale story.

But by the end of 2017, only three months into Cara's reign, the Miss America Organization had descended into turmoil. An article on *Huffington Post* revealed email exchanges involving the CEO and executive chairman of Miss America, Sam Haskell, slut- and fat-shaming former Miss Americas. Following Haskell's resignation, massive changes came to the Pageant in 2018.

Those changes, spurred by the #MeToo movement, paved the way for the installation of Miss America's first all-female leadership team, helmed by former Miss America 1989, Gretchen Carlson. In June 2018 Carlson announced that for the first time since it began in 1921 swimsuit would no longer be a category in the Miss America *competition* (the word *pageant* became verboten). Additionally, contestants would now be referred to as *candidates*, and they would no longer have a *platform* but rather a *social impact initiative*.

In the midst of this transformation, and the press surrounding it, Cara was noticeably absent. Just before she crowned her successor, Cara publicly accused Carlson of workplace harassment and bullying. As she put it, her childhood dream had become a nightmare.

Cara's Miss America experience—both the good and the bad—encapsulates what many people find fascinating about beauty pageants. Each pageant has inherent drama, thanks to the winner-take-all structure of the competition itself along with behind-the-scenes drama.

Then there is the ritual of a beauty pageant. Some of this involves traditions that are more formulaic, like an annual event held in the same location at the same time of year with the same competitive elements. Other rituals are more symbolic, like crowning a winner.

The drama, ritual, and tradition of pageantry are not limited to beauty pageants. *Pageantry*, broadly defined, refers to any elaborate ceremony. You can see it in political events like the US president's annual State of the Union speech or a military commissioning ceremony, in religious events like a Catholic mass, and even in academia like at commencement ceremonies. Some of the biggest events in popular culture, like the Academy Awards, Super Bowl, and opening and closing ceremonies of the Olympics, have many elements of pageantry to them. These richly symbolic competitions have audiences with specific expectations about attire, songs, and actual physical awards. Because the contestants tend to be associated with a geographic location or group, it helps audience members identify with and feel invested in particular individuals or teams during the competition.

Beauty pageants have all those elements of pageantry and more. Pomp and circumstance transform into glitz and glamour at a beauty pageant, which I define as a contest with a winner selected by judges who make subjective evaluations of contestants' physical appearance and poise. That winner is nearly always someone who identifies as a woman, and, historically, that woman has tended to be white, heterosexual, able-bodied and thin, and Christian.

Cara Mund fits that description. But in other ways she did not conform to the traditional stereotype of national beauty pageant winners: that pageant queens are ditzy, out-of-touch blonde-haired and blue-eyed Southern girls. While Cara does have blue eyes, in all other ways this Midwestern woman was not typecast, especially because when she won Miss America she had already graduated from one of the most academically selective universities in the country. She planned to use her $50,000 Miss America scholarship to pay her tuition at the equally selective law school to which she had already been admitted.

And, yet, to access that money she had to discipline her body to appear in a swimsuit in a way that judges in Williston, North Dakota, and Atlantic City, New Jersey, found acceptable. Cara, and all those she competed with, had to worry about their weight and appearance on their way to the Miss America stage.

As it turned out, Cara and her fellow contestants were the last group required to compete in a swimsuit to win the title of Miss America. This was a change that had been decades in the making. In 1928, just seven years after it began, the Miss America Pageant ended largely due to concerns, led by women's groups like the League of Women Voters, that the swimsuit contest was simply too risqué and immoral for any respectable woman. A woman who publicly showed her body in that way was considered by many to be too outré. When the pageant returned seven years later, so did its feminist critics, though their content changed. The 1968 protest of the Miss America Pageant, led by New York Radical Women (a group associated with the women's liberation movement), and similar subsequent pageant protests in the 1980s, focused on the ways in which beauty contests not only objectified women's bodies but also opened up the possibility of eating and exercise disorders in order to maintain that body.

In the wake of the #MeToo movement and events like the 2017 Women's March, Miss America finally scrapped tradition, eliminating the swimsuit competition. This time protests were internal. Most of the dissenting current and former contestants said that they personally felt empowered by the swimsuit competition. Many also said that preparing to compete in a swimsuit, perhaps counterintuitively, made their bodies healthier because of what they learned about nutrition and fitness. These women felt that if they were proud to display their bodies, then criticisms of that display were unfair as they were not cultural dupes.

As this brief history of the swimsuit competition at Miss America shows, beauty pageants have long been connected to broader changes affecting women's place in American society. Over the next six chapters I tell a much more detailed story of the complicated reign of the American beauty pageant. This story, and its connections to women's history, unfolds in three parts, which correspond to the three waves of American feminism.[1] Defining the first two waves of feminism is not difficult. Both are characterized by major public events that have links to pageantry—women's suffrage parades in the 1910s and the protest outside the 1968 Miss America Pageant.

The First Wave brought women into public life, culminating in the right to vote in 1920. In 1921, the first Miss America event co-opted the sashes women wore in suffrage parades and protests to identify the geographic home of contestants and, ultimately, the winner. The Second Wave brought women greater educational and professional opportunities, opening the doors of employment in nearly all areas, powered by access to a range of safe and legal contraception. It was no accident that the platform of the Miss America Pageant was used to bring Second Wave feminism the public attention it needed to attract others. This time feminists usurped the popularity of pageantry.

The Third Wave has until recently been amorphous, defined without a clear goal or public event. Some have pointed to the 1991 Clarence Thomas confirmation hearings at which Anita Hill testified, as hallmarks of a third wave, especially because they were situated within the rise of identity politics as an African American woman appeared before the nearly all white and all male United States Senate. But the intersectional 1980s and 1990s should be thought of as a continuation of the Second Wave. Instead, the 2016 presidential election of Donald Trump (former owner of the Miss USA and Miss Universe Pageants), and the subsequent Women's March in 2017, followed by the #MeToo movement, mark the beginning of Third Wave feminism.

In defining the three waves in this way, each is divided into roughly fifty-year periods. If the First Wave was about getting women into the public sphere through the politics of suffrage, and the Second Wave was about getting women into the public sphere through employment and education, the Third Wave is about making it safe to be female in those public places. Third Wave feminism has focused on preventing sexual harassment and assault (especially in the workforce, where equal pay remains an issue) and on electing more feminists to public office to protect the rights women have gained over the past century—and to continue to advance them. Making work and public life safer for women also means promoting policy that supports their continued education and employment at various life stages.[2]

In case it is not obvious by now, this is *not* a how-to book about becoming a pageant queen. It also is not about the nitty-gritty of what happens backstage at any particular pageant in a given year. This is a different take on beauty pageants than you may have seen before, providing a new way to think about women's *herstory*. Overall, it is neither an indictment of beauty pageants nor a paean, instead showing that beauty pageants have never been all bad or all good—for participants, for women, or for feminism.

Of course, the criticisms of beauty pageants are valid. These critiques generally fall into two sometimes overlapping categories. The first is that pageants *objectify* women (primarily for male consumption) by prioritizing physical appearance, which opens up the possibility of unhealthy practices, like eating disorders and overexercising, to obtain an "ideal" body. Relatedly, beauty pageants are *exclusionary* in a number of dimensions, including but not limited to race and ethnicity, sexuality, religion, class, and disability.

Let me be clear: For most of the past century, participating in a national beauty pageant, like Miss America or Miss USA, was quite simply one of the whitest and most ableist and heteronormative things a young woman could do. While I argue that in the nineteenth century beauty contests helped bring women into the public sphere, the national beauty pageants that started in the twentieth century reinforced limiting and exclusionary gender, racial, and sexual norms. The original intent of Miss America, invented in 1921 by male businessmen, was to use women's bodies to titillate a crowd to stay longer in Atlantic City so that the businesses, owned by the men, could make more money. Starting in the 1930s the Miss America Pageant was explicitly racist and ableist, implementing a rule saying that all contestants must be "of good health and the white race."

The veracity of the critiques of pageants is undeniable, but there is another dimension to these events, particularly for individual participants. After the 1968 Miss America protest featuring "bra burners," there was backlash within the growing feminist movement because of the perception that women were attacking other women. As Second Wave pageant protestors learned, it is more useful to criticize misogynistic and patriarchal structures that lead to beauty pageants than to attack individuals who choose to compete in them for their own personal reasons.

Many women who compete in pageants cite feelings of empowerment as they develop skills, like speaking in public, that help them advance themselves. Moreover, they point to educational scholarships they have won as a way to advance themselves personally, which can lead to greater class mobility and a larger engagement in the public sphere. This is true not just for Miss America, which has changed substantially from its 1921 origins, but also for the wide variety of American pageants that have developed since the second half of the twentieth century in an effort to make the beauty ideals promoted by pageants more inclusive.

In addition to personal skill development, some individual pageant participants, both historically and in the present, choose to compete in beauty pageants simply because they enjoy them—in the same way that some women like to cook, knit, paint their nails, watch *The Real Housewives*, or read "chick lit." Many of these "women's" activities or hobbies are demeaned as light, fluffy, or frivolous. If activities are put down mainly because they are seen as feminine, that is insidious and can harm women, just as objectifying them does (though the ways in which some of these activities may reify harmful stereotypes of women is certainly grounds for critique).

Overlooking pageant participants and fans, and viewing them as "less than," certainly brings political implications. Donald J. Trump embraced pageants as an owner and fan. Trump understood the importance of appearance and form, a reality that pageants address directly. Many dismissed him as all form and no function, but much as those who dismiss beauty pageants as all form, they underestimated the power and importance of these forces.

Even though the beauty industry market earns over a half-trillion dollars each year, it too is often disparaged as all form. Part of this stems from dismissing feminine things as unimportant, and a large share of this critique comes from many who would like to turn away from the notion that how humans look matters. But a great deal of research across the social and hard sciences shows us that various aspects of appearance have significant implications for social life.

Economist Daniel Hamermesh has studied the impact of good looks—for both men and women—on political success and income, and the resulting book title summarizes his findings: *Beauty Pays: Why Attractive People Are More Successful.*[3] This notion also applies to criminal defendants, who get lighter sentences the better looking they are.[4] Kids do not escape the beauty bias. Elementary school teachers assume that cuter boys and girls are more intelligent and that their parents are more interested in their education. This has ripple effects for educational attainment based on popularity in school and even athletic performance.[5]

The rough pattern here is that facial beauty and body shape lead to visual attractiveness, regardless of gender, which leads to social dominance, which ultimately leads to greater life success (mainly money but also status). While this is true for men, the demands are far greater for women. The expectations become even more onerous for women of color and anyone who identifies as part of a nondominant group.

What components of beauty matter, especially for a woman? It is useful to separate the face from the body. More specifically, when it comes to the face, we can delineate four areas: hair, makeup, skin, and teeth.

Hair is powerful because it helps identify our gender, class, religion, and politics, without us saying a word. Two ideals have long been associated with women's hair: that it should be long and smooth and that it should be blonde.[6] The length is related to fertility, being a presumed marker of health. The color blonde is also seen as a symbol of youth, since tresses darken later in life—not to mention race, since only Caucasians have blonde hair.

Fertility and youth also come into play when thinking about makeup. Some studies have found that women wear more makeup when they are ovulating. Makeup itself serves to highlight features related to fertility and sexual arousal. At the point of climax, women have larger eyes (which eyeliner and mascara help accomplish), flushed cheeks (blush), and darker or red lips (lipstick).[7] Both men and women often see women who wear makeup as more confident, more competent, and more likeable.[8]

Skin itself can be a sign of general health, and hence fertility, but today it serves more as a marker of class. As Joan Jacobs Brumberg describes in her classic *The Body Project: An Intimate History of American Girls*, skin came to be seen as a sign of respectability and cleanliness. For some this meant no acne, and for others it meant trying to actually lighten their skin. Parents invested in skin treatments for daughters, understanding that "good looks were an important vehicle of social success for their daughters."[9] Those who could afford to have good skin did.

The same is true for teeth. Straight teeth, usually achieved through orthodontia, became a clear class marker.[10] Having all your teeth is also a sign of health, but having straight teeth is an indication that you are likely from a family that had money to afford braces. The same could be said for contact lenses, plastic surgery, weight loss camps, and more.

In these cases, appearance has become a proxy for wealth, and hence to many, intelligence. People do not wear their IQ number, credit score, or IRS refund amount on their person[11]—or at least most do not—so certain aspects of appearance substitute for that information.

The more recent development of a variety of weight loss programs, and other efforts to control the body through exercise, indicates the crucial role of the body in attractiveness as well. Facially disfiguring diseases (like smallpox) have largely died out, which means that while there is some variation in facial beauty today, the range has become smaller. Hence, the body project became increasingly important to social status throughout the twentieth century. Bodies matter because they are visible signs of class, morality, sexuality, and more.[12]

This is most obvious when it comes to weight and fitness. Beautiful women are expected to be thin. This is a relatively recent development, as it used to be that thinness was a sign of poverty and malnourishment, whereas now being overweight is class laden. Peter Stearns writes in *Fat History*: "Over the past century, a major addition has occurred in Western standards of beauty and morality: the need to stay thin. . . . Failure to live up to the new, standardized body image entails at least an appalling ugliness, at most a fundamentally flawed character."[13] Today being thin is not enough. A woman must also be lean, toned, and muscular, which requires even more time and commitment than "simply" being thin.

Other bodily elements that are now regulated and expected in ways that were barely true in the last century include making the body hairless and tanning the skin.[14] Spray tanning is a common choice today—though it should not be too dark, indicating that the sun should only leisurely touch the presumably white skin. These practices involve investment of time, money, and often discomfort. The impetus behind these "beauty" practices seem to be more societal than biological.

In the end, both nature and nurture play a part in physical attraction. Evolutionary psychologists argue that when it comes to facial beauty and bodily attractiveness, humans are still very much animals. Our brains quickly and subconsciously respond to certain signals like clear skin, healthy hair, and flushed cheeks, which helps explain the efforts people undertake to enhance features that signal fertility.

Still, it is undeniable that some beauty and fitness practices are socially constructed, and they change over time. This is especially true when it comes to expectations for women. Feminist thinkers, like Naomi Wolf, argue that as women have acquired more power both inside and outside the home, they have simultaneously been saddled with higher expectations about their looks. Those expectations take up women's time and money, inhibiting their abilities to engage with work and activism in the same way as men.[15] Coloring hair on the head, removing hair from the body, and coloring the skin on the body are just a few ways in which the "beauty myth" affects women today.

Beauty pageants reinforce both the biological and the sociological perspectives on women's physical appearance by unabashedly embracing the notion that looks matter. Beauty pageants are not about smashing the patriarchy. Some women who participate may be complicit in the patriarchy, while others may be using their pageant experience to understand how structures of oppression work so they can get inside the system (either to succeed within it or to change it from within). But, to date, there have not been any attempts by pageant winners to completely change how that system works.

Interestingly, the audience for beauty pageants—whether in person or on television—is mainly women and not men. Ditto the judges, who have been predominantly female at both the Miss America and the Miss USA Pageants over the past several decades. In other words, pageant contestants *perform* primarily for other women.

This has been true for at least fifty years. In his 1971 book *There She Is*, Frank Deford explained that "the hand that rocks the cradle also turns the TV dial [to Miss America]."[16] Deford's take on the history of Miss America continues to be one of the most popular books on the topic, despite its age and the sex of its author.

I situate my updated version of Miss America's story, along with that of her sister pageants, firmly in women's history. The history of beauty pageants' complicated reign in the United States begins seventy-five years before Miss America's birth, at the start of the organized women's movement in Seneca Falls, New York.

PART I

The Birth of American Pageantry and the Feminist Movement

CHAPTER 1

America's Handsomest Suffragists

The Start of the Woman Movement and Beauty Culture

IT ALL STARTED with a locked door.

On a sweltering July morning in the town of Seneca Falls—nestled in the Finger Lakes region of western New York—a group of people, mainly women, gathered outside Wesleyan Chapel. They were there to attend a two-day meeting addressing the injustices American women faced.

But first they had to get in.

In their excitement, the organizers had forgotten to get a key to the church. Eventually someone stepped up to enter the building through a window and open the doors.[1] Once inside, for the first time ever in an organized and public setting, American women came together to speak out about their lack of rights.

The Seneca Falls Convention, held July 19–20, 1848, is regarded as the first public event of the women's rights movement. The idea, generated over a tea party only a few weeks prior, helped spur many other conventions, like the first National Women's Rights Convention, which was held in October 1850 in Worcester, Massachusetts. These conventions helped create and support female speakers and activists, part of the First Wave of (what we would today call) feminists fighting for rights for American women.

These mid-nineteenth-century women were often heavily criticized for presenting themselves in public in large crowds—let alone for speaking and sharing their thoughts and opinions in front of an audience of any size. Historian Sally McMillen explains, "Female actresses and singers came onstage with bare arms and necks and garnered much praise. But when a demurely dressed woman stood before the public and demanded the right to vote, people labeled her masculine and denounced her for moving beyond her assigned sphere."[2] Because of intense and early criticism, by the mid-1850s many women stopped feeling comfortable speaking publicly.

This view that women should not be on public stages grew to affect the entertainment industry, including the newly organized world of beauty contests. Beauty contests were part of a contest trend in the 1850s. P. T. Barnum, most often remembered for his collection of "oddities" and his circus, organized many of these public contests. Barnum sponsored dog, flower, and poultry contests beginning in 1853.[3] While competitions focused on female beauty had existed at local and folk festivals since colonial times—like May Day festivals, which had both religious and civic significance—Barnum devised the first commercial event in 1854. But the contest for women was a rare flop for the great showman, as women in the 1850s felt uncomfortable being evaluated in public.

The year 1854 also brought the first American "baby show." Held at the Clark County Agricultural Fair in Springfield, Illinois, over 120 babies vied for the top four prizes. The winner ("the finest baby, two-years-old and under") was a ten-month-old girl born to Mrs. Romney of Vienna, Ohio.[4] She received a tea set valued at $300.[5] The contest swiftly attracted national attention, and by 1855 many other baby contests had sprung up across the nation, including a version popularized by—you guessed it—Barnum the following year.

These two 1854 events, Barnum's American Gallery of Female Beauty and the Springfield baby show, seem different on the surface. One was about adult women; the other about infants of both sexes. But they are linked in two ways. The first is that both events are precursors: the former, to the "Miss" beauty pageants we know today, and the latter, to contemporary child beauty pageants. Second, baby contests helped make it acceptable for in-person, adult beauty contests to develop. Because women had to carry their babies onstage to be judged, it became acceptable for the female body to appear in public as well, especially if it was associated with motherhood.

Female and baby beauty contests in the nineteenth century were far from disconnected to political and social movements of the time, particularly the protofeminist movement of the mid-nineteenth century. It is no coincidence that just as women were beginning to find their (public) voices, female beauty culture began to develop in the late nineteenth century. The renewed focus on motherhood as part of the separate spheres of men and women confounded women's public efforts. Child-saving initiatives placed the onus on women in the private sphere of the home, which meant that women's worth was mainly determined by their children. While these ideas influenced all American women, only white women participated in these major public contests that gave rise not just to baby shows but also to Better Baby contests, baby parades, and more. Because infants and toddlers could not "perform" publicly on their own, their mothers had to help them. At one 1867 baby show in Savannah, Georgia, the newspaper reported young men attending a baby show to gaze at the women and not the babies.[6] Slowly these baby shows helped enable the transformation of the female body into something to be publicly and formally evaluated, a gateway to more "respectable" beauty contests.

STEP RIGHT UP: BARNUM'S AMERICAN GALLERY OF FEMALE BEAUTY

Following Seneca Falls in 1848 and the Worcester Convention in 1850, national women's rights conventions were held nearly every year until 1860. By 1860 New York state had passed a bill that gave women who lived in the state the right to own property, collect wages, and sue in court. Leaders like Elizabeth Cady Stanton and Susan B. Anthony were among the vanguard of women to use the speakers' circuit to bring attention to these issues, and they used the power of the petition to generate public support for women's causes more generally.[7]

The public nature of their work drew consternation. Suffrage historian Ellen Carol DuBois explains, "To women fighting to extend their sphere beyond its traditional domestic limitations, political rights involved a radical change in women's status, their emergence into public life. The right to vote raised the prospect of female autonomy in a way that other claims to equal rights could not. . . . Most obviously, woman suffrage constituted a serious challenge to the masculine monopoly of the public sphere."[8] It is often forgotten that at Seneca Falls, Lucretia Mott's husband, James, chaired the convention because it was simply too scandalous to have a woman chair a public event.

It was in this shifting time for women that P. T. Barnum came up with the idea for a women's beauty contest. Barnum, who started his decades-long show business career running lotteries as a young man in his native Connecticut, knew how popular public contests could be. Add in a participatory element—that is, the viewing public likely knew one of the competitors—and you had a pop culture winner. In the winter of 1853 he started his National Poultry Show.[9] The flower and dog shows soon followed. They were successful and made money because "everyone in the family had to stop by to admire Mother or Uncle Charley's handiwork, and all were welcome so long as they paid 25 cents each."[10]

Barnum assumed that a Handsomest Lady contest would be an instant success as well. His idea was that women would appear at his New York City American Museum to compete against one another, not unlike the chickens and the dogs. He was shocked when enrollment was low. Why? Because, according to a contemporary, "no mother or husband—no matter how liberal—would allow a daughter or wife to thus appear in public."[11] Barnum uncharacteristically misread the zeitgeist when he thought both males and females would have little moral opposition to women's faces and figures being judged in public.[12]

Unfortunately, we do not know much more about this first failed attempt at a women's beauty contest. Barnum did not write about it in any of his three autobiographies—which is not surprising given it was not exactly a rousing success. Plus, he had a terrible habit (for historians) of destroying incoming letters after he had read them.[13]

Barnum regrouped in 1855 with a different version of the beauty contest. This one was based on the new technology of daguerreotypes, or early forms of photographs. Daguerreotypes had become extremely popular by the 1850s, so when Barnum heard of a Parisian contest about the most beautiful women in the world, he saw an opportunity to resurrect his women's beauty contest. Instead of welcoming women to his museum in the flesh, the American Gallery of Female Beauty reduced women to a static image, and only of their faces.[14] He reasoned that if a physical female body was considered immoral in public, a frozen image, focused on the face, was significantly more acceptable.

To reach the general public, Barnum used newspapers, like the *New York Tribune* and the *Poughkeepsie Journal*, to emphasize how respectable this beauty contest was.[15] S. L. Walker wrote in the August 11, 1855, edition of the upstate newspaper, "Mr. Barnum's advertisement appeared for the first time in the Tribune of July 12, 1855. . . . The advertisement which is lengthy, is high toned and full of the spirit of the great American Genius. No one with propriety can take exceptions to it, and if its provisions are complied with, it will be both honorable and creditable to America."[16]

Similarly, Barnum spoke to daguerreotypists directly in their circular *Humphrey's Journal.* A July 15, 1855, ad explained his motivation to hold the contest: "In order to obtain such specimens of American beauty as will compare favorably with any that the Old World can produce . . . and at the same time encourage a more popular taste for the Fine Arts . . . and laudably gratify the public curiosity."[17] In this case, Barnum's impulse was not just commercial but also nationalistic.[18]

Barnum directed the thousand contestants—single or married—to galleries that would take their pictures for free or at a discount.[19] All entries had to include details on the subject's eye and skin color, along with a lock of her hair. For anyone still concerned about propriety, Barnum said proper names did not have to be used. All entries were to be numbered and displayed for one full year at Barnum's New York museum—from October 1855 to 1856—so that the (paying) visiting public could vote. Price of admission was twenty-five cents, and with it came one hundred votes in the first round and twenty votes in the second.[20] The images were displayed by state of origin, foreshadowing not just the nationalism but also the regionalism that beauty pageants would later embrace (though not the entire nation, as women of color were not included).

We know, thanks to a February 1856 ad in *Humphrey's Journal*, that voting was ongoing just after Barnum sold his American Museum.[21] But we know nothing about whether the gallery was ever completed—and no word on how American beauties may or may not have fared against their European peers. Unfortunately, due to multiple fires in the Barnum museum in the 1860s, none of the portraits are known to have survived.

Though the 1850s contest appears to have never selected a winner, the yearlong success of Barnum's event inspired newspapers to create their own photographic beauty contests. These became especially popular post-Civil War and into the twentieth century by focusing on the "best" of regional beauty. They also were a commercial bonanza for local newspapers.[22]

Barnum's goal was to make pop culture respectable. One strategy was to make it "feminine" for middle-class women, and, of course, for white women exclusively. The gallery was one example of how he did this, both expanding women's roles and relying upon traditional ones at the same time. The message was clear that for a woman who wanted to appear in public, she should do so either in pursuit of marriage or as a wife.[23] This attitude set the tone for in-person beauty contests in the nineteenth century. These contests brought women out of the domestic sphere into a much more public setting even as they reinforced more traditional gender roles.

BEAUTIFUL BATHING BEAUTIES

The 1860s were a slow time for both beauty contests and the women's rights movement as the nation focused on the Civil War, but over the next few decades both saw growth. The conclusion of the Civil War, and especially the passage of the Fifteenth Amendment, which granted black men the right to vote, clarified that the goal of the women's movement should be suffrage (before that the organizationally decentralized movement could not agree on their ultimate purpose).[24] Unfortunately, the pathway to achieve suffrage was long and hard—with respectability again a key part of the debate. In May 1869 the women's movement split between the more radical National Woman Suffrage Association and the more respectable American Woman Suffrage Association over the nature of acceptable tactics to secure women's suffrage.[25] The organizational division lasted until 1890, with the creation of the National American Woman Suffrage Association, though the debate among women's rights advocates over "proper" feminist tactics would persist into the twenty-first century.

During this time of division in the women's rights movement, a variety of beauty contests began. These contests emphasized respectability while being a bit radical by placing women's bodies in public in a competitive setting. Many were associated with existing civic or regional festivals. For example, New Orleans's Mardi Gras crowned its first queen in 1871, and San Antonio's Fiesta celebration had its first queen in 1896.[26] Others were associated with carnivals and expositions—Chicago's World Fair, held in 1893, featured a Congress of Beauty.[27] But the most successful were held at seaside resorts.

Beach resorts, which developed in postbellum America not only on the East Coast but also along the Gulf Coast, were the perfect host for beauty contests. These locations had already waged battles over how much of any body could be seen in public, becoming sites where all bodies, including female bodies, could be on display in public.[28] They were also sites of leisure, where adults could relax and enjoy their limited time away from work.

An 1880 bathing beauty contest held in Rehoboth Beach, Delaware, is recognized as the first American bathing beauty contest. This "Miss United States" event has also come to be seen as the first "beauty pageant" because of its use of a bathing suit—until 2018 the sine qua non of major American beauty pageants. We can be almost certain the winner was not showing much skin (form-fitting suits did not exist before the 1910s). But it still was very adventurous for a woman to be judged in public, especially because it was now her *body* and not just her face being assessed.

The winner of that contest was a young woman named Myrtle Meriwether. Myrtle went to Rehoboth Beach, "the Nation's Summer Capital," from Shinglehouse, Pennsylvania, as part of a woman's business league that was holding its convention there. While in Delaware she saw a poster advertising the Miss United States competition. She fit the contest's specifications—"single, not more than 25, minimum height 5 foot 4 inches, maximum weight 130 pounds"—and was attracted by the prizes, which included a complete bridal trousseau worth $300.[29] The emphasis on marriageability and appearance in this first contest is clear. Myrtle was selected the winner after a week of being judged by an illustrious panel, which reportedly included Thomas Edison.[30]

Following Rehoboth Beach's success, in the late nineteenth century several other beach resort towns held bathing beauty contests. In the midst of a postbellum protofeminist schism over how women fighting for enfranchisement should pursue their objectives in public, women started entering the public sphere to be judged on their appearance. While the women's rights movement was stalled in this moment and the women's beauty contests were still nascent, it was kids' contests that grew rapidly.

SHOWING BABIES

The inaugural 1854 baby show in Springfield, Illinois, attracted quite a bit of press coverage, which is what drew Barnum's interest. Because the Midwestern organizers' purpose was to increase attendance at their agricultural fair, they wanted as much attention as possible. To that end they invited famed abolitionist and women's rights leader Lucretia Mott to judge, thinking she would be a draw and generate press coverage.[31] While Mott declined, she sent a letter—which was reproduced in the newspapers—criticizing the contest for only including white babies.[32] The popularity *and* controversial nature of this first event foreshadowed struggles child pageantry would face over the next two centuries.

While Barnum cannot lay claim to hosting the first-ever baby show in the United States, he can say he created the biggest one. According to the *New York Times*, over forty thousand people saw his 1855 show at the American Museum.[33] Of all the contests he introduced in the 1850s, the baby shows were Barnum's most successful.

Barnum started his baby show during the summer of 1855, between his failed Handsomest Lady contest and his more successful American Gallery of Female Beauty. Evaluating babies was part of his strategy to make the American Museum, and pop culture more generally, a welcoming place for women. He did this by heavily policing morals so that it was acceptable for unescorted women to appear in public. Barnum famously had a sign outside the entrance proclaiming, "No Admittance for FEMALES OF KNOWN BAD CHARACTER."[34]

Babies were one way to do this. Some critics railed that a baby show sullied the sanctity of home life by bringing it into the public sphere. But the sheer number of people who came to see the over one hundred children (from a few months old up to age five) shows how noteworthy bringing babies, and their mothers, into such a public space was at that time. Females dominated at these public events—both onstage and in the audience.[35] Babies made the space safe because they were so tied to traditional notions of womanhood.

The 1855 National Baby Show was the most popular participatory event in the history of Barnum's museum.[36] This, despite extreme June heat, meant that on the second day Barnum had to close the doors because the space was too full, with close to eighteen thousand visitors. The *New York Daily Times* reported that over the four days of the show more than sixty thousand visitors went to the museum, earning Barnum over $17,000 in tickets[37] (approximately half a million in today's dollars[38]).

Riding the huge wave of interest, Barnum quickly took his baby shows on the road. He first went to New England and then moved west throughout the fall of 1855. By the time Barnum's baby show reached Cincinnati, Ohio, in October 1855, opponents to the shows had organized. A community leader, writing under the pen name "Pater Familias," attacked the upcoming local baby show in the paper. This critic, along with others, thought it was not acceptable for "family life" to be commercialized in public—especially when it was associated with prize money.

This line of moral argument worked especially well in Cincinnati during the fall of 1855. Residents there were already upset about women appearing in public at a women's rights convention, which happened to take place in the same location as the planned baby show.[39] Because of the public negativity, only twenty of eighty-three registered babies showed up for the show.[40] Cincinnati marked the end of Barnum's tour of 1850s baby shows.

Much like his women's contest, Barnum's baby shows set the stage for many imitators. Churches, hospitals, and other civic organizations began to run their own baby shows, especially as fund-raising events.[41] While money was involved, those shows were not about individual profit but rather about raising money for an institution (and one that presumably did good community work), so people were less uncomfortable mixing kids and money. Virtual contests also began to develop, led by magazines and newspapers, in the later nineteenth century and into the twentieth— similar to the women's photographic beauty contests that Barnum had pioneered.

May Day festivals are another event that show the rise of competitive in-person events without of the intrusion of money. May Day festivals have medieval roots. At a spring festival a May Queen, who was transitioning from youth to adulthood, would be selected. This young woman would represent temporary royalty within her locality.[42] The tradition moved beyond folk meaning in the nineteenth century when Catholics began to appoint a "Virgin Mary" as May Day queen.[43] May Day contests were especially popular at girls' schools.[44] Sometimes the most popular friend was crowned, sometimes the one considered most beautiful. Perhaps because of the folk and religious origins—as opposed to anything commercial—there was no public opposition to these crowning contests.[45]

In the postbellum years and into the Gilded Age, May Day rituals continued to evolve, especially with the popularization of the May Queen festival. In 1881 artist and social critic John Ruskin held a contest for schoolgirls at a woman's college in London. His event, focused on much younger girls as a way to honor their innocence, was so popular it spread to the United States in the 1890s.[46] This iteration was more aligned with child contests than adult beauty contests.

PARADING (BETTER) BABIES

Around the same time, baby parades started popping up in Coney Island and up and down the Jersey Shore. These parades were updated versions of baby shows, with the added component of movement. The babies did not stay in one spot to be evaluated; they moved. So, the possibilities for maternal display also grew. Not only were children decked out but their carriages were too—like miniparade floats.

The Asbury Park baby parade became the most famous of the baby parades and contests that began in the late nineteenth century. The event was the brainchild of the first mayor of Asbury Park, James A. Bradley, who founded the city along the Jersey Shore in 1871. At the first event, on July 21, 1890, two hundred mothers wheeled their babies on the Boardwalk. According to the *New York Times* it was "the most unique parade ever known here . . . a baby show on wheels."[47] Carriages—decorated in flags, lanterns, and even a hammock—carried many happy babies (the paper was careful to note that only one baby cried).

The Asbury Park baby parade immediately became an annual event. By 1895 the parade had over eight hundred participants, with forty thousand witnesses.[48] The top prize getter, one of forty to receive awards, rode in a carriage covered in nearly three thousand yellow roses. Each participant received a photograph of themselves to mark and remember their participation in the event.

The event was so popular that Thomas Edison selected the Asbury Park baby parade as the subject of one of his first movies. The movie shows children of various ages dressed up and decked out as mothers walk beside them. A large, patriotic audience was also shown, well protected by many community members and police officers. Part of Edison's motivation in filming the Asbury Park baby parade was to show the patriotism that was so strong outside the major cities.[49] According to the *New York Times*, in 1904 the Asbury Park baby parade had over five hundred participants marching in front of over one hundred thousand spectators.[50] The fame of the Asbury Park baby parade set off a string of imitators in Hoboken, Jersey City, Newark, Long Island, and Coney Island. Atlantic City began its own version, thirty years before Miss America, in 1891.[51]

Baby shows and baby parades were obviously becoming big events. Soon, some social reformers wanted to capitalize on that popularity to introduce science and education to childhood and parenting. Hence, the birth of Better Baby contests. From the beginning, these events focused on getting the "right" start early in life. What is recognized as the first Better Baby contest took place in Louisiana in 1908.

Mary De Garmo, a former classroom teacher, organized that first Better Baby contest at the state fair in Shreveport.[52] It was purposely held five days after the fair's traditional baby show, as a way to distinguish the two events. Mrs. De Garmo billed her event as the first time that "physical perfection" would play a role equal to or greater than "merely facial beauty."[53] These "scientific baby shows" quickly took off, born out of the very real Progressive Era concern about child mortality.

Iowa held its first event in 1911, Boston and Philadelphia in 1912, and New York City in 1913.[54] That year was the peak for Better Baby contests, not coincidentally a high point of the Progressive movement, with its focus on improving the health of infants. These contests both evaluated and celebrated mothers, who used the events as a way to make their private work public.

At most Better Baby events, babies were stripped naked and then judged by physicians according to a "meticulous point system like that used in cattle judging."[55] Measurement tried to make clear that the aim was not just looks but also physical perfection—while tying this activity to the growing eugenics movement. Communities competed with one another to find the "most perfect" baby, in service of improving health for all. However, many of these contests were rooted in the racist belief that all children needed to look and act like white and more affluent babies to be considered healthy.

Photographic baby contests were also incredibly popular, which is not surprising given the success of similar events for women in the late nineteenth century and into the twentieth. Major national publications offered their own "American Babies," including *Ladies' Home Journal* and *Good Housekeeping*.[56] Smaller regional and local newspapers also offered versions.

The connection between babies' and women's photo contests has largely been overlooked, but they were clearly related. Baby shows, parades, and contests all helped pave the way for women to appear in public and have their bodies judged. At a San Francisco baby show in 1873 an award was presented for "handsomest mother."[57] Bringing a baby onstage meant a mother was presenting her body in public as well, perhaps even to be judged. It was in presenting children in public that it became acceptable for women themselves to appear publicly, leading to a new investment in beauty culture.

THE WOMAN MOVEMENT OF BEAUTY CULTURE

While the "Woman Movement," as it was then called, was seen as being in "the Doldrums" from 1896 to 1910, women's beauty culture was going through a lively developmental period.[58] Civic festivals that crowned queens thrived in this time: St. Paul's Winter Carnival began in 1885, Pasadena's Tournament of Roses in 1889, and the Order of the Alamo in San Antonio in 1909.[59] And everywhere in the late nineteenth and early twentieth century saw extensive development of beauty industries like makeup, skin care, dieting, and women's fashion magazines. There was also a transformation from local, service-oriented beauty culture, dominated by individuals, to national systems of mass production, marketing, and distribution, dominated by companies.[60]

This was especially true when it came to hair and skin care. In the 1870s women turned to their hair as a specific way to express themselves. They started styling their hair in elaborate fashions, which helped lead to the creation of hairdressing as a profession. In 1878 the first trade magazine, *American Hairdresser*, began, which shows how quickly the profession expanded.[61] The number of hairdressers doubled from 1890 to 1900, and nearly again by 1907, with thirty-six thousand women identifying as hairdressers.[62]

Cosmetics followed a slightly different path, though it ended up in a similar place. Women had long used some "natural" makeup to enhance particular features—like the lips, cheeks, and eyes. At different times in American history the acceptability of "painted ladies" has gone up and down. When hairstyling was so popular in the 1870s, cosmetics were in a down moment, but by the turn of the twentieth century both aspects of beauty culture were becoming increasingly entrenched, particularly with the establishment of beauty parlors.[63] While beauty was considered a small business in 1914, compared to what it would become, it was still estimated to be worth $17 million. And with only one-fifth of American women using cosmetics then, there was room for growth by female entrepreneurs, like Madam C. J. Walker, considered the first female, African American self-made millionaire, who made makeup and hair-care products for black women.[64]

In the early twentieth century, upper- and middle-class parents invested in skin-care ointments and creams for their daughters, particularly because skin is publicly visible, like clothes. So those with money invested in products to make the skin clear, smooth, and (often) whiter. Joan Jacobs Brumberg, in her groundbreaking work on the history of young women's bodies, explains, "American parents cooperated with a body project like skin care because they understood that good looks were an important vehicle of social success for their daughters."[65]

As an outgrowth of this focus on public appearance and its ties to social class and future prospects for girls, the body itself became a beauty project. This applied to the removal of body hair, which began to grow in popularity at this time.[66] And the body as beauty project especially applied to size. The 1890s reversed a generations-long preference for "plumpness."[67] This was the time when preference for a thinner body began to develop, which was tied to middle-class restraint and respectability. In his history of how thinness came to dominate as a preference in the US, Peter Stearns argues that "constraint, including the new constraints urged on eating and body shape, was reinvented to match—indeed to compensate for—new areas of greater freedom."[68] Those freedoms included being in public more for leisure and to fight for rights as women, thanks to the Woman Movement.

Not only were women's bodies more often in the public sphere but women's knowledge found a home in the women's magazines that started in this historical moment. Between 1885 and 1910 the top women's magazines, like *Ladies' Home Journal*, *McCall's*, and *Good Housekeeping*, were founded.[69] These magazines became a way for women to find out about all aspects of beauty culture—hair, makeup, skin, and body care. They also became a way for advertisers to reach many women across the country. Because of increased literacy and purchasing power, not just upper- and middle-class women could consume these magazines. Working-class women could as well, and that started to democratize American beauty. Naomi Wolf, the noted feminist thinker, has observed that at the same time women were fighting for more rights in the public sphere, the circulation of women's magazines doubled, suggesting a connection between more public freedom and more bodily constraint (in the form of standards of beauty).[70]

By the 1910s, the borders of the beauty industry in the United States had become clear. Consumers were female, and they could be reached through magazines that promulgated a particular ideal regarding hair, skin, and body type.[71] This set the stage for massive development of the beauty industry in the 1920s, and beyond.

PERFORMING FEMALES

The story differs when it comes to other forms of performed femininity, like burlesque and the circus. Burlesque, a somewhat ribald form of variety show, came to the United States from Europe in the 1840s. Women who performed burlesque were often disparagingly linked to "painted ladies." But the development of dime and theater museums helped make burlesque performances more acceptable. Burlesque reached an apex of feminine spectacle in the 1890s, before declining popularity led to the development of the striptease, taking it out of the mainstream.[72]

Female circus performers, on the other hand, enjoyed growing respectability throughout the nineteenth century, even when it came to their bodies. Despite often performing in tighter-fitting outer garments for safety reasons, public advertisements depicted them in "proper" clothing, including corsets under their dresses.[73] Circus women's performances also often demanded more intense training than that of burlesque performers. Of course, Barnum was famously involved with the circus—and part of the reason we remember his name so well today is because of the 1880 merger with Bailey's circus. Barnum's circus posted stringent female-conduct rules, which showed how policed femininity was in the space.[74]

Circus women were often linked with public activism, especially regarding temperance, leading to prohibition, and suffrage.[75] One famous female circus performer, the bareback rider Josie DeMott Robinson, played a big role in the suffrage movement. At suffrage parades she posed on top of her horse for pictures and frequently led the parades.[76]

It was not only female performers who started presenting themselves in public at this time. Debutantes, from the upper classes, also started "coming out" in public beginning in the late nineteenth century.[77] Some of these same women would go on to participate in the fund-raising fairs that became so popular around the turn of the century (including to support suffrage).[78]

Many women of the Progressive Era also took part in community pageants, performances that mythologized some aspect of town history and life, which were enormously popular in the 1910s. Some community pageants were tied to suffrage and other popular political issues of the time, like child labor legislation. In 1913 a group of "pageant-masters" formed the American Pageant Association, which had roughly equal numbers of women and men, unusual for the time.[79]

In all these public events—from debuting to community pageants—it was wealthier (and hence white) women who tended to participate. This had been true since Seneca Falls, but it became especially significant to the Woman Movement as the suffrage fight heated up. It was then that nascent feminism became fashionable in two senses, popularity and sartorial choices.

PARADING SUFFRAGISTS

When extremely wealthy women began advocating for women's right to vote around the turn of the twentieth century, it gave the movement currency—financially and culturally—helping make it more acceptable to mainstream society. One celebrity leader was Alva Belmont Vanderbilt, who organized and advocated out of her New York City and Newport, Rhode Island, mansions. Women like Vanderbilt were the first celebrities to endorse a political cause in the new century. Johanna Neuman christens them "Gilded Suffragists," in her book of the same name, who risked their social position to fight for a cause.[80] However, it is important to note that while these mainly white, affluent, and well-educated female leaders were publicly putting themselves out there in fighting for suffrage, they were not arguing for universal suffrage, rather for the women's vote to be a marker of educated and privileged women only.

Vanderbilt and her set added glamour to the movement. They saw fashion as a way to help the suffrage efforts, mainly by eliminating one of the biggest criticisms of the Woman Movement: that the movement and its fight for suffrage was making women too masculine.[81] Inevitably, their focus on clothes made some dismiss the gilded suffragists as frivolous, but the wealthy women's suggestions seemed to help, especially when it came to parades.[82]

Parades have a long history in the United States. Historically and in the present, they have many militaristic overtones.[83] Neuman explains, "Of all the tactics women now employed in winning the vote, few were as controversial—or as upsetting to the mannered civility that had settled on relations between American men and women for more than a century—as the public parade."[84] In response, gilded suffragists promoted two changes in public parades and protests. One was to make sure "beautiful" women were prominent. This meant putting glamorous women at the front of the parade to quell fears that getting the right to vote would harden women and emasculate men. At protests this meant, under the influence of makeup maven Elizabeth Arden, having women paint their mouths with bright red lipstick.[85] The other change was to be organized. Women were instructed to wear white and to march in choreographed groups. This also helped lessen the other major criticism of women who marched in suffrage parades—that they were "streetwalkers," "ladies of the night."[86]

Feminism and physical appearance had been linked since the beginning in Seneca Falls, when Elizabeth Cady Stanton talked about the need for exercise and healthy living.[87] Amelia Bloomer, famous for her, well, bloomers, and dress reform more generally, was active in the Woman Movement of the nineteenth century. The focus on fashion and feminism was also strong in the American South. Newspaper reports always tended to emphasize the "beauty and femininity of suffrage leaders."[88]

A lot of this feminine advocacy was a result of the increasing number of women seeking higher education in the United States around the turn of the twentieth century. The numbers grew quickly. In 1870 about 11,000 females ages eighteen to twenty-one attended college. By 1890 that number had grown to 40,000, and by 1920 the number was 283,000, or about 47 percent of the collegiate population in the United States.[89] As part of this expansion, three interrelated things occurred. First, schools began to track the bodies of their female student bodies. In 1885 the newly formed Association of Collegiate Alumnae published a report on women's health and physical education, which reported their body measurements, like height and weight, along with details on other parts of the body.[90] Second, women's sports teams formed. For example, Smith College held the first women's collegiate basketball game in 1893. Athletic opportunities continued to expand for women into the twentieth century, centered in schools and especially on college campuses. Finally, women's fraternities (soon to be called sororities) began in the 1870s and 1880s. While initially focused on academic performance, by the 1890s "female fraternities" started to place a premium on physical appearance and sociability (both among the same sex and across the sexes).[91] Even as (almost exclusively) white women progressed with higher education, their bodies were heavily policed and regulated by others and themselves.

What started with a locked door in 1848 ultimately led to more education for women and more women in the public sphere during the second half of the nineteenth century. It also led to a greater emphasis on physical appearance, with the growth of beauty culture, and a sustained interest in women's role as mothers. None of these things had to, or have to be, mutually exclusive. But as women fought for more rights in public, they were constrained in other ways, namely, through bodily expectations. Some of those expectations involved a focus on physical appearance (which required both restraint and embellishment) and on motherhood. That same focus on beauty provided commercial opportunities for some women as business owners, but also additional restraints by changing expectations about how women should look in public.

Ultimately, this time was marked by growing options for women to engage in the public sphere. In particular, by engaging with their children to be judged by strangers—at baby shows, Better Baby contests, and baby parades—women ultimately laid the groundwork to be publicly judged themselves. Women could not be locked out or silenced, whether in Seneca Falls or elsewhere. They simply had to find new ways to parade themselves, showing off increased education, beauty, and feminine motherhood. To members of the growing Woman Movement, opening that church door in Seneca Falls revealed a platform from which to showcase different types of feminine expectations in public.

CHAPTER 2

Sashes and Suffrage

After the Vote

M ARION, OHIO, was decked out on July 22, 1920. Almost every store had patriotic bunting hanging, and nearly every home had a window boasting a photo of Senator Warren Harding, their hometown hero. It was "notification day" for Harding, the Republican nominee in the 1920 presidential campaign, and the event was a "strange mixture of political wedding, coronation, homecoming parade, and Fourth of July celebration."[1] Notification day was when a presidential nominee was formally announced by political party representatives, who ceremoniously traveled to his hometown to notify him of his official selection.

Between fifty thousand and one hundred thousand visitors descended on Marion on that hot Thursday, but not all were as enthusiastic about the occasion, or welcome for that matter. Alice Paul, chairwoman of the National Women's Party, had sent word that she needed bodies to pressure Senator Harding to fight for women's suffrage. The final state needed for ratification of the Nineteenth Amendment, Tennessee, hung in the balance. More than one hundred suffragists from fifteen states answered Paul's call.[2]

That morning the women who had assembled in Ohio donned their white dresses, chosen to symbolize purity and virtue, and their tricolored "Votes for Women" sashes. They marched in a single line, grouped behind pennants held aloft naming their states, until they reached Harding's front porch.[3] There, two sashed suffragists stepped up onto Harding's porch to speak with him. The representatives of the National

Women's Party requested that Harding call on all Tennessee Republicans to vote for suffrage in the special legislative session to begin in a few weeks.

The protest by these "Suffs" forced bands and marchers to slow down, and then halt completely, in front of Harding's home. The candidate knew he had to move the Suffs along so the parade could continue. To do so, Senator Harding dodged the women's demands by saying his position would be forthcoming in his afternoon address. In his speech that afternoon, Harding supported suffrage, but did not commit to any action in Tennessee. Paul and her team of sashed Suffs vowed to follow Harding anytime he left his front porch to campaign until ratification occurred. They were not deterred by the recurring disappointment of male politicians.

To achieve suffrage, women of the time took public action in ways and numbers never before seen. The women were directed by leaders like Alice Paul and Carrie Chapman Catt, who led (sometimes conflicting) pro-suffrage organizations. Suffrage parades, pageants, and protests were one way to get large numbers of supporters visibly engaged. For example, Paul helped organize the first national suffrage parade in 1913, on the eve of Woodrow Wilson's inauguration, along with an extremely popular suffrage pageant on the steps of the Treasury Department. More than twenty thousand people watched the suffrage pageant performance, which featured over one hundred women and children dressed in costumes representing Charity, Freedom, Hope, Justice, Liberty, and other themes.[4]

At suffrage events, particularly parades, American women donned sashes. In much the same way as women borrowed the public parade from the military, so too did they borrow the sash, which had been a popular part of the American military uniform since the Civil War.[5] In the armed forces, most often during the nineteenth century in both Europe and America, the sash was worn with formal uniforms from the shoulder to the opposite hip by draping fabric over the head and across the body.

Suffragists usurped this practice to fight their own war, conveying their own distinct message. The sash was especially popular because it did not cover much of women's dresses. Keeping the dress, a symbol of traditional femininity, visible reassured men that even with the vote women would remain respectable and ladylike. The addition of the sash made a woman's progressive allegiance clear through its carefully selected colors, words, and symbolism.

Sashes were commonly worn as the suffrage battle climaxed over the summers of 1919 and 1920. It was at this point—the height of the suffrage campaign—that the word *feminism* began to be used with much greater frequency.[6] The term had a rapid ascendancy. In 1910 it was rarely used, but by 1914, just after the first national suffrage parade, it was common parlance.[7] While no one called it this at the time, this was the peak of the First Wave of feminism, the rising tide of millions of women speaking out and acting to secure their right to vote.

Following over nine hundred local and state women's suffrage campaigns, a serious fight at the national level (which culminated in Congress passing a joint resolution on June 4, 1919), and then a fight in over forty states for ratification, Tennessee became the thirty-eighth state needed to ratify the Nineteenth Amendment on August 18, 1920.[8] Eight days later, on August 26, 1920, the following words entered the Constitution of the United States of America: "The right of citizens of the United States to vote shall not be denied or abridged by the United States or by any State on account of sex." Only a few months later, on November 2, 1920, ten million women voted in the presidential election that resulted in Warren Harding becoming the twenty-ninth president of the United States—some of whom had stopped the notification day parade in front of his Marion, Ohio, home.[9]

A year after ratification, the sash that suffragists had usurped from the military was usurped again, this time by pageant promoters. And not by *suffrage pageant* promoters. Instead, 1921 saw the (re)birth of the bathing beauty contest and the establishment of an American institution: the Miss America Pageant. Over the next four decades Miss America became one of the most recognized events in the United States, and it did so by helping women transform from commercialized objects into educated, individual women—who, of course, still wanted to become wives and mothers.

INTER-CITY BEAUTIES IN AMERICA'S PLAYGROUND

For the first half of the twentieth century, Atlantic City, dubbed "America's Playground," was seen as the apex of leisure for middle-class America.[10] It was a city with the largest hotels in the world. It also had the country's longest boardwalk—a wooden walkway built over sand—which made sense as Atlantic City had created the first one. Atlantic City also created saltwater taffy, rolling chairs, Monopoly, and, of course, Miss America. But the shore town wanted to continue to grow, and to do that they needed to get more tourists, and for them to stay longer periods of time.

H. Conrad Eckholm, owner of the Monticello Hotel—an Atlantic City hotel *not* on the famous Boardwalk, which meant he had to fight harder to get visitors' attention—came up with a way to keep tourists down the shore after Labor Day, the traditional end of the summer season.[11] His idea was to create "Fall Frolic," a festival to be held after Labor Day to attract visitors later in the season. Eckholm convinced his friends at the Atlantic City's Business Men's League that this Fall Frolic needed a special event to anchor it. Drawing from the success of the Asbury Park baby parade and two unique features of Atlantic City since the 1870s and 1880s—the Boardwalk and its rolling chairs—the men came up with the idea of the Rolling Chair Parade down the Boardwalk.[12]

Rolling chairs were covered and cushioned wicker chairs on wheels that someone pushed. Tourists rented rides down the Boardwalk, and the activity was considered a must-do tourist attraction in Atlantic City. The Rolling Chair Parade elevated the activity by inviting women to decorate a rolling chair and then be pushed in it. For an hour on September 25, 1920, about 350 women in decorated rolling chairs were pushed down the Boardwalk by men. The parade was led by a young woman dressed in flowing white robes, identified as "Peace."[13]

This was almost exactly a month after American women secured the right to vote.

While the Rolling Chair Parade was not a rousing success—estimates varied from 50,000 spectators to 125,000—it was successful enough to show that the idea of a large event on the Boardwalk to keep tourists around after Labor Day had promise.[14] In February 1921 Sam P. Leeds, the president of the Atlantic City Chamber of Commerce, appointed a planning committee of ten businessmen to design the program for the 1921 Fall Frolic. The men—who included several hoteliers, a dry cleaner owner, an advertising man, among others—decided to keep the Rolling Chair Parade *and* add two more events imagined to draw larger crowds: a beauty contest and a bathing revue.[15]

The beauty contest got an extra boost that winter when Harry Finley, a newspaper publisher in Atlantic City, took a page from P. T. Barnum's book and suggested that local newspapers run a "popularity" photo contest to determine a beauty to represent them on the Boardwalk.[16] Just like it did for newspapers in the nineteenth century, the beauty contest was meant to boost circulation.[17] Harry Godshall, the member of the organizing committee in charge of the Inter-City Beauty Contest, named off the top of his head the cities Atlantic City would invite to send queens for a "vacation."[18] They included Washington, DC; Camden, Newark, and Ocean City, New Jersey; New York City; and Harrisburg, Philadelphia, and Pittsburgh, Pennsylvania. While there is some disagreement among historians over how many cities sent "beauties," most agree that eight young women ended up vying for the top prizes (after Miss Atlantic City withdrew, due to the perceived advantage of representing the host city).[19]

How were these women identified to the public? They wore sashes over their attire. Unlike the Suffs, those sashes did not say "Votes for Women" but rather the geographic location they represented, like "Miss Camden," or "Miss Philadelphia." They also were not worn over white dresses. But the style of sash—over the shoulder, with the words in front—were the same as the suffragists'.

In 1921 Miss Washington DC, Margaret Gorman, a tiny sixteen-year-old,[20] won both the Inter-City Beauty Contest *and* the Bathers Revue in the beauty category at the Fall Frolic.[21] Because of Gorman's dual victory the two contests—one in a bathing suit and one in a dress—have become conflated over time. Without question, from the start Miss America was a bathing beauty contest. But relatively little skin was shown in 1921, especially compared to present-day swimsuits. Gorman wore her bathing suit with tights, and the suit went down to her knees. Nonetheless, it was still titillating for a young woman to be so clearly presented in public and judged by strangers based on her face and figure. Things had surely changed since Barnum's failed contest in 1854, when a respectable woman would not physically appear in public to be judged, but American society was still coming to terms with women being more fully in the public arena.

Since the 1860s Atlantic City had staked its success on skirting the line between respectability and titillation. It wanted to attract the middle class, but it did so by going a bit beyond everyday life. This meant allowing the female body to be more visible, while still regulating it. The city's 1907 Mackintosh Law made it illegal for anyone "to bathe in the ocean or to appear on the beach front . . . in a bathing suit which does not reach at least four inches below the knee."[22] Atlantic City also had a law that people could not walk on the Boardwalk in a bathing suit without being covered up from below the knees up to the shoulders. The body was out there, but only by so much.

Just three days before the first Inter-City Beauty Contest in 1921, a woman was arrested on an Atlantic City beach for baring her knees.[23] Louise Rosine was visiting Atlantic City from her Los Angeles home when she rolled down her stockings on the Virginia Avenue beach. A beach policeman informed the thirty-nine-year-old novelist that uncovering her knees was against city regulations, to which Rosine replied, "The city has no right to tell me how I shall wear my stockings. It is none of their darn business. I will go to jail first."[24] And so she did.

Monitoring women's bodies on the beach was something that the leading feminist organization of the time, the League of Women Voters, supported. Many feminists today promote women's freedom of expression when it comes to bodily display, but the league was associated with the more conservative Suffs, including those who did not support passage of the Equal Rights Amendment. Carrie Chapman Catt, founder of the League of Women Voters in 1920, had been the president of the National American Woman Suffrage Association (NAWSA), which was the more "respectable" suffrage organization (NAWSA, for example, did not participate in any pro-suffrage hunger strikes and supported America's entry into World War I). Given the less liberal focus of the league and overall older composition of its members, it is not entirely surprising that the league supported restricting women's bathing suits in Atlantic City.[25] This early feminist battle against women's bodies foreshadowed later feminist protests in Atlantic City.

Still, the Fall Frolic seemed to hit a sweet spot—a young (presumably innocent) girl wins a bathing beauty contest, but she is still very covered up. This was in keeping with the role of women in 1921: they could vote, but not govern; they could work, but only until they married. Given how successful the first "Miss America" was, preparations quickly began for 1922.

MISS AMERICA IN THE ROARING TWENTIES

Atlantic City committed more money to put on the Fall Frolic in 1922 (the amount jumped from $1,000 to $12,500[26]), and the number of participants in the Inter-City Beauty Contest went up substantially (from eight to fifty-seven). Contestants now came from as far away as California, Washington state, and Canada.[27] The organizers added a separate preliminary competition to reduce the number of contenders on the final evening.[28] Individual winners were announced in the bathing suit and evening gown categories at the preliminary, a practice that continues today.

Mary Katherine Campbell, the red-headed Miss Columbus, was selected the 1922 winner by twelve judges, including one woman (Anita Stewart), and male celebrities like Norman Rockwell and Flo Ziegfeld.[29] Campbell was sixteen years old, like her predecessor, the outgoing queen Margaret Gorman (whom she defeated, as the reigning Miss America was expected to come back to defend her title).[30] Frank Deford, in his 1971 history of Miss America, recounts the following story from Campbell: "I came home and told my mother, 'I was chosen Miss Columbus, and they said it's because of my figure. Mother, what's a figure?' My mother said: 'It's none of your business.'"[31] While young Mary Katherine's figure was revered, part of her charm was in not knowing what that was.

Campbell was the first winner to be referred to as "Miss America" in an article in the *New York Times* about a trip to Canada when she met with the mayor of Montreal.[32] The paper again referred to her as "Miss America" when she successfully defended her title in 1923 against seventy-four other contestants, making her the only two-time winner.[33] That year Campbell once more bested the 1921 winner, Margaret Gorman, and at eighteen turned some heads when she cast aside her bathing skirt for a much more clinging (and au courant) bathing suit.[34]

That was not the only "scandal" at the 1923 contest. It turned out that Miss Brooklyn, who won several awards, was actually not a "Miss," as she was married. Ditto Miss Boston—who actually showed up with her husband and infant in tow, suggesting that it was not an underhanded attempt to win but a rules oversight on the part of the organizers.

Given concerns about respectability (which seemed to be a code word for virginity or maidenhood), it might have made more sense for married women to compete. Instead, because Miss America was about bringing women into the public (more than ever since the start of the Woman Movement), it offered an opportunity to women who were not already committed to a husband and family. Miss America presented a rare, public opportunity for young, single women. The official rule stating that all Miss America contestants must be unmarried was made explicit the following year.

Another rules change would become necessary when Miss Alaska turned out to live in New York City.[35] But, proof that scandal can be good publicity, 1923 was the first year that the winners were announced nationwide via radio.[36] The next few years brought more contestants—almost one hundred in 1927—and more rules.[37] For example, after Miss America 1924, Ruth Malcomson, Miss Philadelphia, declined to defend her title in 1925, the pageant organizers decided a contestant could win only once.[38]

The rapid, early development of Miss America was due in large part to its organizers seizing on recognized tropes about respectability. This also helps explain why this event held in Atlantic City, a location already identified as more aspirational and middle class, triumphed over beauty contests held in, for example, Coney Island, which was identified more with working-class leisure. Take the name "pageant," which in the Progressive Era had been associated with community historical events, often set in small towns. Historian David Glassberg, who has written about community historical pageants, explains that the 1920s Miss America creators and promoters knew they were exploiting small-town moral respectability when they started using that term.[39] He argues that the notion of a "pageant" itself—a procession of people in elaborate, colorful costumes or an outdoor performance of a scene—has always been both progressive and conservative.[40] These events celebrate the past, while trying to create something new for the future. It was for just this reason that suffragists also put on "suffrage pageants."

In this context, it is uncomfortable to recognize that shortly after women get the right to vote, a national ritual develops—a "pageant" no less—that basically said "the pursuit of beauty ought to be a woman's primary goal."[41] Moreover, that beauty could be exploited by men for commercial purposes, like extending the tourist season. Sure, women had been somewhat liberated politically with the vote and socially, in terms of dress (corsets were largely gone), but the cost was the commercialization of their faces and bodies. The hair and cosmetics industry became increasingly dominant in the 1920s, reinforced by popular magazines and events, like Miss America. As young, single women became more public, they were exploited in new and different ways.

While only six young women earned the title of Miss America during the 1920s, the "Miss America Pageant" almost immediately took on outsized significance. Over those six years more women made the journey to Atlantic City each September to seek the title. It was a haphazard system, with each town, city, or state selecting its representative—sometimes through a pageant or photo contest, other times by simply appointing a young woman to compete on behalf of a geographic entity. Already a Miss New York City? No worries, welcome Miss Bronx and Miss Manhattan, for example. As the number of contestants grew, the number of days of competition did as well, along with the size of the audience.[42]

Given the rapidly growing popularity of the contest it is not surprising that many detractors emerged. Women's and religious groups took particular umbrage with the 1927 Miss America Pageant, claiming it damaged morals and exploited girlhood. Catholics, Methodists, and a variety of Christian churchwomen found the business of profiting off swimsuit-clad bodies upsetting.[43]

Tensions bubbled over when only two members of the 1927 winner's court wore swimming stockings (and two also had bobbed hair, considered "unnatural," though they were not the same two women sans stockings).[44] Some of the very Atlantic City businessmen who supported the event in 1920 and 1921, as a way to raise the city's tourist profile, now saw it as hurting the reputation it had worked to expand. They feared the city had begun to be associated with tawdriness rather than respectability. On March 3, 1928, by a 27–3 vote, the all-male pageant organizers voted to discontinue the event.[45]

What is remarkable about the Miss America Pageant of the 1920s is not only its swift popularity but also how quickly it became a site for people to project their concerns about women. The hundreds of women who competed in Atlantic City as bathing beauties were bold. They were appearing in public, and their bodies and looks were clearly assessed. This was forward and daring in many ways. And, yet, they were totally silenced. They did not do anything except stand, smile, and look pretty.

In a just-after-the-passage-of-the-19th-Amendment moment, the only reasonable interpretation is that this was reactionary. As women began to be subjects with voices, they were put on a pedestal as silent objects.

Nonetheless, much like the term *feminist* in the 1910s, it is striking how swiftly the term *Miss America* entered popular usage and consciousness in the 1920s. People surely had a lot to say about both feminism and Miss America, but in the midst of so much attention and change, no one was quite sure where either was going after their momentous starts in 1920. Both needed to regroup during the 1930s—and beyond—to clarify their mission and structure. In the meantime, other events centered on motherhood (and girlhood) evolved over the next several decades.

THE PERSISTENT PAGEANTRY OF GIRLHOOD—AND MOTHERHOOD

Baby parades continued to be popular in the early twentieth century. The suffrage movement, which utilized both parades and pageants to get their message into the public in a "feminine" way, used baby parades as well. In a New York City parade in May 1911, suffragists had women push their babies in carriages to show that good mothers could be publicly and civically engaged.[46]

Given the deep roots of baby parades in pop culture, and politics, it is not surprising that from the start, Atlantic City's Fall Frolic had its own version. In 1925 the baby parade portion was so popular that the organizers had to add a Juvenile Review, for children older than five, in conjunction with Miss America.[47]

The Coney Island baby parade continued to thrive into the 1920s. The annual event regularly boasted four hundred entrants who wore a variety of outfits.[48] A three-year-old girl won in a harem costume, a two-year-old won as a "Vanity Girl," and a six-year-old won dressed like a "Show Girl."[49] The *New York Times* reported that the 1929 Coney Island baby parade had five hundred thousand spectators.[50]

Asbury Park's event also continued to flourish, sometimes capitalizing on the new Miss America Pageant down the shore. In 1927 over 150,000 spectators saw five-year-old Norma Dreyer crowned Little Miss America. She bested the winners of twenty-six other baby parades at the thirty-sixth annual event. Many more children, dressed as princesses and dolls, won smaller awards.[51]

By the 1930s these popular baby parades were criticized in ways similar to that of Miss America—namely, that they were commercialized and exploitative. In September 1932 the chief of the preschool division of the Pennsylvania State Board of Health condemned baby parades "as a deplorable exploitation of childhood."[52] It also did not help that mothers started to vehemently disagree with judges' decisions at baby parades. This headline sums up a trend in the 1930s: "Gloom Spreads Like Hurricane Among Mothers at Wretched Taste of Coney Judges."[53]

Health concerns developed as well. The publisher of *Parents Magazine*, George J. Hecht, declared in 1930 that baby parades "subjected babies and children to physical dangers and unwholesome mental and spiritual reactions," though he did not specify what those were.[54] Hecht argued that baby parades should be replaced by Better Baby contests, which were focused on establishing science-based standards regarding babies' growth and development rather than how they looked.

While many Better Baby contests were over by the end of World War I—especially after the 1918 influenza pandemic—a few stayed on, and new ones popped up.[55] For example, Indiana built a Better Babies Building at its state fair in 1920, where it put on annual contests through 1935. The first Indiana event attracted seventy-eight babies, and ten years later the number had grown to 1,301 entrants.[56] Though Better Baby contests were meant to promote health, such large crowds, crammed into smaller spaces like a building at a state fair, did not necessarily lead to orderliness and cleanliness. With the advent of World War II, links—sometimes implicit and sometimes explicit—between Better Baby contests and the eugenics movement made many uncomfortable. This was especially true when it came to the "improvement" of immigrant (sometimes Jewish) children in the wake of news of the Holocaust.[57]

In the end it was health concerns that hastened the end of both baby parades and Better Baby contests. The last annual Asbury Park baby parade, for example, was held in 1949. While it was a huge success with over one thousand children participating,[58] a polio outbreak meant no parade was held in 1950, and the hiatus lasted longer than anyone anticipated—until 1973.[59] At roughly the same time, Iowa's Better Baby contest—one of the earliest states to adopt the events, in 1911—ended in 1952.[60]

Virtual baby contests continued during the polio scare, as they did not face the health risks that large in-person events presented. Groups who were barred from participating in some events, mainly on the basis of race, like black mothers, organized their own contests. For example, in the 1920s the NAACP used pictorial baby contests to fundraise via their national magazine, *The Crisis.* In addition to magazines, African American churches and settlement homes ran their own black baby shows in the 1910s to arouse "race pride."[61] Famed journalist Ida B. Wells judged a black baby show at the Clotee Scott Settlement in Chicago.

These contests—both virtual and in real life—continued to focus on the mother along with the child. And mothers, riding the wave of the successful campaign for women's suffrage, started to organize themselves. For example, the modern form of today's National Parent Teacher Association, more commonly known as the PTA, was born in 1924.[62] In addition to issues of education, women also organized and advocated for issues related to children's health. So, while women were much more engaged in public life, the ways in which they engaged were still gendered and rooted in conservative ideas about women's "work" and areas of expertise—namely, the domestic sphere.

Another group of organizations that promoted orderliness, femininity, and competition for their girls developed contemporaneously: the scouts. A product of the Progressive Era, the first scouting organization in the United States came to boys, in 1910. Organizations for girls quickly followed. Camp Fire Girls began in 1912, followed by the Girl Scouts in 1917—both squarely in the time of suffrage and rising feminism. The Girl Scouts, the organization that would ultimately prevail of the two, brought together many strands of the Woman Movement in the quest to standardize the health of the girl while also educating her (yes, on homecraft, but in other areas as well). Both the Boy Scouts and the Girl Scouts focused on community service and outdoor activities, but each was run exclusively by the same sex, which led to different signature programs. For example, only Girl Scouts sold cookies, associated more with femininity and the domestic sphere, a fundraising scheme that began in 1917.

Pageants were a part of the mix as Girl Scout camps in the 1930s staged their own historical pageants.[63] And, of course, like both the parading suffragists and the beauty contest winners, Girl Scouts also made use of sashes in their uniforms, but they did so to display patches earned in specific activities. While the sash became a regular part of the uniform a bit later in time, it undeniably connects the simultaneously conservative and progressive Girl Scouts to a long history of women's organizing efforts.[64]

The All-America Baby and Juvenile Review remained a part of the Miss America pageant week through at least 1941, when it was included in the official program for the week's post–Labor Day festivities. The Boy Scouts were a key part of the event, held a day before Miss America was crowned. They helped lead the parade that culminated in the selection of both a baby and a Junior Miss America (age five to ten). Scouting and pageantry were publicly linked through this Miss America youth parade, even as Miss America underwent its most momentous change—one that would influence the image of American womanhood in serious ways.

THE "NEW" MISS AMERICA (AKA LENORA SLAUGHTER)

With Miss America on an indefinite hiatus beginning in 1928, and the Great Depression settling in, a variety of smaller communities in the 1930s decided to hold beauty pageants. College campuses were one site where pageants had grown in popularity during the 1920s, which continued for the next several decades. Campus pageants took many forms in different locales, but included homecoming, prom, fraternity, and even academic department queens. These pageants were common at historically black colleges and universities, which offered young women of color opportunities to wear a crown.[65]

Rural communities, especially in the South, developed crop (also known as commodity) pageants, often corresponding to festivals. The most common crop pageants were for tobacco and cotton. Danville, Virginia, hosted one of the first tobacco queen contests in 1934.[66] Throughout the 1930s and 1940s young women in states such as North Carolina, South Carolina, and Tennessee vied for titles like Queen of the Smoke Flower and Golden Weed while fashioning elaborate outfits out of tobacco leaves. Cotton titles were also common, but one rose above the rest: Maid of Cotton. Each December, beginning in 1939, in advance of the Cotton Bowl, women ages eighteen to twenty-five who had never been married and who hailed from one of the cotton-growing states traveled to Memphis, Tennessee, to vie for the Maid of Cotton title.[67]

Meanwhile at the national level, with Miss America on an extended break, a variety of pretenders tried to lay claim to the title of "top" queen.

In March 1930 the Miami International Beauty Pageant Association crowned Miss Texas "Miss America." But it was an extremely inauspicious start for that pageant, because its winner turned out to be a divorcee, and its first runner-up, Miss California, did not live in the state. In June 1930 the Miami association crowned a new winner, the second runner-up, who was never heard from again.[68] A few months later, in August 1930, Miss New Orleans became Miss United States of America in Galveston, Texas, at the International Pageant of Pulchritude—a title that did not stick around long.[69] Getting closer to the Miss America model we know today, in September 1932 another New Jersey Shore town, Wildwood, held an event for thirty-six area contestants, in which a nineteen-year-old from Camden, New Jersey, was crowned the winner.[70]

A year later, Atlantic City's Miss America made a lukewarm return to bat off these pretenders. But due to lack of funds and fanfare, only thirty contestants tried to become Miss America 1933 in Atlantic City.[71] Instead of being sponsored by newspapers, the contestants were sponsored by amusement parks. Prior to the pageant the parks insisted the contestants go on a seven-week vaudeville tour to cover expenses. As a consequence, the young women arrived in Atlantic City exhausted and tainted by the whiff of impropriety still associated with circuses. After a week of mishaps (including but not limited to forgotten bathing suits, an infected tooth, a case of appendicitis, and the usual verboten marriages and nonresidencies), fifteen-year-old Miss Connecticut, Marion Bergeron, was crowned the winner.[72]

Miss America did not return in 1934.

But when the pageant staged one more comeback, in 1935, it finally stuck. Part of the reason the 1935 pageant went so well was because of the arrival of a young, daring woman. Twenty-nine-year-old Floridian Lenora Slaughter was gifted with a name that reflected her unique blend of fighting femininity. And with her iron-fist-in-a-velvet-glove approach, meant to attract the "right" kind of girl, she would forever change Miss America.

Slaughter was born in Florida, but following a family move she graduated from high school in Newport News, Virginia. Slaughter enrolled at the College of William and Mary in 1926.[73] Before her sophomore year began she was forced to leave school because she could not afford tuition. This experience was formative in young Lenora's life—and one that would ultimately shape the lives of thousands of young American women.[74]

After her year of collegiate study Lenora Slaughter had to do what other young, unmarried women did: work. She found her way back to Florida where she took a job in St. Petersburg for the chamber of commerce. One task of the chamber was to organize the weeklong spring civic celebration, which also marked the end of the winter season in Florida. The event featured a Parade of States, with each state (and sometimes a country, like Canada) providing a float for the parade. To cap it all off, there was also, of course, a festival queen.[75] It became Lenora's job to run that event.

In the early 1930s a local article about the successful Parade of the States got picked up by the Associated Press, and it gave credit to Slaughter for her organizational prowess. As the story goes, in the winter of 1935 John R. Hollinger, an Atlantic City hotel owner, read that article declaring "Lenore [sic] as being the only girl in the country to direct a parade. He asked the St. Petersburg Chamber of Commerce to loan her to Atlantic City and permission was granted. She came to Atlantic City as assistant to pageant director Eddie Corcoran as associate director of pageant specifically to coordinate civic forces here to aid the pageant."[76] A rather hefty $1,000 stipend covered Lenora's six weeks in Atlantic City "on loan" from St. Petersburg (about $19,000 in today's money).[77]

Hiring a woman in this key year of transition was a strategic decision. Women's groups had come down hard on Miss America in the late 1920s for exploiting women in an indecent way, so placing a woman at the helm took some wind out of the detractors' sails. Contracting Slaughter was explicitly about attracting the "right" kind of girl to compete at Miss America. She was meant to find ways to make this popular culture event respectable for the middle class, in much the same way Barnum did for women and popular culture in the nineteenth century.

As soon as Slaughter arrived in Atlantic City, she got to work, making three big changes. First, she brought back the parade—not surprising, given her background. But she got rid of the home-grown rolling chairs in favor of cars, marching bands (which had been popular in Florida), and floats sold to merchants as sponsors.[78] This latter change helped the pageant move toward financial solvency. Second, she introduced an optional talent competition. While only about half the contestants competed, the addition showed that the young women competing were more than just a body in a bathing suit. Finally, Slaughter came up with the idea of chaperoning the contestants. Beginning in 1935, the contestants had to be with their female chaperone from nine in the morning until midnight, to help keep them away from "scandal."[79]

Things went so well at the 1935 pageant, which crowned seventeen-year-old Miss Pittsburgh, Henrietta Leaver, that Slaughter was asked to stay on as associate director. She was offered a salary of $3,000, which was not quite as great a deal as her short-term contract but was still a good amount during the Great Depression.[80] She would end up staying for thirty-two more years, making Miss America her life's work.

For the rest of the 1930s Slaughter continued to push two of her initial initiatives—chaperoning and talent—with the goal of making Miss America more respectable and thereby attracting the "right" kind of contestant. To Slaughter, respectability meant white, middle class, and educated (more on Slaughter's views on race will be addressed in chapter 4). In 1937 she expanded the chaperone concept and formed a hostess committee to welcome contestants. Since many women's clubs were critical of Miss America, saying it degraded American women, Slaughter decided to "out-women's club the women's clubs."[81] When she created the Hostess Committee, she drew from the ranks of many of those clubs comprising Atlantic City's Quaker elite. Moreover, Slaughter continued to institute restrictions on what the contestants could and could not do during the week of competition. Miss America 1937, Bette Cooper of New Jersey, literally flew the coop post-crowning, disappearing overnight with her escort. Slaughter consequently banned all contestants from nightclubs and bars and ruled that contestants could not be seen talking to any men—including their fathers and brothers—during pageant week.[82]

In 1938, partly in continued reaction to the Cooper scandal, Slaughter made the talent competition mandatory. This further legitimized Miss America as a public event for respectable females by making it a showcase for amateur, aspiring talent.[83] This helped lessen complaints about objectification. The talent competition showed what women could do with their bodies, as opposed to just being bodies for display or reproduction. Yes, it was still about the body performing (most successful talents were related to the performing arts), but it was still a step away from earlier iterations of the pageant when the measurements of women's body parts were the primary details reported in the press.[84]

That year Slaughter convinced Vyvyan Donner, a Hollywood director of fashion news features, to do a segment on the pageant, which made its way into Movietone News, the newsreels that ran before feature films.[85] An estimated 112 million moviegoers saw the tap-dancing, twenty-one-year-old Miss Ohio, Marilyn Meseke, crowned Miss America 1938. Interest surged and the pageant finally found itself on firm financial footing.

The changes Lenora Slaughter instituted in the 1930s played a big part in establishing Miss America as a civic event filled with respectable young women who could serve as role models. Slaughter's leadership helped the pageant become extremely popular across the country. It also explains the rise of girls who competed to be Little Miss America and Little Miss Atlantic City at baby parades, many of whom aspired to become Miss America themselves one day.[86]

But those same changes also show the push and pull of womanhood post-suffrage. Lenora Slaughter was brought in to lead, but a man was still the executive director. Women were judged in part on their talent but still largely on their (bathing-suited) bodies. They could present themselves and compete in public, but their bodies were heavily policed by chaperones and hostesses who surveilled almost all their actions.

THE TRANSFORMATIVE TEA

The 1940s did not resolve this tension as the pageant continued to grow. During this decade many lasting traditions were established, along with the imposition of even more structure and rules. In 1940 the pageant made its move from the Steel Pier to Convention Hall on the Boardwalk in Atlantic City.[87] It also officially became a nonprofit civic corporation, with eighteen male business leaders on its board.[88] The not-for-profit status helped lessen earlier complaints about commercialization of women's bodies—since currency was not explicitly involved—but men were clearly still in charge. Finally, the official Miss America sorority, Mu Alpha Sigma (with M standing for modesty, A for achievement, and S for success), also began in 1940.

In the wake of such success Lenora Slaughter was promoted to executive director of the Miss America Pageant in 1942.[89] While there was still a male president and chair, Slaughter ran the day-to-day operations. In the 2002 PBS *American Experience* episode on Miss America, Ric Ferentz, considered a historian of the Miss America Organization, described Lenora Slaughter as "a woman that was well ahead of her time. She was tough when she had to be. But knew how to get by on a Southern drawl."[90] When a pageant judge asked Slaughter what she would like to see in a winner, Lenora reportedly replied, "Honey, just pick me a lady."

The number of contestants grew in the 1940s. Those women now had to be between the ages of eighteen and twenty-eight, to represent a geographical place not a festival or carnival, and to declare they had never been married.[91] Interest in Miss America exploded during World War II, when it became a symbol of patriotism to participate in Miss America. Though the federal government shut down most public events during the war, Slaughter convinced public officials that the pageant must continue, explaining, "Miss America is emblematic of the nation's spirit and that spirit [continues] through war and peace, good times and bad."[92] While the parade was canceled in the war years to conserve materials needed for the war effort, like gas and rubber, the government said the pageant could continue so long as Miss America sold war bonds.

And sell she did. Miss America 1943, Jean Bartel, from California, sold more Series E bonds than anyone else that year—$2.5 million worth (more than $35 million today). Bartel mainly sold in increments of $25 and $50, but a few were larger (including one man in Hot Springs, Arkansas, who supposedly bought $5,000 worth of bonds in exchange for her stockings).[93]

Significantly, Bartel was the first Miss America to attend college. From 1941 to 1942 she was a music student at the University of California, Los Angeles.[94] While there, she pledged Kappa Kappa Gamma, which soon would become especially significant. Between Bartel's September crowning until just after Christmas, she toured twenty-four states on behalf of the War Finance Committee. Slaughter was Bartel's near-constant travel companion. That November they were in Minneapolis selling war bonds near the University of Minnesota when Bartel met some of her sorority sisters at an event and they invited her over for afternoon tea.[95] It was over Earl Grey that the game-changing idea to award Miss America a college scholarship came about.

Bartel and Slaughter have told different public stories over the years about who exactly came up with the idea for the scholarship. In one account it was Bartel herself, in another it was Slaughter,[96] and in another altogether Lenora Slaughter declared, "The scholarship idea actually came from those kids, from the student council of the University of Minnesota in 1943. I don't know any of the names, but I remember that an ugly little girl with spectacles was the head of it,"[97] showing that a "non-beauty" could be involved in pageants. (Based on her negative description of the young Minnesotan's looks, it is clear that Slaughter noticed and valued physical appearance, but she was still eager to include education as a priority of the Miss America Pageant.) Whatever the true story, both Bartel and Slaughter agree it was that afternoon tea with the Minnesota Kappa Kappa Gammas that gave birth to the notion that Miss America should be a co-ed rewarded with money to continue her education.

While that tea may have been the public impetus, encouraging educational achievement was something Slaughter had been thinking about since she was forced to leave college in 1927 due to a lack of money. In a 1946 *Redbook* article about the introduction of brains *with* beauty at Miss America, Slaughter revealed that part of the reason she left school to work was to put a relative through college, so she "vowed that some day she would be rich and establish a means for talented girls who wanted higher educations to get them."[98] Now she had to convince the board of directors of the Miss America Pageant.

After another successful Miss America Pageant in September 1944, where Miss District of Columbia, Venus Ramey, was crowned, Slaughter got to work. On November 10, 1944, she submitted a six-page, single-spaced, typed letter to the board. The letter, addressed, of course, to "Gentlemen," urges them to "carefully read this report, and then discuss my recommendations regarding Miss America not with other men, but with your own daughters, or other young women of similar social and intellectual status, to arrive at an opinion which affects American girls." All the male board members appear to have been white and financially well-off, attributes that shaped their worldviews on how a successful and proper young woman should appear and act in public.

Slaughter's letter goes on to identify two major problems that she believed needed to be addressed now that the pageant was on solid financial ground with strong local support. She defines them as, in all caps: "1) BETTER LOCAL CONTESTS THROUGHOUT THE NATION 2) BETTER DISPOSITION OF MISS AMERICA AFTER SHE IS SELECTED." Of course, Slaughter explains in the letter, these two problems are linked. If a young woman knows what she can attain by winning Miss America—including but not limited to a college scholarship—more women will want to become contestants at the local level. More local contestants would then bring in better sponsors, who could reach a larger audience, which in turn would continue to attract more local contestants, and on.

To address the first problem, Slaughter proposed officially affiliating state and local pageants with junior chambers of commerce. This was another nonprofit organization, also known as the Jaycees, formed at roughly the same time as Miss America (though in St. Louis in 1920). Members in the 1940s were white men between the ages of eighteen and thirty-five with an interest in civic leadership. The Jaycees often partnered with other volunteer organizations, and in many communities local Jaycees chose to sponsor preliminary competitions to Miss America.

Slaughter thought the Jaycees to be "our finest type of sponsor," presumably because they were men with business and community connections who could afford to run local and state pageants, bringing some measure of her desired respectability to each event. She was not specific about why she admired them so much that she proposed formalizing a relationship with them. Given that Miss America was a program only for young women, it is noteworthy that Slaughter does not mention any women's organizations as possible sponsorship partners in her 1944 letter.

Slaughter does have quite a lot to say about young women, though. In the letter to the board she wrote, "Higher education has not yet been made available to the average American girl, and yet it can certainly play an influential part in her life. If the Miss America Pageant lent its good influence to equipping one girl each year to achieving her goal, the nation would soon learn to respect us and be more willing to support us." Her proposal, to interest "the finest type of American girls," was for Miss America to be awarded a $5,000 scholarship to a college, university, conservatory of music, or dancing or dramatic school. On that note, Slaughter finally mentions female leaders, suggesting that a scholarship board be appointed, "composed of perhaps five local women, preferably university women, and the Chairman of the Hostess Committee."

While Slaughter wanted to attract the "right" kind of contestants, who were, naturally, ambitious, she is careful in how she portrays them to the all-male board. She wrote in the proposal, "I sincerely believe the average young American girl has two primary ambitions by the time she is 18. The first is a happy and successful marriage. The second is proper education to develop whatever talents she might possess. The second ambition will certainly better equip her to attain the first ambition." This practice of promoting achievement but still pushing women to marriage is part of what drove Betty Friedan a generation later to pen *The Feminine Mystique*—but perhaps most interesting of all, when Slaughter wrote those words she was a thirty-eight-year-old single woman. To be palatable to men, the idea of an educated woman had to be couched in terms of marriage, especially if it was being suggested by an accomplished single woman.

In her final pitch, Lenora Slaughter articulated her vision for the future of Miss America: "In five years, think what a reputation the Miss America Pageant could build in the schools of this country. Girls would no longer look upon the Pageant as a beauty contest, but would respect the title for its genuine value to them and its rating in the nation." At its next meeting, on December 20, 1944, the board approved Slaughter's plan.

Over the next several months Lenora Slaughter handwrote hundreds of letters to potential sponsors, hoping to get five companies to cover $1,000 each. To do so she approached over two hundred companies before she finally had her $5,000, so, clearly, pageant naysayers remained. On March 29, 1945, Slaughter happily reported to the board that she had secured the necessary funds, though not everyone in the organization was as enthusiastic as she was. In the 1946 *Redbook* article she reveals that Miss America's publicity men asked, "How're you gonna get the papers to run pictures of an I.Q.?"[99]

But word spread that brains were now highly valued at Miss America. This occurred during a time when women had entered the workforce in ways never before seen during World War II, so women being outside the private sphere was a notion being (briefly) embraced. In the 1945 pageant twenty of the forty-three contestants were college students, and six had already graduated, so over 60 percent were considered co-eds.

One of those graduates, Miss New York, Bess Myerson, was crowned the winner. In the official program book Myerson the contestant appears with three other contestants. Those women—Miss Birmingham, Miss Texas, and Miss North Carolina—all are pictured in pinup type poses. But the top prize went to the covered-up contestant in her mortarboard. The time was right to be smart at Miss America.

Bess Myerson, Miss New York City and recent graduate of Hunter College, was a first in several ways—she was the first Miss America to be a college graduate, the first to receive a scholarship, and the first (and as of 2020 still the only) Jewish Miss America. Myerson had her own take on what Slaughter did for the pageant: "She picked up the pageant by its bathing suit straps and put it in an evening gown."[100] The preferred gown remained full and sparkly, not academic and black.

By the end of the decade the pageant stopped referring to "bathing suits" altogether, instead calling them "swimsuits." Catalina, the swimsuit company founded in 1907, became a Miss America sponsor in the 1940s.[101] In 1946, the story goes, Slaughter heard Catalina president E. B. Stewart roar, "It's not a bathing suit, dammit. You bathe in a tub. You swim in a swimsuit."[102] Slaughter was sold, because she remained committed to making things as respectable as possible for "her girls." She briefly allowed two-piece swimsuits in competition, but only from 1947 to 1949.

In 1947 the pageant also added a formal interview element to the competition. Though the interviews were not one on one—they were group interviews over breakfast with rotating judges—they put a bigger focus on the brains element than before.[103] This was a feminist transformation given that the event promoted education at a time when not many women were attending college—especially as women were being pushed back into their homes after working during the war effort. In 1940 about 5 percent of eligible women had completed a four-year college degree. Women were now speaking instead of being silenced, like earlier in the century, on runways big and small.[104]

The following year, 1948, was a big one for Lenora Slaughter personally. That August she married Bradford H. Frapart.[105] Frapart, a Tennessee native, was the business manager of the Miss America Pageant, further emphasizing the central role that Miss America played in Lenora's life. She married at forty-two and never had children, but always referred to each of the Miss Americas, both publicly and in private correspondence, as "my girls."

For nearly two decades Miss Slaughter (as she continued to be called, even after her marriage) worked to construct the ideal American woman, a woman with brains, looks, talent, and ambition. This was during a decade when women were not encouraged to pursue higher education but rather to do what they could for their country, mainly from the confines of the domestic sphere. If Miss America had started the year after suffrage to silence women as they entered the public sphere, Slaughter helped give them their voices back several decades before that became mainstream for American women—although Slaughter had specific ideas about what that ideal American woman should look like (spoiler alert): able-bodied and white.

Winners who embodied this new, vocal Miss America ideal could still expect a degree of privacy, as most Miss Americas were not recognized as they walked down the street. With the arrival of television in the 1950s that was about to change for many beauty queens.[106]

HERE COMES A COMPETITOR: THE BIRTH OF MISS USA

The decade of the 1950s started off with a bang for Miss America—and set the stage for the introduction of its biggest rival. The first change was relatively minor, but it makes the history of Miss America more confusing than it has to be. In 1950 the pageant introduced "postdating" of the crown, which means that the winner named in September of a given year is crowned the Miss America for the following year. When you look at a list of Miss Americas you will notice it jumps from Miss America 1949, Jacque Mercer of Arizona, to Miss America 1951, Yolande Betbeze of Alabama. The pageant did *not* skip 1950—Betbeze was crowned in September 1950—but Miss America organizers wanted it to be clear that the year referred to the time when the majority of the queen's reign took place.

Betbeze's reign was a catalyst for a major change in the pageant landscape: the Miss USA/Miss Universe Pageant. The morning after she won, the Alabamian declared that she would not appear in a bathing suit at appearances during her year as Miss America. She said, "I'm a singer, not a pinup."[107]

On the one hand, this was not shocking as this was clearly the direction the pageant was moving in under the aegis of Lenora Slaughter.

Miss America 1943, Jean Bartel, the scholarship suggester, had also said she would not wear a swimsuit during her year. The last Miss America to be crowned in a bathing suit was Miss America 1947, Barbara Jo Walker of Tennessee.

On the other hand, Catalina, the swimsuit company, was a pageant sponsor by 1950. Obviously, they were not pleased.

No one has written an extensive history of Miss USA, so the history presented here is based on a collection of Miss USA/Miss Universe program books, newspaper coverage (especially of the original Long Beach contests in the 1950s), and selected secondary sources. In reflecting on the start of Miss USA, Betbeze later recalled, as detailed in a 2016 obituary, "a man representing Catalina stood up and fumed [after she announced she would not appear in a swimsuit]. He looked at me and said, 'I'll run you off the news pages. I'll start my own contest. You'll see.' I said, 'That's splendid. Good luck to you.' . . . Anyway, he did indeed start the Miss USA and Miss Universe pageant. So people can thank me—or blame me—for that."[108]

Slaughter was pleased with Betbeze's declaration, as she wanted to continue to move the pageant further from its swimsuit roots, the area subject to the most public criticism.[109] When it came to criticizing the physicality (and hence sexuality) associated with Miss America, even the Roman Catholic Church got in on the action. They instituted a ban, which continued into the 1960s, on female congregants competing in the bathing suit contest—including denying the offending queen's family members the sacraments.[110] It made sense for Betbeze, who competed in the Miss America Pageant shortly after leaving a Catholic convent school, to make such a public stand regarding not appearing in a swimsuit as Miss America.

Slaughter was less pleased when she found out that her outgoing queen, Jacque Mercer, had spent time with Catalina president E. W. Stewart and encouraged him to start that new pageant. Apparently, Mercer even suggested a name: Miss United Nations.[111] Stewart, along with Catalina Swimwear and its mother company Pacific Knitting Mills, acted quickly to start a rival to Miss America. And by the time their first, new contest was held in Long Beach, California, on June 27, 1952, they had also convinced Miss America 1941, Rosemary LaPlanche, to crown the winner.[112]

The location of the first Miss USA Pageant—Long Beach, California—was very deliberate. The West Coast location for the new Miss Universe Beauty Pageant, Inc., was meant to provide a Pacific Ocean alternative to the strong links between the Jersey Shore and Miss America.[113] Like Atlantic City, Long Beach had endured local debate over just how covered up a woman should be in a bathing suit. In 1920 the city passed a regulation that "adult swimwear must, among other things, 'completely conceal from view each leg from the hip joint to a line around the leg one-third of the way to the knee.'"[114] The rule was soon repealed (over the objections of local clergymen who pleaded that Long Beach not "abandon the traditional standards of civic righteousness"), paving the way for Long Beach's first "bathing beauty parade."[115]

About 350 young women participated in the Long Beach Amusement League's beauty parade and contest on August 9, 1925. Despite the strong initial numbers, the West Coast town just could not compete with the activities of its East Coast counterpart in Atlantic City. The beauty parade and contest in Long Beach were short-lived.

But Betbeze's stand at Miss America changed things for the future of West Coast pageantry. When Catalina went out to bid for host cities for Miss USA/Miss Universe, Long Beach readily agreed to pay a $30,000 fee to host the "glamour tournament" and put itself on the map. An October 20, 1951, *Long Beach Independent* article explained, "It will be an annual event that can make this city the Atlantic City of the West and will bring thousands of tourists here the year round."[116] Pan-Am airlines became a pageant sponsor, getting all the contestants to the West Coast city.

Miss New York, twenty-two-year-old Jacqueline Loughery, bested forty-two contestants to be crowned the first Miss USA.[117] One day later she appeared before the same panel of eight men and two women, most of whom worked in Hollywood and some of whom hailed from outside the United States, to compete in the first-ever Miss Universe contest. Along with contestants from twenty-eight countries, Loughery wanted to be named the "most beautiful girl in the world," though she finished in ninth and Miss Finland won the title.[118] Connecting the two pageants—Miss USA and Miss Universe—was a smart business move for the newly formed Miss Universe organization. It helped distinguish between Miss America and Miss USA, adding a layer of glamour and prestige to the upstart Miss USA Pageant.[119]

The Miss USA/Miss Universe contestants, and winners, showed off their bathing suits. Even in the program book, most contestants were pictured in their suits, many like pinup girls. This was a contrast to head-shots that appeared in the Miss America programs, especially when it came to contestants like Bess Myerson who chose to be depicted in their college graduation regalia. The unabashed embrace of being a bathing beauty contest, combined with an international flair, along with strong local financial support, made Miss USA/Miss Universe a success from the start.

Miss USA borrowed some of the most successful elements of early pageantry. In the 1954 program book then mayor of Long Beach George M. Vermillion declared that the pageant was the "Greatest Show on Earth," using a phrase made famous by the earliest US pageant inno-vator, P. T. Barnum. Long Beach also included popular Atlantic City features—namely, the parade (which boasted one million spectators in 1953) and the hostessing program, to help ensure the contestants stayed "safe."[120] They even borrowed TV presenter Bob Russell, who served as the emcee the first five years of Miss USA (Russell emceed nearly every Miss America Pageant in the 1940s).

It is unclear how many contestants from the 1950s competed in both Miss America and Miss USA at the state level. But even winners were not always immediately clear on the distinctions between the two pro-grams. Terry Huntingdon, Miss USA 1959, was recruited when she was a student at UCLA (she represented California). She wrote in her 2013 memoir that she was surprised when she arrived at the Miss California event and discovered there was no talent competition.[121] The inclusion of talent and scholarships at Miss America, and not at Miss USA, would remain the biggest difference between the two pageants until 2018. One minor difference was that for its first eight years Miss USA was not al-ways held at the same time of the year, like Miss America (the first week-end after Labor Day). Miss USA started in June, then bounced around to different weekends in July.

While Miss Universe did not have a major pageant to define itself in opposition to, like Miss America and Miss USA, it did have a few com-petitors. Miss World was one. Miss World started in 1951 in the United Kingdom, one year before Miss Universe. It began first as a bikini contest, but after one year, bikinis were banned in favor of one-piece swimsuits to make the event more respectable. Twenty-eight women competed the first year, and the event continued to grow. An appealing part of Miss World was that it was all for charity, unlike Miss Universe, which was primarily associated with the for-profit company Catalina.[122]

Another rival was Miss Europe, which began in 1948. Miss Europe, which first welcomed seventeen national competitors to the Festival of Elegance and Beauty, was the first post–World War II international beauty contest on the continent.[123] In December 1954 organizers from Miss Universe and Miss Europe reached an agreement that each country would send one representative to both pageants, helping to eliminate confusion over who was the "real" Miss France, Miss Italy, and so on to send to the United States to compete for the title of Miss Universe.

READY FOR PRIME-TIME CROWNING

The success of Miss USA/Miss Universe in the United States, and beyond, influenced the decision Lenora Slaughter and other Miss America leaders made about televising the Miss America Pageant. According to an internal publicity report in 1954, "There was at least a 20% increase in world-wide newspaper publicity on the recent Miss Universe Beauty Pageant over the previous year. This would bring the total *world-wide* newspaper lineage to approximately seventeen million lines. This publicity has definitely put the Miss Universe Beauty Pageant on a par with the Olympic Games, which is the only other event receiving that much world-wide newspaper publicity."[124]

If Miss USA/Miss Universe garnered the most newspaper coverage, Miss America would simply have to take to the airwaves. It was the Golden Age of Television, and live programs were a huge draw. Given the popularity of Miss America it is no surprise that television executives wanted to get it on air.

ABC made a serious offer in 1953, but balked when Miss America executives insisted on a media blackout for Philadelphia and neighboring communities. Slaughter and others thought that the TV broadcast would negatively affect in-person audience size. The pageant depended on ticket revenue to support production costs, so no blackout meant a live televised pageant was a no-go.[125]

But three things changed in 1954. First, Miss USA was continuing to gather steam. Second, so many Americans had TV sets (an estimated one thousand for every twenty-six thousand homes) that a TV broadcast began to seem as inevitable as radio and movie reel coverage.[126] Third, ABC offered to pay $10,000 for the broadcast rights, which would more than make up for any lost ticket sales. This led to an additional $12,500 from corporate sponsors.[127]

On September 11, 1954, with eighteen thousand audience members packed into Convention Hall, the first televised Miss America Pageant aired. ABC went live at 10:30 p.m., showing the last three talents, the naming of the five finalists, and the announcement—by Bob Russell— that Miss California, nineteen-year-old Lee Meriwether, was Miss America 1955.[128] While in-person attendees were annoyed that only those at home saw the announcement live (Meriwether was announced the winner backstage before coming out to walk the long runway), at-home viewers were thrilled. The first televised Miss America was a hit, earning 39 percent share of the TV audience.[129]

The next year, 1955, brought two changes to the telecast. Per feedback, the winner was announced onstage and in front of the cameras simultaneously. The person who announced Miss Colorado, Sharon Ritchie, as the winner was Bert Parks, a television personality who would become synonymous with Miss America. Parks had been a television game show host since the 1940s, and he had hosted an eponymous variety show. He was a natural fit for Miss America after the previous emcee, Bob Russell, deepened his involvement with Miss USA/Miss Universe. Parks serenaded winner Ritchie, as she walked on air down the runway, with the song that would soon enter the pop-culture lexicon, "There She Is."

ABC began broadcasting Miss USA in 1955, continuing the nascent rivalry. Miss USA may have been a bit behind, but she was definitely nipping at Miss America's high heels.

Within a few years, with television ratings continuing to rise (for both pageants), CBS made a play. In 1957 CBS started airing Miss America, and it did so well that the network extended the length of the broadcast to two hours in 1958.[130] By 1960 CBS was also airing Miss USA/ Miss Universe, which had just moved to Miami.[131] In 1965 Miss USA and Miss Universe began to air as two distinct events, with months between them.[132]

On CBS, Miss America reigned supreme. Slaughter and Albert Marks—who served as chairman and executive producer of the Miss

America Pageant for twenty-five years, negotiating television contracts with ease—were no longer concerned about dwindling in-person attendance.[133] Television proved lucrative to Miss America, with the contracts funding larger scholarships. The relationship between the networks and Miss America was mutually beneficial; the national broadcast garnered a whopping 72 percent of the viewing audience in 1960 and 75 percent in 1961.[134]

QUEENS ACROSS AMERICA

With Miss America at its zenith, Miss USA made a big change in 1960: it left Long Beach. This ultimately was a business decision by Catalina. Catalina thought that Long Beach should be paying a higher hosting fee, given the publicity it received in the media, but the city was not interested in spending more. Long Beach was partly reacting to rising, outside conservative pressure. Many countries were becoming more vocal about female modesty and refusing to send delegates to Long Beach.[135] It did not help that the 1957 Miss USA turned out to be a Mrs.[136] The combination of these two factors took Miss USA/Miss Universe to Miami, Florida, for the next eleven years.

Long Beach was not ready to give up its identity as hosting an international beauty pageant each summer. In August 1960 it started a new event, the International Beauty Congress, which would crown a Miss International. In its first year, fifty-three contestants from around the world came to Long Beach. Nearly everything was the same as in the Miss Universe days, save for one major difference: the swimsuits were gone. NBC aired Miss International in 1964, but interest never rivaled Miss USA (perhaps because of those missing swimsuits). Due to a shortage of funds, no pageant was held in 1966, and though it reemerged in 1967, the pageant folded in Long Beach the following year. As one journalist explained, "Long Beach had stayed too long at the ball. . . . The world had changed with the times: the Kennedy assassination, the feminist movement, the Vietnam war, and Long Beach would change also."[137] While Miss International is still held today, with its headquarters in Japan, Long Beach has since stayed out of the pageant game.[138]

Given the popularity of pageants in the 1950s it is not surprising that other long-running pageants began at the same time. The Jaycees, whom Slaughter had singled out in her 1944 scholarship letter to the board, started two national beauty pageants that continue to this day, Miss National Sweetheart and America's Junior Miss (now known as Distinguished Young Woman of America). In 1952, the same year as the first Miss USA, the first National Sweetheart was crowned in Hoopeston, Illinois. The pageant was part of the National Sweetcorn Festival, which had been organized by local businessmen to promote their important (and delicious) crop in 1938. After World War II, the local Jaycees began sponsoring the festival, which featured a Miss Sweetcorn.

National Sweetheart is significant for two reasons. First, it symbolizes the local, and often rural, festival tradition of beauty pageants. Away from the TV glitz and glamour of the coastal pageants like Miss America and Miss USA, festival pageants are the first exposure and experience many participants and spectators have with pageantry. Sometimes these festival pageants are preliminaries for a state or national pageant, and sometimes they stand alone as major events in a local area.

In the early 1950s, in an effort to increase the stature of the National Sweetcorn Festival, the local Jaycees got the idea to invite the first runners-up from both the state and the major city Miss America competitions. It was an idea that benefitted everyone: the almost-winners got a chance to hone their pageant skills (the competition was modeled directly after the Miss America competition), while being treated like celebrities at the Sweetcorn Festival, and the Hoopeston event had a group of qualified contestants who would bring national press attention to rural Illinois.[139] In short order, competing at Sweetheart became an honor, and for many an important stopping point on the way to successfully competing in Atlantic City. Not coincidentally, Sweetheart is held over Labor Day weekend, the weekend before Miss America is traditionally held. The start of the National Sweetheart Pageant embodied and reinforced the strong links between the Jaycees, small towns, and Miss America.

The Jaycees played a similar role in Mobile, Alabama, in the 1950s with what began as the America's Junior Miss pageant. Like Sweetheart, the pageant had roots in an earlier local festival. In the 1920s the newly formed Mobile Junior Chamber of Commerce wanted to draw attention to the azalea flowers that grow on the Gulf Coast. This led to the development of the Mobile Azalea Trail, where each spring area debutantes would serve as hostesses along the trail.[140] The Mobile Jaycees grew what was originally "a local beautification project into one of the nation's best-known floral extravaganzas."[141]

Then, they went further. In 1949 the first Azalea Trail court was named, made up of two senior girls from the four area high schools who were called Azalea Trail Maids. These local girls were rewarded with college scholarships by the Mobile Jaycees.

When the Azalea Trail Festival (or "Azalearama") was born two years later, pageantry played a key role. The reigning Miss America served as Queen of the Azalea Trail among the Maids, who themselves were increasingly Southern girls, and not just from the Mobile area. Contestants were coming from all around Alabama and neighboring states as word about the availability of college scholarship money spread.

As regional interest grew in the Azalea Trail Festival, the Mobile Jaycees realized they had an opportunity to expand their program. In 1958 they introduced a whole new competition affiliated with the Azalea Trail Festival: America's Junior Miss. It was born out of the desire to reward high school senior girls, from anywhere, seeking higher education. Eleven Mobile businesses underwrote the cost of the first pageant that March, and eighteen states sent "their ideal high school senior girl" based on the "man-to-man" recruiting that went on between Jaycees in different cities and states (the Jaycees did not go co-ed until the 1980s). That first year a very out-of-town contestant representing West Virginia won a $5,000 scholarship award—and one of her judges was Miss America 1954, Evelyn Ay.[142] Though the senior high girls did not compete in swimsuits and instead performed a fitness routine onstage, all other major phases of the competition were taken from Miss America.

By 1961 girls from all fifty states were represented. In 1965 the Junior Miss pageant was televised on NBC—and in color (though all the high schoolers wore white dresses, reminiscent of debutante balls and weddings).[143] By that point the event was the largest scholarship program of its kind for high school girls. The 1963 winner, a young woman from Kentucky by the name of Diane Sawyer, would soon help show just how successful an America's Junior Miss could be by becoming an award-winning journalist.

While national pageants, aided by television, were popular and growing during this time, the history of events like Sweetheart and America's Junior Miss show that pageants were fundamentally rooted in local communities. Many of those pageants, especially festival pageants, were intensely followed and coveted by locals, making them competitive annual civic events.

Miss Subways was another local pageant with an avid resident fan base that is often overlooked. Unlike the small town and rural festival pageants, Miss Subways was as urban as they come, as it was a contest meant to cover all New York City's boroughs. But unlike in Mobile and Hoopeston (and even Atlantic City and Long Beach), the Miss Subways competitors did not have to wear a swimsuit to win the title. They also did not have to do anything musical. In fact, they did not even have to present themselves physically in public to win. This was a true photo beauty contest, harkening back to the days of Barnum's first beauty contest, started nearly one hundred years before.

Miss Subways began in May 1941, a few months before the United States entered World War II. Like all the twentieth-century pageants described, Miss Subways was the brainchild of men, in this case two legendary American men: the advertising agency executive J. Walter Thompson and the modeling agency executive John Robert Powers. The idea was that the image of the new, beautiful "career girl" would beautify the subway cars and bring attention to other advertisers' posters nearby.[144] Young women (or, in some cases, their friends and family) submitted a photograph and a brief biography. Powers himself often picked the winner each month, the woman whom he found most photogenic. The first Miss Subways was a fourteen-year-old girl who lived in Westchester—and who had never before ridden the subway—named Mona Freeman.[145]

Ultimately, over two hundred women were awarded the title of Miss Subways, one per month throughout the 1940s, switching to a winner every two months beginning in the 1950s. Given the population base and the cultural importance of New York City within the United States, Miss Subways mattered. Within a decade the winners were reflecting the diversity of the city. Thelma Porter was referred to as the "Jackie Robinson of the subway" when she was the first black woman to win the title in 1948.[146] The 1950s saw Asian and Latina winners—decades before many of the major beauty contests had a nonwhite winner. Some Miss Subways mentioned Miss America, along with airline stewardess dreams, as aspirational and inspirational, very much situating the contest in the beauty context of its time. Of course, almost all also mentioned as a priority their desires to become wives and mothers.

The proliferation of local pageants, like Miss Subways, was everywhere in the decades following the suffrage victory and the start of Miss America. Some local festivals added more queens, like the addition of Miss Fiesta in 1950, for college students in San Antonio, as part of the Order of the Alamo Coronation.[147] College campuses also added more pageants. For example, in 1956 the University of Connecticut added not one, not two, but three new campus queen contests, crowning Miss Fashion Plate, Miss Dairy Queen, and Queen of the Arnold Air Society.[148] Even high schools got in on the act.[149]

Pageant expansion was not always tied to a locality or specific festival but sometimes to a group. Mrs. pageants began in the late 1930s and a national child beauty pageant, Our Little Miss, began in 1962.[150] Sometimes beauty contests popped up in unexpected places—like the 1932 contest at the Amateur Athletic Union's women's basketball national tournament featuring a "parade of basketball beauties."[151] Thanks to the model of Miss America seen on newsreels and then on television, followed by Miss USA and similar contests like America's Junior Miss, beauty pageants were seemingly everywhere by the 1960s. Pageant culture and its accompanying beauty culture were deeply embedded in the feminine psyche by the end of the 1950s at the trough of First Wave feminism.

THE PAGEANT MYSTIQUE

The 1950s have a specific cultural reputation. Some consider it an idyllic time—a time of suburbs, intact families, neighborhoods where children could play freely. For many white women it was a time where they were perceived to rule their homes and children's schools with a feminine ease and authority. Private life was still a focus, even for those who ventured into the public sphere—just like Lenora Slaughter reassured her all-male board it would be when she proposed college scholarships for Miss America contestants. Women simply did not have many opportunities to distinguish themselves outside the domestic realm, and it was difficult to pursue and fund an education without family support. While women appeared in public more by themselves in this time than ever before, thanks to suffragists and others who fought for that space, their public presence was not often based on education or achievement but rather on feminine appearance.

Fittingly the Barbie doll was born at the end of the 1950s, and it was seen by many as *the* symbol of female oppression. With her unrealistic figure she has endured many of the complaints about women's body image issues. Barbie-like physical expectations found real world expression in events like debutante balls, sorority rush, prom preparation, cheerleading tryouts, and stewardess application restrictions. None of these events are pageants, but they are undoubtedly pageant adjacent, as women are evaluated and selected for activities based in large part on how they look. In most of these realms, the primary goal for women was matrimony, but women also wanted to be seen, and heard, in public.

In the post–World War II period the mass beauty industry was a major sector of the economy, affecting the everyday life of the American woman.[152] As feminine beauty became simultaneously time intensive and expected, few to no public complaints were made by women.[153] Yet, of course, discontent was growing, especially among a minority of educated women frustrated that they were still expected to master feminine culture, even if it was not publicly expressed. This group found a voice in 1963 with the publication of Betty Friedan's *The Feminine Mystique*.

Pageant and beauty culture emerged in the four decades following women's suffrage partly as a reaction to the First Wave of feminism, which brought women into the public sphere. Women's bodies in public were now much more acceptable, but sometimes at the cost of silencing their voices. The term *feminism* and the experience of Miss America both enjoyed rapid rises in popular culture, but both needed help articulating just where they were going next. They had enjoyed a symbiotic relationship from the beginning of this period, starting with the sashes.

As First Wave feminism receded, feminism and pageantry had an interesting and, to some, unexpected relationship. By the end of this era, pageantry was much more feminist than ever imagined as it placed women squarely in the public sphere, pursuing higher education and professional opportunities. It was never a zero-sum relationship between the two—nor did they simply run on parallel tracks or co-opt one another. Instead, they pulled elements from one another, especially heading into the 1960s in the United States.

With the rise of Second Wave feminism some women turned to Miss America as a platform upon which to mobilize, much like the suffragists did on notification day in Marion, Ohio, in 1920. It turns out that the town of Marion, Ohio, which hosted the sashed Suffs in 1920 when its native son Warren Harding was running for president, has an interesting distinction. It is the only town to produce both a president and a Miss America. Miss Ohio 1938, Marilyn Meseke, won the national title, aided by a top-notch talent routine in the first year that talent was made compulsory by Lenora Slaughter. News of Meseke's win was shown for the first time via movie newsreels, again thanks to Slaughter. The town that helped usher in a new era for women in politics also did so for women in beauty pageants. Over the next few decades the spheres of politics and pageants began to move closer together, especially during the next major feminist wave.

PART II

The (Second) Wave of Bras and Beliefs

CHAPTER 3

Burning versus Padding Bras

The Establishment of Second Wave Feminism

Miss America 1968, Debra Barnes, from Kansas, had a fairly typical year as Miss America. As a twenty-year-old contestant, the brunette won the preliminary swimsuit competition and impressed the audience with her piano skills. As Miss America she traveled tens of thousands of miles attending festivals, conventions, auto shows, and more.

While Barnes's year as Miss America may have been typical, the year had been a tumultuous one for the country. By September 1968 Martin Luther King Jr. and Robert Kennedy had been assassinated, the Civil Rights Act had passed, and riots had occurred outside the 1968 Democratic National Convention in Chicago. Unbeknownst to Barnes she was about to have a front-row seat for another newsworthy 1968 moment.

As was custom, before the new Miss America was crowned, the outgoing queen gave a speech. She then took a final walk down the long runway in Convention Hall in Atlantic City. It was often a teary moment filled with reflections by an exhausted Miss America, with lots of applause by an appreciative crowd.

But Barnes's speech, broadcast to tens of millions on NBC, was interrupted.

A small group of protestors purchased tickets to attend the live Miss America Pageant. When they entered Convention Hall, they smuggled in a banner. As Barnes took her final walk, a few members of the extreme feminist group known as New York Radical Women unfurled the banner that read "Women's Liberation." They then began yelling, "No more Miss America!" and "Women's liberation!"[1]

That was disruptive enough to induce pearl clutching at the staid Miss America Pageant, but then the protestors threw "smell bombs," using Toni perm solution. Toni, a corporate sponsor of Miss America, made hair-care products, including an odiferous permanent-wave solution. The protestors used the product of one of Miss America's own sponsors to highlight the commercial aspects of the pageant, which they believed promoted the oppression of women by focusing too much on physical appearance, like a particular and time-intensive hair style.

To television audiences at home, the disruption was a minor blip. Inside Convention Hall arrests were quickly made and the pageant continued without interruption. Barnes soon crowned a new Miss America, Judi Ford from Illinois. When Bert Parks asked Ford her final question—how people could live together more peacefully—the eighteen-year-old trampolinist replied, "I think a person has to learn that he is not better than his neighbor and that all people are equal and should be given equal opportunity." Viewing men and women as equal and ensuring equal opportunity were at the core of Second Wave feminism. Yet Ford immediately distanced herself from the message of the protestors. In her post-crowning remarks she was much more interested in clarifying that she was a *natural* blonde; Ford was the first blonde winner in ten years, which some took as a sign of diversity at the lily-white Miss America Pageant.[2]

Until September 7, 1968, pageantry and feminism had been marching along together in US society on a parallel course. But on this night the two paths intersected as women's liberationists, erroneously and derogatorily dubbed "bra burners," used the immensely popular platform of the Miss America Pageant to help spark a movement that would affect more than half the population. It publicly marked a growing divergence between the Miss America Pageant and the typical young American woman, accelerating the emerging irrelevancy of beauty pageants among the baby boom generation.

MISS AMERICA CATTLE AUCTION

Sunday, September 7, 1968, dawned with perfectly temperate weather as women from across the country gathered on the Boardwalk for the annual Miss America Pageant. A few were there to compete in the pageant, some to escape into glamour for a few hours by watching the event, and others to protest the existence of Miss America and women's inferior place in the United States more generally. The latter group mainly comprised protestors from New York who identified themselves as women liberationists.

The women's liberation movement had emerged, in part, from the 1963 publication of Friedan's *Feminine Mystique*. The next step was the 1966 founding of the National Organization for Women (NOW). Friedan joined twenty-seven others who were attending the same national conference of the Commission on the Status of Women, including the African American author, lawyer, and Episcopal priest Pauli Murray, to start an organization dedicated to bringing women into full participation with men in American society. NOW quickly developed a pyramidal structure, with local, state, and national chapters that met together at an annual conference.

Unlike the more federalist and bureaucratic NOW structure, the women's liberation movement (aka "women's lib") focused on convening intimate groups of women. Those small groups engaged in consciousness-raising by discussing issues in their own lives. These women often pursued radical actions as a result of those conversations.

New York Radical Women (NYRW) was one such liberation group. At an August 1968 consciousness-raising meeting in New York City, NYRW members watched the 1965 American avant-garde film by Gunvor Nelson and Dorothy Wiley, *Schmeerguntz*, which included images of the Miss America Pageant. After seeing the pageant images, group leader Carol Hanisch asked members to share how they felt about the Miss America Pageant. It turned out that everyone in the meeting had strong, negative feelings about the event and about the beauty expectations experienced by American women more generally. In particular the women believed that such stringent beauty ideals, as personified by Miss America, limited opportunities for women to advance educationally and professionally by reducing them to their physical appearance. Hanisch later explained, "From our communal thinking came the concrete plans for the action. We all agreed that our main point in the demonstration would be that all women were hurt by beauty competition—Miss America as well as ourselves."[3]

Quite quickly Hanisch and other members of New York Radical Women produced a mimeographed flyer titled "No More Miss America." A copy was released on August 22, 1968, to attract protestors to Atlantic City.[4] In explaining the motivation for the protest, the NYRW wrote, "Miss America represents what women are supposed to be: inoffensive, bland, apolitical. If you are tall, short, over or under what weight The Man prescribes you should be, forget it. Personality, articulateness, intelligence, commitment—unwise. Conformity is the key to the crown—and, by extension, to success in our society."[5]

Robin Morgan, another leader of New York Radical Women, worked hard on the last-minute logistics. She said of the experience, "I can still remember the feverish excitement I felt: dickering with the company that chartered buses, wangling a permit from the mayor of Atlantic City, sleeping about three hours a night for days preceding the demonstration, borrowing a bullhorn for our marshals to use."[6]

In an August 29 letter to Richard Jackson, the mayor of Atlantic City, Morgan explained the purpose of the demonstration:

[Miss America] projects an image of woman that many Americans find unfortunate: the emphasis being on body rather than brains, on youth rather than maturity, and on commercialism rather than humanity. At this time of crisis in the world and in our nation, we feel we must miss no opportunity to call attention to the basic issues that concern us all—problems which must be looked at and worked on if humanity is to survive.[7]

Mayor Jackson replied to Morgan less than a week later, on September 4, with the news that the NYRW was permitted "to demonstrate in a lawful, peaceful manner," without loudspeakers.[8] Morgan later reported to Charlotte Curtis, a *New York Times* reporter, that in her conversations with the mayor he expressed concern about the group burning anything on the Boardwalk: "He said the boardwalk had already been burned out once this year. We told him we wouldn't do anything dangerous—just a symbolic bra-burning."[9]

Three days after receiving the mayor's letter approving the protest, a large group of women, just shy of one hundred, boarded a charter bus at 9 a.m. in Union Square. They paid five dollars (for a few more dollars a protestor got food for the day as well).[10] When the passengers arrived in Atlantic City they were joined by fellow women's liberationists from Florida, Michigan, and several Northeastern states, who showed up after reading the "Miss America No More" flyer. By early afternoon, with TV cameras on, the group, which had swelled to more than one hundred women, began their radical "zap" action.[11]

The protest had five major components. The first, already mentioned, was the protest of Toni Company, one of the pageant sponsors, inside Convention Hall during the outgoing Miss America's final walk, which led to arrests. The second was traditional protest fare: signs along with singing and chanting. Many of the signs became iconic, especially those referring to Miss America as a "cattle auction."

It might have been difficult to get a cow on the Boardwalk, but a sheep was doable. The NYRW brought one to the protest, crowning it Miss America 1969 in a ceremony that constituted the third major component of the zap. This mock pageant highlighted the group's belief that the women competing at Miss America were treated no better than animals, who were often bought and sold for their body parts.

The next part of the zap action is what gained, and has continued to gain, the majority of the press coverage of the watershed 1968 Miss America protest: Freedom Trash Cans. In planning the event, the NYRW urged women to "bring old bras, girdles, high-heeled shoes, women's magazines, curlers, and other instruments of torture to women!" to the Boardwalk on protest day (an earlier planning document included false eyelashes and makeup, but those items were dropped in later planning materials and not mentioned in press coverage).[12] In that same early document, which has Robin Morgan's handwritten edits and notations on it, the demonstration named "Bonfire" is crossed out and renamed "Trash Basket."[13] Given Atlantic City mayor Jackson's explicit directive not to burn anything on the Boardwalk, the change to trash cans was necessary. By protest day, they had been renamed Freedom Trash Cans, a nod to the receptacles used for the burning of military draft cards, happening contemporaneously.

Of the items thrown into the Freedom Trash Cans, bras got the most attention. Why? The first explanation is simple: they were listed first on internal planning documents, the public call to arms, and the official press releases. Second, the alliterative phrase *bra burning* or *bra burners* appealed to journalists and the public. Finally, simply put, bras, linked to breasts, were more titillating than girdles and curlers.

But the story that popularized the phrase *bra burners*, by *New York Post* journalist Lindsy Van Gelder, was written and filed before the event had concluded. Van Gelder did not know that nothing in fact would be burned in the Freedom Trash Cans. Art Buchwald, a *Washington Post* columnist, used Van Gelder's reporting five days later in his opinion piece titled "Uptight Dissenters Go Too Far in Burning Their Brassieres."[14] If someone had not yet heard about the bra burning, they now knew about it, as Buchwald was a popular syndicated columnist. Buchwald's negative coverage helped make the phrase *bra burners* synonymous with radical feminism and quickly transformed the term into a negative epithet.

That a female journalist came up with the ultimately pejorative expression is ironic given the fifth and final component of the NYRW 1968 Miss America protest. Robin Morgan and the other organizers decided they would only speak to female members of the press. The August 22, 1968, "Miss America No More" release simply declared, "Male reporters will be refused interviews. We reject patronizing reportage. *Only newswomen will be recognized.*"[15] A subsequent planning document goes into more detail on this press relations decision and how the act itself was about consciousness-raising, explaining, "Insistence on women reporters. Then, engaging those women in a rap about their 'restricted' use."[16] The work of female journalists like Van Gelder was frequently limited to society pages; the NYRW wanted to elevate the work of female journalists through their Miss America action by having them cover news.

Thanks to the combination of all five components of the NYRW protest, the birth of the Second Wave of feminism burst onto national headlines. In fact, that night's protest received ten times the newspaper coverage allotted to the actual winner, Judi Ford, from Illinois.[17] This is remarkable given that 63 percent of the television viewing audience watched Judi Ford be crowned Miss America.[18] Those watching the broadcast saw little of the Toni-inspired NYRW protest. (It was truly a blink-and-you-miss-it moment, as the cameras were trained on the stage and the sound of the kerfuffle was brief and muted.)

While the 1968 New York Radical Women's zap action put women's liberation on the map as a major social movement, it also brought negative impacts to the nascent new iteration of the women's movement, especially regarding the term *bra burners*. Protestors suggesting women stop wearing bras was a marked turn in the organized feminist movement; when the First Wavers picketed the White House as they were fighting for passage of the Nineteenth Amendment, they had gone out of their way to look conventionally attractive.[19] Opponents of women's equality saw the bra burners complaints as sour grapes because the protestors lacked the erotic appeal (busts) of Miss America contestants.[20] An additional concern for the women's movement was that the term *bra burner* came to represent a woman who criticized other women, since that became the overall feel of the anti–Miss America protest.

Even with a complicated legacy, the 1968 Miss America protest provides a symbolically rich origin story for Second Wave feminism. Robin Morgan reflects on the protest being an endpoint of a process that had begun on a smaller scale in the early 1960s: "If it was the birthdate, conception and gestation had been going on for a long time; years of meetings, consciousness-raising, thought, and plain old organizing had taken place before any of us set foot on the boardwalk."[21] It was a splashy beginning for the women's movement of the 1970s, exploiting the glamour of heels and sequins—even if it ignored another Atlantic City protest featuring black women that same night. (The first Miss Black America was a positive protest pageant designed by the NAACP to celebrate black beauty and call attention to the continued exclusion of black women at Miss America and beyond, which will be discussed in chapter 4).

One major focus of 1960s and 1970s Second Wave feminism was women's access to higher education and a wider range of professions. This is not surprising given that the initial Second Wave feminists were themselves educated. In an early study of the movement, a sociologist found that 90 percent of the over one hundred activists she interviewed had at least a bachelor's degree, and a third held PhDs, MDs, or law degrees. She also identified more than 90 percent as middle- and upper-middle-class white women.[22]

Of course, the Miss America Pageant had been an early mover in promoting women's higher education and subsequent career opportunities in the 1940s under the reign of Lenora Slaughter. The 1968 radical feminist protest, which used the stage of Miss America as a springboard for public mobilization, occurred less than one year after Slaughter retired, in October 1967. Albert Marks, a local investment broker involved with Atlantic City's chamber of commerce, replaced Slaughter. Without a strong female at the helm, Miss America seemed to falter, paradoxically at the hands of protesting women focused on public achievement, much like the achievement Slaughter had wanted for "her girls" in the Miss America Pageant.

THE (PAGEANT) PERSONAL IS POLITICAL

One of the most distinctive features of Second Wave feminism was "its embrace of the maxim 'the personal is political,'" especially related to consciousness-raising.[23] In the aftermath of the 1968 protest, the women's liberationists started to plan an even larger protest for the 1969 pageant. In an August 1969 letter explaining why they were encouraging protestors to attend, the group wrote, "People will be coming from all over the country to watch this most ancient and barbaric display. This atrocity pits sister against sister, and then debases and uses us all for the seller's own means. THE MISS AMERICA PAGEANT HAS TO BE DESTROYED."[24] This is where the political gets personal for me, as that is the year my mother competed at the Miss America Pageant.

My mom, Pamela Anne Eldred, was born in Detroit, Michigan, in 1948, the third of four children. She attended parochial school for her entire education and found a creative outlet in ballet, where she displayed precocious aptitude. By age fourteen Mom was a principal dancer with the now defunct Detroit City Ballet, to the consternation of the nuns at her all-girls parochial school, who heartily disapproved of her appearing in public in a leotard and other form-fitting clothing. Between her junior and senior years of high school she trained at the American Ballet Theater in New York City. But Mom's hopes of a professional ballet career ended when she injured her knee during her sophomore year of college.

Still wanting an outlet to perform, Mom signed up for a modeling class at the Patricia Stevens Finishing School, where she excelled, combining a very proper upbringing with bodily awareness from dance. As fate would have it, Patricia Stevens was sponsoring the Miss Detroit pageant in 1968—a year after the 1967 Detroit riots. Teachers at the modeling school thought Mom had a real shot at winning the title. It was the perfect opportunity for her to dance again, even if it was not at the highest level, and put her new modeling skills to use. Sure enough, she was crowned Miss Detroit and was soon off to the Miss Michigan pageant.

At Miss Michigan in 1968, Mom was the first runner-up. Immediately after crowning, the judges suggested she come back the next year—with a less technical and more crowd-pleasing talent. She was not sure she would be back, but she was excited to travel to Hoopeston, Illinois, to compete in the National Sweetheart Pageant a few weeks later. While Mom was not crowned the winner there either, she did win the talent award and felt like a queen at the Jaycees-organized National Sweetcorn Festival. That experience helped inspire her to return to the Miss Michigan pageant in 1969, where she won the title.

During 1968, a year that truly rocked America, Mom was not concerned with politics. She was, of course, concerned about her older brother, who was voluntarily fighting in Vietnam, but school, dance, and modeling were her main focuses. The 1968 Miss America protest barely registered for her—it simply was not something that was discussed in her home or in her small, all-female Catholic college classes. It also was not something the Miss Michigan pageant itself directly addressed, especially during the competition.

Mom was driven to compete by the desire to perform while earning scholarship money to help fund her education, an opportunity the Miss America Pageant almost uniquely could provide. She saw having a pageant title as an achievement, and winning as an accomplishment—something that she felt was not so easy for her to do in other aspects of her life, which seemed more focused on young women's domesticity than professional feats.

When Mom arrived in Atlantic City in September 1969 to compete for the title of Miss America 1970, she was completely shielded not just from protests but also from men. Contestants were closely chaperoned. Not only were they unable to see any boyfriends, they were not even allowed to see fathers and brothers alone during pageant week. Not surprisingly, Mom had no clue what was happening on the Boardwalk the day of the competition.

Unlike the Miss America contestants, the women's rights protestors were decidedly *not* chaperoned, by choice, and they were in touch with both politics and the opposite sex. Following the highly publicized 1968 protest, Robin Morgan helped form the Ad-Hoc Committee for the Miss America Demonstration, as the NYRW had disbanded a few months after the 1968 protest. A press release by the new committee went out on August 28, 1969, in advance of the September 6 pageant, celebrating movement victories of the past year (like NOW's success in getting the *New York Times* to stop listing job postings separately for men and women).

The protest invitation was similar to that of the previous year's with two exceptions. The first was that there was no mention at all of Freedom Trash Cans, bonfires, or bras. Second, in addition to again only speaking to women reporters, the committee declared that in the case of arrests, protestors should "demand arrest by policewomen only (in Atlantic City, policewomen are not even allowed to make arrests)."[25]

In 1969 the Miss America Pageant was ready for the protestors—and prepared for arrests. On September 4, Albert Marks, the relatively new chairman of the Miss America Pageant, filed for and was awarded a restraining order against the Ad-Hoc Committee. The restraining order specified that the protestors could not, among other things, "[burn] material and clothing in public." The restraining order lasted for thirty days, and anyone arrested for violating it would be released on one hundred dollars bail.

The day Judge A. J. Cafiero of the Superior Court of New Jersey issued his decision was the same night my mother won a preliminary award for her swimsuit presentation.[26]

Because of the restraining order, Robin Morgan led a smaller than originally expected gathering of radical women on September 6 outside Convention Hall. No arrests were made. Though the 1969 protest was more muted than 1968's, feminists noted that the previous year's protest had already made an impact at Miss America. For example, in October 1968 Pepsi announced it was no longer a sponsor of Miss America.[27] A company spokesman explained that it was "because the pageant no longer has big-city appeal. It is a waste of time, for instance, to try to do anything with Miss America in New York City."[28] In other words, companies now knew that Miss America was out of touch and not keeping up with changes in women's lives.

Losing Pepsi as a sponsor was a wake-up call for Miss America. In 1969 contestants' dresses could be shorter than in 1968, and the outgoing queen, Judi Ford, (gasp) bared her midriff on television. With the 1970 pageant's theme of "The Sound of Young," more contemporary music was incorporated into the production.

Still, progress only went so far. Albert Marks, the new Lenora Slaughter, explained that Miss America stood for

the great American middle class, the nonvocal middle class, for normal, average, young American womanhood. . . . We are for normalcy. We have no interest in minorities or causes. SDS [Students for a Democratic Society] has its thing. We have no thing. If that is a crime in today's society, so be it. Our youngsters are interested in plain American idealism.[29]

Marks was not wrong when it came to the apparent conservative and status quo interests of contestants, as would become clear during the Top Five's final questions. First Miss New Jersey approached the legendary master of ceremonies Bert Parks. She answered a question about her decision to pursue special education for "brain injured" children—a new specialty at the time for teachers and a pink-collar profession. Next up was Miss California, who stunned Bert Parks with a short answer to her question. When asked at what age a girl should ideally marry, she quipped, "Heavens only knows!" Miss Ohio gave a longer reply to her question about what she would do if her brother dated a girl whose "character she had reason to question."

Then it was Mom's turn. Every time I watch Bert Parks call her up by saying, "There she is—the blonde, lovely Miss Michigan," my heart starts to beat a bit faster. After some small talk, Parks asked her the following question: "Your little sister, Melanie—that is her name?" to which Mom says, "Correct." Parks continued, "Who is fourteen years old—see what we know about you. What are some of the rules, the guidelines you give to all young girls about to enter the 'Now' generation?"

The pageant knew about my mom and her siblings, along with her favorite foods, activities, and many other tidbits, because each contestant had to fill out a long biographical questionnaire before pageant week began. Two of the other Top Five contestants were also asked about siblings, so it was a popular topic. But even with that long questionnaire, there was something pageant personnel did not know about my aunt Melanie.

Mom stopped smiling, licked her lips, and said, "Well, unfortunately, my little sister Melanie is brain damaged, so I really couldn't give her any information. But I think a young girl entering the 'Now' generation to-day, I'd just tell them to be themselves and enjoy life by being themselves."

There was a momentary hush from the crowd after Mom revealed that her sister had severe mental delays. In 1969 this was a taboo topic—she even received some death threats because she openly talked about a mental handicap on national TV (in addition to many kudos, thank-fully). Mom always felt an added familial responsibility because of her younger sister. Melanie was often assaulted by neighborhood kids; once they even tried to set her on fire. Mom wanted to be perfect so she could "make up for" Melanie to her parents, which is part of the reason she spent so much time in the dance studio as a child. This is also why earning scholarship money to cover the cost of her own college educa-tion would help her parents, since the out-of-pocket costs of Melanie's care were a lot for my grandfather, who worked in a Chrysler car fac-tory. In other words, Melanie was a huge part of the reason Mom ended up competing for Miss America at all. And there she was, about to be crowned Miss America, her little sister with her in spirit on the Miss America stage.

But first Miss Minnesota had to answer her final question. The young-est member of the Top Five, at nineteen, she was asked arguably the hardest question: When will the United States have a female president and why might it take so long? Of course, fifty years later it still has not happened, so Miss Minnesota should not be fully blamed for her awk-ward, fumbling answer. While she was right in her assessment of "not anytime soon," her halting explanation that women are "too emotional" and "might be distracting" on the Senate floor did not fly, even in 1969.

Soon it was time for the crowning ceremony. Honestly, Mom's goal in competing at Miss America was to make Top Ten so she could dance on national television. Making Top Five was a bit of a shock to her, and nerve-wracking, because it meant answering an unknown question on live TV in front of millions. Having done that, she was pleased. She did not think she would win, and if you watch the telecast when it is down to the final two—Miss Michigan and Miss Ohio—you can see Mom lean over and say to her competitor, "Congratulations." Miss Ohio apparently also thought she herself would win, since you can see her mouth on the tape, "Thank you."

That is how I know the expression on Mom's face when she is announced the winner is one of true shock. Her long-gloved hands grab the sides of her face as her mouth hangs open, her eyes wide.

In that moment, her life has changed forever.

One of the most immediate changes is that she will now be asked publicly about those women's liberationists, among many other topics . . . though she may not always answer. A United Press International article titled "Miss America Speaks Up for Authority on Campus," published the day after she won, captures this shift. The journalist wrote, "Looking pert and refreshed after only three hours sleep, the 110-pound, 34–21½–34 beauty said she had 'no political convictions as yet' and then went on to express a whole range of political opinions." When asked about student militancy, for example, she replied that "there is a right time and a right place to do everything. . . . There should be authority. As soon as we do away with authority, we're going to have troubles." When she then was asked "whether she agreed with the position of the radical ladies that the pageant 'exploits' women," pageant officials prevented her from answering the question, protesting that this was "irrelevant," and moved on.

Avoiding the question of women's liberation, or only referring to it indirectly, was not uncommon among those associated with Miss America and with pageantry more generally. Marjorie Ford, the mother of Miss America 1969, Judi Ford, wrote a 1971 book called *Sharing the Crown*. In it Mrs. Ford obliquely writes,

> Obviously, the very fact that millions watch the national pageant, televised each September, is a strong indication of the large number who have placed their stamp of approval on a program that encourages wholesomeness and discourages the moral decadence so prevalent in our contemporary society. . . . If some of the activities I observed outside of Convention Hall during Pageant Week the past two years are examples of so-called sophistication, then I am indeed grateful that Judi was on the inside being corny rather than on the outside being sophisticated.[30]

In 1969 America's Junior Miss put forward a similar message in their program book, which begins with the following headline: "No Riots . . . No Protests . . . Just Solid Americanism!" The article goes on to explain that many thought Junior Miss would not succeed as a pageant, because without the swimsuit category it was "too square," but clearly that view was wrong.

While bathing suits would continue to be an issue at Miss America over the next several decades, no subsequent feminist protest, in size or media coverage, has yet reached the level of 1969, let alone 1968. Still, much change was in store for American women in the 1970s, especially at the start of the decade.

ORGANIZING THE FEMINIST MOVEMENT IN THE 1970S

Much like their First Wave sisters, Second Wave feminists used popular culture and public engagement to build organizations. The organizations helped spread the message that women should have access to all the same higher educational and employment opportunities as men. The most significant and enduring of these organizations, as mentioned, is the National Organization for Women. NOW was the first women's rights organization to "stick" since those started by suffrage leaders approximately a half century earlier.[31]

NOW was formed in 1966 on the back of a napkin at the national conference of the Commission on the Status of Women in Washington, DC—the first year that the Miss America Pageant was broadcast in color.[32] Betty Friedan was the first president and she helped to define its purpose, articulated as "to take action to bring women into full participation in the mainstream of American society now, exercising all privileges and responsibilities thereof in truly equal partnership with men."[33]

A year later, in 1967, the first widely recognized women's liberation groups (like the NYRW) formed.[34] These groups tended to be smaller and more radical than NOW. If NOW often worked within the political system to achieve its goals for women, women's lib groups generally wanted to blow up the system and start over.

The push and pull of radical action versus pragmatism was a longstanding division among feminists. There had almost always been complementary (and at times oppositional) organizations in the women's rights movement, some filled mainly with activists and some filled mainly with advocates. For example, in the 1870s there was the National Woman Suffrage Association, largely led by Susan B. Anthony, and the American Woman Suffrage Association. These eventually merged in 1890 to form the National American Woman Suffrage Association (NAWSA), of which Elizabeth Cady Stanton took the lead. Later, in the 1910s, Carrie Chapman Catt took over leadership. With Catt at the helm, NAWSA later butted heads with the National Woman's Party, largely directed by Alice Paul. Paul would eventually receive the lion's share of credit for the passage of the Nineteenth Amendment, and subsequent generations of feminists would honor her by referring to the Equal Rights Amendment as the "Alice Paul Amendment."

In the 1960s, leaders like Betty Friedan and the NYRW's Robin Morgan continued this push and pull tradition of advocacy versus activism. In 1967, as many women's liberation groups came into being for specific action before dissolving rather quickly, NOW was establishing its organization, a sort of grassroots bureaucracy. At the second annual NOW convention, Betty Friedan laid out a list of issues NOW would advocate for: paid maternity leave, tax deductions for child care, educational aid, job training, access to contraception, passage of the Equal Rights Amendment, and, most controversially, the legalization of abortion.[35] This list guided the work of the organization, and the feminist movement as a whole, through the 1970s and beyond.

While NOW became established under Friedan's presidency, there were also problems with her leadership. By 1969 Friedan had alienated two important groups, lesbians and black women, which made her position as the leader of NOW untenable. In her farewell address Friedan shocked many when she declared that on August 26, 1970—the fiftieth anniversary of women's suffrage—there would be a women's strike. In the fifty years since women had won the right to vote, they had not gained any other significant rights, with *Roe v. Wade* and Title IX still a few years away. The strike was a public way to declare that major inactivity in the fight for women's equality must soon change.

The women's strike was a bigger success than imagined, with twenty thousand women marching in New York City and many more across the country. Its most famous slogan became "Don't iron while the strike is hot." Strikers came in for heavy criticism, but like many suffrage parades of the past, the public event showed how much momentum there was in the fight for women's rights.

One woman who did not strike in August 1970 was Miss America 1970 (aka my mom). She had just returned from a USO tour in Vietnam entertaining the troops, which she considered to be the highlight of her year as Miss America.[36] She was also getting ready to celebrate the fiftieth anniversary of the Miss America Pageant, a little over a week after the women's suffrage celebration.

Another woman who did not strike was the woman my mother crowned, Miss America 1971, Phyllis George, from Texas. In her 2003 memoir, *Never Say Never*, George, who went on to have a career as a broadcaster, businesswoman, and actress, describes her take on Miss America protestors:

> Then the final day of the competition arrived. A group of women from the women's liberation movement were burning their bras on the Boardwalk outside Convention Hall. They were proclaiming their independence from social restrictions and protesting that we contestants were being exploited, especially by having to parade around in swimsuits. I had mixed feelings about the protest. Even though I'd won the swimsuit competition, I despised that part of it; most of the other contestants did as well. But in spite of those reservations, I saw the pageant as an opportunity, a way to earn scholarship money and a springboard to new possibilities.[37]

While Mom and her successor did not consider themselves women's liberationists, many other Miss Americas and Miss America contestants at the very least saw themselves as pursuing similar goals to those of the feminists, even if their methods were different. One of the biggest differences between feminists and Miss America feminists was that the latter were opting to work for change for women from within the system rather than outside it. They understood that "the system" still forced women to prioritize performing femininity, especially when it came to a focus on physical appearance, and they were able to play along more easily than others in that aspect, while trying to push women forward in other ways.

Patricia Hill, who like my mom was Miss Detroit and then Miss Michigan, was named second runner-up at Miss America in 1942. In 1969, only a few months before Mom became Miss Michigan and then Miss America (but over two decades after Hill herself had competed), Hill founded Michigan's first chapter of NOW and served as president of the state chapter. She also went on to serve on the national NOW board. Hill took particular pride in showing that beauty queens could be strong, public feminists during the height of Second Wave feminism in the 1970s, still favoring more of a within the system approach to the women's movement.[38]

Other prominent feminists of the time were not as critical of beauty pageants as one might expect. Take Gloria Steinem, a feminist known for working both inside and outside the system. She could be radical but also mainstream. Her long hair and fashion choices helped make her acceptable to the masses; her physical attractiveness also helps explain her ability to go undercover as a Playboy bunny to write an exposé on how women were treated in Playboy clubs.

Steinem competed in a beauty pageant in her native Ohio in the early 1950s, at the height of Miss America's popularity. In her own words, Steinem described her motivation to compete:

> Beauty contests are ways that if you live in a poor neighborhood, you can imagine getting ahead because it is a way up. It is a way to scholarships, to attention, and it's one of the few things that you see out there as a popular symbol. When I was living in a kind of factory working neighborhood of Toledo, the K-Part television Miss TV contest, something like that, was advertised. And I decided I would try to enter the contest even though I was underage. I think I was 16 and the limit was 18.[39]

Of the experience of being a pageant contestant, Steinem had this to say: "It wasn't a terrible experience. It was a surrealistic experience. You had to put on your bathing suit and walk and stand on a beer keg. I did three or four different kinds of dances. . . . It seemed glamorous. It seemed to me in high school like a way out of a not too great life in a pretty poor neighborhood."[40]

Miss America 1967, Jane Jayroe, came to her feminism a few years after her reign, pursuing an unexpected within-the-system approach to women's rights. Jayroe, who represented Oklahoma, won the title at nineteen years old. While she said she would never have burned a bra, Jayroe sympathized with many of the goals of the protesting feminists, especially when it came to a lack of professional opportunities for women.[41] Nonetheless, after crowning Miss Kansas Debra Barnes Miss America

1968 (the Miss America whose farewell walk would be interrupted by the NYRW a year later), Jayroe returned to Oklahoma City University as a music education student, where she made it her priority to fall in love and get married, wanting to emulate her own mother's path.[42] Fewer than two years after giving up her title of Miss America, and with a year left in her undergraduate studies, Jayroe married the student body president from the University of Oklahoma.

After marrying, Jayroe focused on being the "perfect wife" as her husband began law school (aided by the $50,000 she had earned for appearances as Miss America, which is almost $350,000 today). A few days a week she would drive about thirty miles back to Oklahoma City University to finish her degree in music education and earn a teaching certificate, neither of which she would ever use. While she sometimes performed in regional musical theater productions and occasionally gave motivational speeches and did commercials, Jayroe described herself as a "desperate housewife." She wanted to start a family but felt alone in her marriage and neighborhood as her husband focused on his career. In her 2006 autobiography she explains that she might have misjudged the bra burners: "I knew little about the women's movement. I had always thought that women activists were radical, attention-seeking, jealous women who burned their bras in Atlantic City. Nothing prepared me for what I was learning. I discovered that the lonely path I was traveling was crowded with all kinds of other women."

In November 1975 Jayroe unexpectedly and happily found herself pregnant. But fewer than two months after her son was born, she had separated from her husband and was living with her parents as a newly single mother. She needed to make money to support herself and her son, so she returned to school to earn her master's degree in the humanities. Jayroe subsequently began working for the Oklahoma State Department of Education, where she hosted a thirty-minute public service program promoting the arts.

That program drew the attention of a news station in Oklahoma City, which hired Jayroe as an evening news anchor. Over the next seventeen years she became a respected television news anchor in Texas and Oklahoma. In 1994, when her son was a senior in high school, Jayroe remarried, and she enjoyed a second career when she joined the governor of Oklahoma's cabinet as the secretary for tourism. Now retired and a grandmother, Jayroe had personal and professional experiences after her year as Miss America that highlight many of the struggles and successes of Second Wave feminists.

During her year as Miss America 1974, at the height of Second Wave feminism, Rebecca King from Colorado represented a new type of Miss America in the wake of the establishment of NOW, the 1968 protests, and the women's strike. King competed at Miss America for one reason, which she was very clear about: to win scholarship money. She had just finished her undergraduate degree at Colorado Women's College and was looking for a way to pay for law school. King, a feminist, was not there for the emotion, glamour, or tradition but rather for the cash to pursue an advanced degree.

When she won—a bit of a surprise, because she did not win any preliminary awards—she did not cry. Why? Because, according to her, she was not a feminine waif but a tough, aspiring attorney. In her own words, "Well, I didn't fall apart as Miss America. Walked over, got the crown on, and I think my mother received maybe a hundred letters because I didn't cry. 'She didn't cry! What kind of Miss America do we have here on our hands walking down the runway not crying?'"[43]

The lack of tears at winning was just the start of the ways in which King surprised people. When asked about the Supreme Court's 1973 *Roe v. Wade* ruling, King was clear. She was pro-choice. The pageant asked her never to speak about it again, but it was apparent that Miss America had crowned someone who publicly identified with Second Wave feminism.[44]

Of course, King was in line with her peers, many of whom had gone on "the Pill" after it became legal in 1960 or read Helen Gurley Brown's *Sex and the Single Girl*, published in 1962 (before Brown went on to top the masthead at *Cosmopolitan* for decades). After her year as Miss America, King graduated from the University of Denver School of Law, the first Miss America to earn a JD. She used the $15,000 scholarship she won at Miss America to pay for nearly half of her law school tuition. Following graduation King became a domestic relations lawyer in Colorado, specializing in divorce. In many ways, she embodied Lenora Slaughter's goal of the Miss America Pageant attracting young women who wanted to be educated, professionals, and leaders, a vision that coincided with that of Second Wave feminism. But, for many feminists, King's arrival as Miss America was simply too late to save the institution.

King was the reigning Miss America when NOW decided to hold its annual convention in Atlantic City to coincide with the Miss America Pageant. Feminists and pageant contestants shared a Boardwalk hotel as NOW tried to "show woman as a full human being—a provider, creator and thinker, not just as an object or a mythical creature as exemplified by the bathing suit clad Miss America."[45] The two groups never formally interacted, despite being in the same place at the same time. NOW staged a parade on the Boardwalk a few hours before Miss America's traditional parade (complete with women dressed up like Little Leaguers, to honor the recent sex integration of Little League, and ambulance attendants for the same reason).

Albert Marks, Miss America's chair, harbored lingering resentment after the 1968 protests and was wary of an organized feminist presence in Atlantic City. He said NOW "will get no trouble from us if we get none from them, and, if they let us do our thing while they do theirs." While NOW extended an invitation to all contestants to attend some of their workshops, Marks explained, "The girls are tied up with a demanding schedule."[46]

One contestant, Miss Missouri, Michelle Marshall, later wrote that a NOW protestor confronted her outside her hotel one day. The protestor asked, "How can you demean yourself like this?" To which Marshall simply replied, "You want to pay for my college tuition?"[47] For Marshall, winning Miss America would in fact have paid for her college education. She was a student at Stephens College in Missouri, where the tuition in 1973–1974 was $3,750. Miss America that year won a $15,000 scholarship, which would have covered all four years of college tuition there. Marshall, like many other contestants, earned only $500 for her efforts in Atlantic City, however, because she did not place in the Top Ten or earn any preliminary awards.[48] In this case, it was the *hope* of college tuition being paid for that drove participation for many—and one in fifty-one odds were not bad.

While the NOW conference drew about two thousand participants, it did not make nearly as big a splash as the one hundred bra burners just six years earlier. If anything, targeting Miss America was old feminist news at that point. If any of the NOW members snuck up to their rooms or into Convention Hall to watch the crowning of Miss America 1975, they would have seen Miss Texas, Shirley Cothran, named the winner.

Given NOW's focus on access to higher education and professional opportunities for women, it seems ironic that Cothran would become the first (and, so far, only) Miss America to earn a PhD, which she earned in education in 1979 from Texas Woman's University. Miss America was changing along with American society, though not nearly as quickly. King and Cothran showed NOW and other feminists that Miss America could be about educational and professional achievement—though the women did still have to wear a bathing suit to access that scholarship money. In the end, the pageant's changes were too little, too late for Miss America to retain its cultural relevancy.

PRESENTING (SECOND WAVE) PAGEANT CONTESTANTS

It is easy to assume that all the talk of scholarship at pageants like Miss America and America's Junior Miss was and is lip service. That at heart these pageants, like Miss USA/Miss Universe, have always really been about how a woman looks in a bathing suit and evening gown. The stereotype of that winning woman is that she is blonde, light-eyed, Christian, and from a small Southern town. In order to see how beauty pageant contestants were officially presented in terms of their appearance and their scholastic and professional achievements during Second Wave feminism, I analyzed the official program books from four major beauty pageants—Miss America, Miss USA, National Sweetheart, and America's Junior Miss. What each pageant chooses to include in its official program books indicates what they value as an organization, while also reflecting changes over time in what American society has valued in young women more generally.

To many, pageant programs are simply pieces of paper tossed into a rubbish can shortly after the event. But they are more than ephemera; they contain the rich details of life showing what is worthy of remembering. For example, the physical measurements listed show how women's bodies have changed over time. Moreover, what is absent or not listed—such as college major, GPA, or professional ambition—and when that information first appears, shows when the organization and society more generally began to care about those things for women. These historical sources open a window onto women's history to help us understand changing ideas about young women's lives.

Popular culture events, especially women's events, have a long history of producing brochures and souvenir books. Suffrage parades put out souvenir books in the 1910s.[49] In 1940 Miss America issued its first souvenir program book. It was glossy, like a magazine, and contained information on all the contestants, events, advertisers, judges, organizers, and volunteers. The producers had previously released a pamphlet, but it had only scheduling information and nothing on the contestants.

Frank Deford recognized pageant program books as a rich source of information. In an appendix to his book *There She Is: The Life and Times of Miss America*, Deford presents data he collected from these books or pamphlets dating from 1937 to 1970. Over thirty-five pages, he reports the body measurements of Miss Americas and contestants, the average ages of contestants, their hair and eye colors, their talents, and the leading names of contestants.[50] I picked up where Deford left off, collecting and analyzing all the Miss America program books from 1972 through 2015, roughly the span of Second Wave feminism. Then I went further by doing the same for nine state pageants, Miss USA, America's Junior Miss/Distinguished Young Woman, and the National Sweetheart Pageant, which no one has looked at before.

My analysis shows that some beauty pageant stereotypes are just wrong. For example, most winners are not blondes with light-colored eyes. In all four national pageants the winner tends to have brown hair (although they do not completely look like Barbie from the face up, they do tend to mirror her from the neck down). On the other hand, some stereotypes are correct. When it comes to race, the majority of pageant contestants are white.

In the 1970s you can tell by looking at the program books that Miss America was searching for its identity at the height of Second Wave feminism. Throughout the decade the Miss America Pageant presented a table filled with details on how each state contestant looked, identified only by her title, not her given name. Nearly all the information conveyed in that table had to do with appearance—the size of the body (both bust-waist-hip measurements along with height and weight) and the color of hair and eyes. Each contestant's talent was included, the only attempt to move beyond looks. While singing was the most common talent choice, a wide variety of talents appeared evident, including a sketching presentation and banjo playing.

In a second part of the 1972 program book—and throughout the 1970s editions—each contestant's picture is shown, along with a few more biographical details. For example, the winner, Miss Wisconsin, Terry Anne Meuwsen, was then a student at St. Norbert College, studying music and drama, and was a graduate of Fox Valley Technical Institute with a degree in psychology. Her birthday was also listed, along with her talent (Meuwsen's was "popular singing," not be confused with "semi-classical singing" or "Country Western singing," like other contestants).

Fast-forward forty-four years and the presentation is quite different. Gone are the bust-waist-hip measurements, which last appeared in 1985, and height and weight, which last appeared in 1992 along with hair and eye color. In the 2016 pageant program book, each contestant got a full page that shared much more information about each of them, including their individual platforms (such as the social issue or cause they wanted to bring more attention to), as well as scholastic honors and ambition, career ambition, two favorites (such as movie, food, place to visit, weekend activity), who inspired them, and their proudest accomplishment. That year's winner, Miss Georgia, Betty Cantrell, said she hoped to perform on Broadway after graduating from a conservatory with honors. Her favorite foods included steak and mashed potatoes and she loved horror movies. The accomplishment of which she was "most proud"?: "As a high school sophomore, I was selected to play my first lead role in the school musical." It should not come as a surprise that her talent was singing (opera).

Cantrell was in good company. From 1972 to 2016, nearly half of all Miss America contestants chose to sing (48 percent). An even higher percentage of Miss America winners were singers, 64 percent. The next two top talents, for both contestants and winners, were dance and playing a musical instrument.

With brown hair, Cantrell also was consistent with the typical Miss America. While the women who win may look alike, their features do not fulfill the *Gentlemen Prefer Blondes* stereotype. Deford found the same result for hair color with the earlier Miss Americas. The found blue eyes to be most common, so a switch to brown eyes came in more recent years.

Deford also calculated a Miss America's composite figure. He found that the average Miss America weighed in at 123 pounds while standing 5' 6.5", with a 35" bust, 23.75" waist, and 35.5" hips.[51] She had been getting progressively smaller through the decades. In the 1920s, Miss America was about the same size as the average young woman (and bigger than most fashion models), but by the 1940s that was no longer the case.[52] This is how Miss America came to look like Barbie from the neck down.

With the 1986 Miss America Pageant, the organization stopped reporting the bust-waist-hip measurements. Albert Marks, still chairman of Miss America at the time, nearly twenty years after the NYRW protest, explained why: "The measurements . . . were superfluous to our operation and, although they've been in there for many years, I don't think anyone is interested in how a contestant is constructed."[53] While some always doubted the veracity of the measurements, others conceded that they were not that important so long as a contestant did not have "anything too outstanding."[54] Marks added that the decision to drop measurements from the program books could be partially attributed to feminists, who focused on the numbers in their criticisms of Miss America. The pageant wanted to give them one fewer thing to complain about.

Marks did not mention the rising concern about eating disorders, especially anorexia. But in the early 1980s, the popular press began featuring stories about young women who were not eating.[55] For Miss America to continue to report the body measurements of young women in this context, while aware of the potential psychological and physical harm a focus on body size could have on contestants and pageant fans, was not acceptable. It would have been in poor taste, given the pageant's stated focus on contestants being role models, including when it came to physical fitness.

I found that, from 1972 to 1986, the average profile of Miss America changed only slightly from Deford's: her waist and hips got a touch smaller but her bust stayed the same. The average Miss America's measurements were 35–23–35. This number remained nearly the same for all Miss America contestants, though as a group they had a slightly larger waist, at 35–24–35. Contestants still needed to wear bras, and not burn them, but there is no word about how much of those busts were natural, whether enhanced with pads (or gel inserts, known as "chicken cutlets") or silicone.

The Miss America Pageant continued to report height and weight for seven more years after bust-waist-hip numbers went away. By 1994 all body measurements had been dropped completely. Compared to Deford's earlier Miss Americas, the average Miss America in my sample is smaller. She dropped from 123 pounds to 116 pounds, but got taller by half an inch, to 5'7". The average Miss America contestants in the same period were essentially the same height and weight as what Deford had found. This puts the average body mass index (BMI) of Miss Americas in the 1970s through the mid-1990s at 18.15, a bit lower than for all contestants (18.34).

Both BMIs are right at the edge of being considered underweight, and far below the national average for American women at the time, which was 23, according to the National Health and Nutrition Examination Survey. The smallest Miss America had a BMI of 16.8, which is considered dangerously low. The highest was 19.1 which is considered a healthy weight, though on the lower end of the range. During the 1980s the average BMI of young women in their twenties actually went up to 24, while Miss America's dropped slightly. What was presented as "There she is, your ideal," was far from the norm. Miss America was actually idealizing unhealthy weights for many, always a concern but even more so in a time when eating disorders among young women were on the rise.

What replaced the height and weight numbers in the program book? In the 1993 pageant program book each contestant's platform was listed for the first time. The part of Miss America known as platform began in 1990, and its origins and implications are discussed more in chapters 4 and 6. What is relevant here is that the name of a contestant's platform (like "Stay in School" and "Drinking and Driving") became a substitute for body measurements. This suggests a shift from looking only at how the body appears to focusing on what motivates the body and mind.

Among all the categories listed for Miss America contestants, besides talent, the only other contestant-specific information listed for the entire forty-four years for which I have data is college major. That college major is consistent each year does suggest a long-standing interest in young women's intellects and not simply their bodies. Given the focus on college scholarships at Miss America since the 1940s, this is not entirely surprising.

In general, since the 1970s more college women have pursued majors in STEM-related fields (science, technology, engineering, and math). Consequently, I expected to find an increase in STEM majors for Miss America contestants over time. In fact, I observed a decrease, from eight contestants with a STEM-related major in 1972 to only five in the 2016 pageant. The total number of STEM contestants in a given year has never been higher than twelve (in 1991, 2007, and 2008). Five Miss Americas out of forty-five had STEM-related majors or ambitions. Two said they wanted to be medical doctors, one a veterinarian, one a nurse, and one a biologist.

The most popular majors for Miss America contestants were business and communications, and the most common scholastic goal was obtaining a master's degree (which appeared as a program book category in the twenty-first century). Professional ambition was first reported in 1986—presumably to replace the recently removed bust-waist-hip measurements, just as platform replaced the height and weight listings in 1993. Among Miss America contestants, the top professional ambition by far was entertainment related, with business goals a distant second. But among Miss America winners, the picture is different; those focused on medical careers number the same as those focused on entertainment. So when it comes to Miss America *winners*, there has been an overall shift toward STEM over time.

It is one thing to want to do something and quite another to do it. For example, of the two Miss Americas who said they wanted to become doctors, one did and one did not. To see if contestants did what they said they wanted to do, I looked at contestants from 1999 to see what they are publicly doing today. Most of them are in fact doing what they said they wanted to do. This includes several doctors, lawyers, professors, teachers, news anchors, and performers. A few appear to have changed tracks completely (like wanting to be a professor of art history but never pursuing a PhD, or wanting to be an attorney but instead going into a singing career), but the Miss America from that year, 1999, Miss Kentucky, Heather French, has worked in fashion design as she desired. She also parlayed her time as Miss America into an advocacy career related to her platform, supporting military veterans. French served as commissioner of the Kentucky Department of Veterans Affairs and ran for secretary of state in Kentucky.

I also looked at contestants from 2001. Fewer from that year are doing what they said they were going to do (for example, at least four wanted to be lawyers, but they have never gone to law school, which is far less likely now that they are in their late thirties or early forties and pursuing business or singing careers instead). On the other hand, many have now achieved their professional goals, including being teachers and ortho-dontists. That year's winner, Miss Oregon, Katie Harman, did not go on to pursue her own scholastic and professional ambitions—to obtain a master of arts in bioethics and work for a health-care organization—but she has gone on to sing professionally (her talent) and to teach music.

Overall, the inclusion of college majors, platform issues, and scho-lastic ambitions in program books shows that the Miss America Pageant has moved beyond how a woman looks. Since the 1990s no details on any aspect of a contestant's appearance have been explicitly reported—either bodily measurements or eye or hair color—though photos of the contestants do appear next to their biographies, so looks are still part of the equation at Miss America.

The Miss USA program books reveal some core differences between Miss America and Miss USA. Pretty much the only information shared about the 2,345 women who competed for the title of Miss USA between 1970 and 2015 was their name, title, hometown, and age. No interests, goals, awards, or anything else, with a few rare exceptions, are presented for the contestants. The lack of details makes the books less interesting to read; it also makes the contestants seem more like images and less like multidimensional people. In the end, the focus of the program book is on how the contestant looks in a photo—though unlike Miss America, contestants' measurements, height, and weight were *never* reported in the official Miss USA program books.

The Miss USA books of the 1970s showed black-and-white images of the contestants, but by the early 1980s color photos were included. Color photos matter because, for every year from the 1970s through the 2010s, eye and hair color are the only things that can be determined about all these contestants (beyond name and state), along with perceived race or ethnicity based on the photo. Unlike the Miss America program books, in those for Miss USA, hair and eye color were never officially listed. By assessing photographs, however, one can see that close to a major-ity of Miss USA winners are brunette, at 48 percent, while 39 percent are blonde.[56] The story is similar for eye color: a slight majority of Miss USAs have brown eyes, at 54 percent, and the rest are 30 percent blue and 16 percent green or hazel. Again, the typical pageant stereotype of a blonde, blue-eyed winner does not hold true, though Miss USA did crown a higher percentage of blondes and blue-eyed winners than Miss America across the same time period.

The Miss USA books through the 1990s, and the contestant information contained in them, are similar to the previous decades. In 2000, for the first time, Miss USA updated how it presented contestants in the program book. That year all contestants were photographed in pink dresses with three-quarters body shots. Of those women, fifteen appeared to be nonwhite contestants. While 2014 had the highest number of nonwhite contestants (eighteen), 2000 is the year that the increased racial and ethnic diversity of Miss USA contestants becomes apparent. Of the fifteen nonwhite Miss USAs crowned between 1970 and 2019, ten have been crowned since 2000.

The America's Junior Miss (AJM) program books tell a very different story about their contestants, and hence what the program values, nearly from the start.[57] As with Miss America, the first published program information in 1958 was more of a pamphlet, and it did not list contestants' names. By 1960 that had changed. A glossy souvenir magazine was produced, with all the contestants' pictures, though with little other information about them.[58] In 1964, organizers added more contestant details: age, height, average scholastic grade in high school, career ambition, religious and other activities, community service, and talent. Clearly, AJM was about more than a face or a figure. That year's winner, Miss Washington, Linda Felber, stood 5'6" and was a Methodist with an A average who wanted to be an actress (her talent was performing a monologue from *St. Joan*). Linda was a cheerleader, a science club member, and much more. All Miss Washington's fellow competitors were white.

AJM has been incredibly consistent with the information it has shared about each contestant, always adding categories and not removing them. While a lot can be learned about contestants at AJM over the years, they tend to be a homogenous group, especially among the winners. For the twelve winners I have data on, all but one was white (and the one nonwhite winner came in 2015, which is also the year with the highest percentage of nonwhite judges). All but one had brown hair and brown eyes as well. One-third of them danced for their talent, and nearly half wanted to pursue a career in medicine, with a fourth interested in entertainment. As a group they stand, on average, at 5'6", two inches taller than the average American woman. A composite Junior Miss winner then is a tall, white girl with brown hair and brown eyes who is interested in pursuing a medical career and dances to stay healthy. Like Miss USA, diversity increased the most at AJM in the twenty-first century, though the highest percentage of nonwhite contestants was only 11 percent in 2015. Overall, America's Junior Miss delivers on its promise of a program that rewards an all-around contestant, at least based on what is presented in its program book.

The information that the National Sweetheart Pageant puts out about its contestants is a bit different. It most resembles Miss USA in that the information is more limited, but the Hoopeston Jaycees chose to highlight talent as one of the three reported facts about each contestant (the others being name and state). This is true starting in 1971, the year of the oldest program in my collection.

From 1971 to 2015, slightly more than one thousand contestants traveled to Hoopeston, Illinois, to compete.[59] During that time Sweetheart and Miss America had an amicable relationship, and Sweetheart proved to be a good training ground for Miss America state runners-up. Nine Sweetheart contestants went on to become Miss America. My mom was the first, followed by Rebecca King in 1974. Five actually won Sweetheart *and* Miss America (all contestants in the 1980s and 1990s: Grace Ward, Debbye Turner, Carolyn Sapp, Leanza Cornett, and Tara Dawn Holland). While state first runners-up were initially the ones invited by the Jaycees to travel to Hoopeston, that changed over time to include any runner-up at a state Miss America pageant.

Given the close ties to Miss America—during this time Sweetheart used the same scoring system—it is somewhat surprising that college major and professional ambition were not reported in the program book.[60] Then again, this is a festival pageant that does not award scholarships but rather cash prizes, so being entertaining is key.

The Sweetheart winners over this time period tend to be much whiter than the other national pageants. There have been only two nonwhite winners—one of whom, Debbye Turner, went on to become Miss America. The year 2007 saw the highest proportion of nonwhite contestants, at 30 percent, but as recently as 2011 that number has been as low as 3 percent. That more blondes participate in Sweetheart is surely reflected in these statistical results. In 2010 a majority of contestants were blonde, at 53 percent, which is in contrast to other national pageants that see brunettes as the majority of contestants and winners.

In some ways, Sweetheart is like a state pageant for the Miss America program. The number of contestants varies from year to year, and the level of pageant achievement and competency varies as well. Each state follows the Miss America competition and judging format, but in the program books, there is wide variation. The information presented in the program books is not uniform across states or within states from year to year.

I gathered program books from nine states for nine specific years, beginning in 1975 and then every five years through 2015.[61] The nine states cover all the major regions of the United States. Listed in alphabetical order they are California (Far West), Idaho (Rocky Mountain), Mississippi (Southeast), New Hampshire (New England), Ohio (Great Lakes), Oklahoma (Southwest), Pennsylvania (Mideast), South Dakota (Plains), and Texas (Southwest). Southwest is the only region with two states, both with large state pageants (I consider Texas more "South" and Oklahoma more "West").

The goal had been to see if state winners could be predicted. Unfortunately, the only data I can report for all nine states over the time period is race and hair color, so that was not possible. But the race result is quite shocking, because until 2000 in these nine states (so, forty-five opportunities) a woman of color did not win the crown. And in 2015, the last year I collected data, all nine states had white winners. Of the nine states, Texas and California had the most diversity among contestants, whereas Idaho and South Dakota had for the most part only white contestants over the entire time period (South Dakota had only two nonwhite *contestants* in these nine years, both Hispanic). Oklahoma, with 362 contestants, saw its diversity among contestants increase during this time period (in 1975, 100 percent of contestants were white, and in 2015, 87 percent of contestants white, still far from the state's overall breakdown of 65 percent white). Yet, all nine of Oklahoma's winners were white.

That Miss America's state pageants would be focused on higher education during Second Wave feminism would not be an unreasonable assumption. But it would be wrong, at least when it comes to the information conveyed in the program books. Of the states in my sample, only three list college major in their program books, and not one of them for the entire time period. Mississippi listed it most frequently, for six of the years.[62] Mississippi is often stereotyped as a state focused much more on how their Southern belles look than on how they think. But the Mississippi program books suggest that education was a big focus of their program, and in these years, contestants' measurements or their height and weight were never listed. While majors related to business and communications were the most common every year in Mississippi, among the winners the most common majors were science related.

For four years of its program books, Idaho listed contestants' college major, for a total of sixty-two contestants (this is one of the smallest state programs).[63] Of those sixty-two contestants in those years, only *eight* had a college major in the hard sciences. The social sciences were the most popular, with twenty-three majoring in this area, and business-related majors were a close second, with twenty-one. Interestingly, in these four years when college major was listed, only half of the winners had a social science major, and the other two were performing arts majors, one of the least popular overall among contestants. This suggests that the onstage talent competition played a big role in securing the crown, and studying something different (or pursuing one's true passion) may help secure a victory, because the talent competition received the largest percentage of the total contestant score.

As with the Sweetheart program books, in many states, talent is likely to be listed. Vocal is the most popular among contestants in all the states with the exception of New Hampshire, where dance takes the top spot.

Texas was the largest state pageant I looked at. Over those nine years, 504 contestants competed, for an average of 56 contestants each year, larger than the Miss America Pageant itself. This state embodies many of the overall trends of the state program books. While racial diversity increased over time, especially after 1995, white contestants won in every year for which I had a program book. Singing was the most common talent among both contestants and winners. Through 1990 Texas reported the measurements and height and weight of its contestants and never reported major or ambition in these years. The first year in which measurements were not included was 1995, also the only year that included the college or university a contestant attended.

Given Miss America's stated focus on education, it is shocking how little the state-level program books emphasize the educational backgrounds and goals of contestants. Also shocking was the lack of diversity at the state level within Miss America. I will detail the racial and ethnic aspects of pageantry in the next chapter.

What I cannot say much more about, at least based on program books, is the social class and religious backgrounds of contestants. That said, it is not difficult to make informed inferences about both. Given that only two Miss Americas have not been Christian, and that America's Junior Miss listed religion for some time, it should not come as a surprise that most pageant contestants are Christian (for context, however, in 1990, in the middle of the date range in the sample I created, about 85 percent of Americans identified as Christian). What may surprise some is the degree of religiosity that many contestants display in their performances onstage and to one another.[64] Public praying, sharing of Bible verses, and references to the Lord and to Jesus Christ are extremely common at pageants. The very public display of religion may only further dissuade non-Christians from competing.

Because it costs money (sometimes a lot of money) to compete in pageants, it should not be surprising that most competitors seem to come from middle-class and upper-middle-class backgrounds. While entry fees vary at the different pageants—in Miss America there is no official entry fee, while in Miss USA it is approximately $1,000—the real costs can be attributed to the materials that contestants need to purchase to successfully compete.

In addition to the entry fee, contestants also have to consider the cost of a wardrobe. Evening gowns, expected no matter the pageant system, tend to run around $1,000. In addition, all the contestants need an interview outfit. Some spend a lot (again, close to $1,000 for a dress or suit and accessories), while others are much more frugal (one recent Miss America winner told me she spent only twenty-five dollars on her interview dress, purchased at a major national chain store). Pageants that expect talent also demand a larger financial commitment from contestants.

For most of them, that means years of paying for lessons to hone their talents, usually since childhood. Then, when they hit the competition stage, they need to be wearing another dress or costume, which can be expensive, regardless of the talent. For example, one pianist reported to me that her custom dress cost $2,750. A singer reported that her talent attire cost $4,000. Additionally, most contestants also have to purchase makeup (or other preferred styling services like spray tanning and manicures), cover travel to local and state competitions, and get professional photos taken.

Clearly, competing in a pageant is not a cheap endeavor. For some the investment is worth it, even for those who do not make Top Fifteen at Miss America. For example, if a contestant makes use of an educational scholarship offered by her state or local pageant, that counts toward her overall winnings. The young woman who spent $4,000 on a dress to sing in, Miss Rhode Island 2015, Alexandra Curtis, was able to earn a scholarship to cover her master's degree, which was valued at $21,860. That scholarship was separate from the $13,000 she earned in additional scholarship money, which she used to cover undergraduate student loan repayment. Others, like the woman who spent $2,750 on her talent dress, earned over $30,000 in scholarship money. But similar winnings did not fully cover the tuition costs for three years of law school for Miss Arizona 2002, Laura Lawless. By her estimates Lawless spent more to prepare to take the Miss America stage than she earned competing on it.[65]

The judges who control the fate of the contestants and their winnings are also featured in program books. Some of what I found out about judges debunks a big pageant myth. One of the biggest pageant criticisms is that it promotes men judging women. However, at least since the 1970s at Miss America and Miss USA, half the judges have been women. In the 1990s, 56 percent of the Miss America judges were women, up from 46 percent in the 1980s. With Miss USA, the decade of the 2010s has the highest percentage of female judges—55 percent—up from 44 percent in the 2000s. While it is not a stretch to say that it would be better to have almost all female panels, that most of them approached parity was unexpected given prevailing common wisdom about pageant judges.

Not surprisingly, with both major national pageants, the percentage of judges of color has increased over time. This change is almost certainly the influence of broader societal changes, like an increase in inclusion and a decrease in overt exclusionary racism, showing up in beauty pageants. The percentage of older judges has decreased over time, also reflecting the acceptance of youth success and achievement. In these cases, the pageants are responding to the social evolution of society, and reflecting it, rather than influencing it themselves.

THE INVERSE RELATIONSHIP BETWEEN
MISS AND CHILD PAGEANTS

Though Miss America reached a record number of television viewers at the start of the 1970s, by the end of the decade it was in decline. Women's rights protests likely hastened the drop, but they certainly were far from the only cause. In a decade that simultaneously saw Title IX massively transform women's and girls' educational and sporting activities in 1972 and the failure of the Equal Rights Amendment in 1979, when it came to images of femininity Miss America was no longer at the center of American society and popular culture.

But pageantry is much bigger than Miss America. Recall that versions of child beauty pageants were on the rise before Miss pageants, and then that flipped as Miss pageants came to the fore and child events took a backseat. In the 1970s we see that switch yet again, suggesting an inverse relationship between the two types of pageants—which are related, but quite different at the same time.

Interestingly, Robin Morgan, who kicked off the (anti)pageant era by leading the NYRW protest, got her start in baby contests when she was less than a year old.[66] Those contests led her to be a child performer and a radio star. Those early experiences helped shape Morgan's personal views on pageantry and performing.

The same year Morgan helped lead the NYRW on the Boardwalk in Atlantic City, 1968, and just two days before the protest, a pageant for girls ages five to ten, called Little Miss America, aired on TV. Like Miss America, this pageant was also run out of New Jersey, specifically Palisades Amusement Park. The *New York Times* ran a scathing review of the event, which they saw as overly commercialized, crass, and uncomfortable—especially for the thirty-nine young girls who did not win.[67]

Little Miss America was not the only New Jersey event to start the resurgence of child events. Asbury Park's baby parade made a comeback in 1973 in anticipation of the city's one hundredth birthday. The resurrected event in Asbury Park was a successful one, with three hundred children ages seven and under participating.[68]

Two national child beauty pageant systems started in the 1970s; Cinderella began in 1976[69] and Sunburst in 1978.[70] Cinderella, which calls itself an international scholarship pageant, and Sunburst, which is a model search, both follow the pyramidal local-state-(inter)national model. While makeup is allowed, along with cosmetic dentistry, it is not encouraged at the younger age levels—namely, those six and under. (That this needs to be delineated is, of course, shocking, even to those who compete at the Miss America or Miss USA level, which highlights that child beauty pageants are an outlier even within pageantry.) These pageants started out more locally in the 1970s—especially in the South— but grew throughout the twentieth century.

Unlike child pageants, which were growing in the 1970s, Miss Subways, like Miss America, faced decline as a result of Second Wave feminism. In the 1960s, Miss Subways moved to public voting (previously John Robert Powers modeling agency had selected the winner), and by the 1970s public interest shifted from negative to uninterested. Maureen Walsh Roaldsen, Miss Subways February–August 1968, explains:

> The contest stopped because of the women's lib movement in the 1970s. At that time Miss Subways was mistakenly lumped in with the other beauty pageants. There was this idea that it was demeaning to women, that there wasn't an audience for it. But we were women who had different interests. We had people from all walks of life. It wasn't, "Oh, she's this height, this weight, this color eyes." No, it was about what we had accomplished and what we hoped to accomplish.[71]

With the major national pageants in decline, several specialized pageants all began in the same year, 1972, likely a reaction to the civil, women's, and gay rights movements of the era. Miss Gay America was established "to enhance the art of female illusion."[72] That year also saw the introduction of Ms. Senior America ("the world's first and foremost pageant to emphasize and give honor to women who have reached the 'Age of Elegance,'" or ages sixty and above),[73] Ms. Wheelchair America ("recognizes the accomplishments of women who utilize wheelchairs for mobility"),[74] and Miss Deaf America (for "young deaf and hard of hearing women from all over the nation to represent their home states and demonstrate their talents, leadership, and character in their quest for the NAD Miss Deaf America title").[75]

The Mrs. America pageant—which had begun in 1938 but stopped in 1968 with declining marital rates and the death of its director—re-emerged in 1977.[76] Gone was the homemaking skills competition that set the Mrs. America pageant apart in the 1950s (even if it was kitschy to iron onstage) and in came a model based on Miss America, just like the other specialty pageants of the 1970s.[77] Interview, talent, and gown were mainstays of these niche pageants, along with the perceived ability of an individual to represent a particular community, which did not tend to be white, straight, and able-bodied women more generally.

Many of these pageants had emcees who tried to emulate Bert Parks, either in admiration or as a parody. Nonetheless, after hosting the 1979 Miss America pageant, Parks was unceremoniously fired, in January 1980. Parks infamously heard the news from an Associated Press reporter rather than from a representative of the pageant he had hosted for twenty-five years.[78] The outcry was immediate, spearheaded by late-night talk show host Johnny Carson.[79] The official reason offered was that, at sixty-five years old, Parks was too old to play host.[80] In the wake of Second Wave feminism, an older man cozying up to and serenading women in their twenties had definitely lost some of its allure. Parks's only consolation was that he outlasted the women's liberationist group, the NYRW, that had mocked him in effigy on the Atlantic City Boardwalk in September 1968.

The NYRW clearly had an outsize influence on Miss America, given the size of the group and the duration of their existence. While the historical record now generally agrees that no bras were burned in Atlantic City in September 1968 (or if they were, it was a very small number),[81] it is also now clear that the legacy of bra burning is complicated. Any bras thrown into Freedom Trash Cans were not ragged ones. These women's liberationists could afford to buy new bras; so they represented a particular type of (mainly white) affluent feminism.[82]

Ultimately, despite a more complicated internal and external message from the group, the feminist critique boiled down to this: pageants objectified (duped) women, which created unrealistic expectations for young girls who watched them, which ultimately led to increased rates of eating disorders (and, soon, plastic surgery).[83] The journalist who coined the term *bra burning*, Lindsy Van Gelder, more recently stated, "I hope it's not my most lasting contribution to the culture," especially because it appears to be largely inaccurate.[84]

Other popular culture institutions weighed in on the pageantry versus feminism debate. For example, Barbie got involved in the counter-protest act in 1972 when Mattel, an organization where "feminist seems to be an obscene word," introduced an official Miss America doll.[85] While that Barbie was not modelled after my mother but rather Miss America 1972, Laurel Schaefer, the Barbie doll resonated with my mother's background and worldview. My mom wanted to achieve something and saw pageants as a vehicle to do so, irrespective of feminism—much like Barbie started to do in the 1960s when she became a nurse and astronaut (though *of course* while assiduously maintaining her unrealistic figure). This became increasingly true for a range of other women who wanted to find new, public platforms to express their identities in the 1980s and beyond—especially when it came to race, ethnicity, and other aspects of identity. For some, pageants were their avenue, but for increasing numbers of women, the ideal became something else as more educational, athletic, and professional opportunities continued to develop for all women, not just those who looked like Barbie from the neck up or down.

CHAPTER 4

Penthouse and Platforms

Identity and Intersectional Politics

O N A HOT NEW YORK CITY Monday in July 1984, in front of over four hundred reporters in a hotel ballroom, Miss America 1984 declared: "The potential harm to the pageant, and the deep division that a bitter fight may cause, has convinced me that I must relinquish my title as Miss America."[1]

The source of the "potential harm" Vanessa Williams could inflict on Miss America were explicit sexual, nude photos of her with another woman, set to appear in the September issue of *Penthouse*.[2]

Vanessa Williams made headlines even before she was crowned Miss America. As Miss New York, the beautiful and talented chanteuse was a double preliminary award winner, for talent and swimsuit, something only a handful of Miss Americas had ever done. But bigger headlines were to come on the evening of September 17, 1983, the final night of competition, when Williams was named Miss America—the first-ever black Miss America.

A little under ten months later she also became the first Miss America ever to resign. While eight more black Miss Americas and two other women of color (one Asian American and the other Indian American)[3] have since won the title of Miss America, Williams remains the only Miss America not to complete her year.

Yet, some would say, Williams is the most successful Miss America ever. After appearing in what became the best-selling issue of *Penthouse* of all time, Williams has gone on to be nominated for multiple Emmys and Grammys and a Tony Award.

Like Williams's reign, Miss America's relationship with race is complicated. Miss America is not alone. Miss USA did not crown its first black winner until 1990 when Miss Michigan, Carole Gist, won the crown. However, Miss USA is the first major national pageant to crown a woman of color; Miss USA 1962 was the first Asian American winner, and she was followed by Miss USA 1985, who was the first Latina winner.

The very titles Miss America or Miss USA imply representation. The winners of these national beauty pageants show which women are included and which are excluded in defining American womanhood. This is true especially when it comes to race and ethnicity but also when it comes to able bodies. Women from these groups are not well represented as winners of national beauty pageants.

Participants themselves have not tended to be representative of the general population. The number of contestants in the Miss America Pageant (from local to the national competition) during the height of its popularity in the 1970s, was seventy thousand, or less than 1 percent of all women ages eighteen to twenty-two in the United States at that time. Nearly all of those women were white and all were able-bodied—women who looked different were not winning because they were not even competing.

Up until now I have primarily focused on white feminism and white pageantry. It was widely understood that both the women's movement and beauty pageantry were segregated activities, at least until the start of Second Wave feminism. After initial attempts to racially integrate pageants in the 1920s that idea quickly went away, much like attempts to link abolition and suffrage did in the 1840s.[4]

Early beauty contests for black women followed a parallel path to pageantry for white women, paths that did not intersect due to continued racism, not just in the South but across the nation. In the late nineteenth century, when newspaper photo contests were popular for white women, *The Appeal*, a black paper in Chicago, offered its own contest for black women.[5] Similarly, the Golden Brown Chemical Company, which made cosmetics for black women, had a national photo contest in 1925, which drew over one thousand entrants. As it turned out, Golden Brown was one of the last national black contests for several decades, although local black contests endured as black women continued to be excluded—sometimes explicitly and sometimes implicitly—from other national and local pageant competitions.[6]

The 1968 Miss Black America pageant was the first national pageant for black women in about forty years. A self-described positive protest pageant, it was held in Atlantic City the same night as New York Radical Women took to the Boardwalk.

Second Wave feminism, from its earliest days through the rise of identity politics and intersectionality in the 1980s and 1990s, helped reshape pageants. This happened not just for black women but also for brown women and differently abled and sized women, as more specific pageants developed to elevate an increasing variety of feminine ideals in America.

RACING MISS AMERICA

From the start, Miss America was nearly an all-white affair. In the 1920s, racial segregation in the Miss America enterprise was not de jure, but it was de facto. Miss America 1926, Norma Smallwood from Oklahoma, presented as Caucasian, though she later identified herself as Cherokee, making her the first and, so far, only Native American winner.

Exclusion of women of color at Miss America became rules based after Lenora Slaughter's arrival. In 1938 when she changed the rules to include talent in the competition, Slaughter added "Rule Number 7." Rule 7 stated that contestants must be women "of good health and the white race."[7] Slaughter added other new rules that made contestants swear that they had never been married, borne a child, or generally committed any acts of "moral turpitude."[8] Slaughter brought her Southern Baptist mentality to Atlantic City about what "respectable" womanhood should look like. That mentality was clearly racist and ableist.

While Rule 7 was relatively short-lived, it has rightly had an enduring impact on perceptions of the Miss America Pageant as racist (few focus on the health portion of the rule, but it was also exclusionary for anyone whose body was different). Due to poor record keeping regarding this issue and not a lot of talk about it at the time, it is estimated that Rule 7 was gone by 1940, though some media reports suggest it was still in existence in 1949.[9] For example, the first paragraph of an October 1949 *New Yorker* article about Miss America reads, "There are thirteen million women in the United States between the ages of eighteen and twenty-eight. All of them are eligible to compete for the title of Miss America in the annual

contest staged in Atlantic City last month if they were high-school graduates, were not and had never been married, and were not Negroes."[10]

It seems that Rule 7 was not on the books when Miss America 1945,
Bess Myerson, won. Myerson was the first—and so far the only—Jewish
Miss America. While Jews have been considered white in America since
colonial times, culturally that has not always been true (for example, the
Ku Klux Klan often targeted Jews, as does today's alt-right), and they
have long been marked as "other."

When Lenora Slaughter saw Myerson compete for Miss New York
City she was taken by her, but had a hard time overcoming her biases.
Myerson later recalled a conversation they had: "Lenora invited Bess
to sit with her in the empty theater for a talk. According to Bess, Lenora told her that she had a good chance of becoming Miss New York
City. . . . She then offered Bess some advice: why not change your name
from Bessie Myerson to Betty Merrick?"[11] Myerson balked and recounts
it as one of the first times in her life that she was directly confronted with
anti-Semitism (though she would encounter more such experiences
during her year as Miss America, especially in the South). Needless to
say, Myerson won Miss New York City, and the ultimate title of Miss
America, under her given name. She went on to be a highly sought-after
speaker for the Anti-Defamation League, an organization dedicated to
fighting anti-Semitism, both during her reign and after.

Years later Slaughter said she did not recall asking Myerson to change
her name, but

> acknowledges she might have out of concern that Bess would encoun-
> ter anti-Semitism: 'I thought it would be a good idea because I knew
> how Atlantic City felt about Jews. I figured that if I could get her name
> changed it would help because she didn't look Jewish or anything like
> that. . . . Those Quakers who organized the pageant did not like Jews,
> but that didn't bother me one way or another because I was a Southern
> Baptist. I didn't know a Jew from a gentile or a Quaker.[12]

Slaughter, in trying to absolve her own apparent anti-Semitism and
racism, drew on pernicious stereotypes about Jewish women's appearances, usually involving large noses and shorter and rounder bodies. She
implies that had Myerson looked more "Jewish," she would not have won
the title of Miss America, regardless of her name.

For anyone who was marked as different from the WASP establishment—either by name or by appearance—it clearly made sense to pursue pageant opportunities separate from Miss America. No serious attempt was made to protest the de facto segregation of the major national beauty pageants until 1968—the same year as the New York Radical Women's protest.

BLACK IS BEAUTIFUL: MISS BLACK AMERICA

While New York Radical Women (NYRW) had included racism as one motivation for their protest, it never took center stage in their messaging or in the press coverage of the event. But the first-ever Miss Black America pageant, held the same night in 1968 as the Miss America 1969 pageant and the NYRW protest, placed racial exclusion and prejudice front and center. The National Association for the Advancement of Colored People (NAACP) organized and sponsored what they referred to as this "positive protest pageant."

Like the NYRW, the NAACP understood that any protest associated with Miss America was sure to resonate and get press because Miss America was a symbol of (exclusionary) representation easily understood by all Americans, regardless of race or sex.[13] One organizer explained, "We're not protesting against beauty. . . . We're protesting because the beauty of the black woman has been ignored."[14] The NAACP saw a black beauty pageant as a way to promote a different view of black beauty, which embraced natural hair, dark skin, and features not identified as traditionally Caucasian.

The NYRW, on the other hand, wanted to get rid of *all* pageants. Robin Morgan summarized this sentiment when she commented on the NAACP protest: "We deplore Miss Black America as much as Miss White America."[15] All forms of beauty ideals damaged women, according to the NYRW, though they were especially harmful to black women who did not conform to either the white or the black ideal.

J. Morris Anderson, a Philadelphia businessman, is credited with founding Miss Black America. He came up with the idea after his two young daughters said they wanted to be Miss America, something that appeared impossible for an African American woman at that time.[16] Anderson reached out to his local NAACP to work on financing a pageant.

NAACP leaders embraced Anderson's idea, booking the ballroom at the Ritz-Carlton, very near Atlantic City's Convention Hall, for the same night in 1968 as the Miss America Pageant. Phillip H. Savage, the tristate director of the NAACP, explained, "We want to be in Atlantic City at the same time that the hypocritical Miss America contest is being held."[17] Like the NYRW, the NAACP understood that their protest could piggyback on the press coverage of Miss America to elevate coverage of their issues.

Instead of directly competing with Miss America, the Miss Black America organizers decided to start their pageant at midnight, after Miss America 1969 was crowned. This was meant to encourage press to walk down the Boardwalk a bit to the Ritz-Carlton once the winner's press conference concluded. And it worked.

The next day, in the *New York Times*, the night's two winners—Judi Ford and Saundra Williams—were pictured side by side. The two women took up the same amount of space in the paper, despite very different access to resources (Miss America had all the money and attention that came with airing live on national television). The length of the articles about each pageant was also the same, despite a big difference in the number of competitors (only eight women competed for the title of Miss Black America, while Miss America had all fifty states, plus the District of Columbia, represented).

The winner, Saundra Williams, was crowned the first Miss Black America at 2:45 a.m., early morning on Sunday, September 8. The *New York Times* described her as a "5-foot-4-inch, 125-pound," "curvy, hazel-eyed co-ed"[18] who "wears her hair natural, does African dances and helped lead a student strike at her college last spring."[19] One of Williams's goals in participating in the positive protest pageant was to "show black women that they too are beautiful, even though they have large noses and thick lips." The *New York Times* article detailed Williams's accomplishments (she was a sociology major at Maryland State College) along with her father's occupation (electrical engineer).

Like Ford, Williams was not simpatico with the NYRW protestors. The paper declared she "looked bored" when asked about the other protest, explaining, "They're expressing freedom, I guess. To each his own."

Miss Black America was about having a separate pageant to celebrate black beauty, but many NAACP members were also focused on integrating the Miss America Pageant. Both objectives seemed to succeed by the early 1970s. Within two years, the first black contestant appeared onstage at Convention Hall. Miss Iowa 1970, Cheryl Browne, competed at the 1971 Miss America Pageant (though unlike Miss Black America 1970, Stephanie Clark, her hair was not natural and her nose was not wide).[20] Five years later, Deborah Lipford, Miss Delaware 1976, became the first African American contestant to make the Top Ten (also without natural hair, but without features traditionally associated with whiteness).[21]

Even with integration happening at Miss America, albeit slowly, Miss Black America continued. The year 1977 was a major breakthrough for the pageant as NBC aired the pageant live, one day before Miss America was shown on CBS.[22] Unfortunately, that was the only year Miss Black America appeared live on network TV; in subsequent years a taped version was shown on alternate channels.

Three years later Miss Arkansas 1980, Lencola Sullivan, became the first black woman to win a preliminary talent award at Miss America and to earn a Top Five finish. In 1984, sixteen years after the first Miss Black America was crowned, the first black contestant won the title of Miss America. Vanessa Williams's win made the aspirations of little black girls like the daughters of J. Morris Anderson realistic.

Little black girls would have to wait a few more years to see anyone like them win in other national pageants. The first black National Sweetheart was crowned in 1988, when Debbye Turner won. Two years later Turner went on to be crowned Miss America, the first black winner since Vanessa Williams.[23] It appears the first black Sweetheart contestant competed in 1973, as Miss Georgia; the first Latina in 1980, as Miss Arizona; and the first Asian American in 1993, as Miss Hawaii.

Racial diversity came much later to America's Junior Miss (AJM), based in Mobile, Alabama. AJM did not have its first nonwhite winner until 1987, when Chuti Tiu, an Asian American, won. Another Asian American winner followed in 1991, and the first black winner was not selected until 1997 (black contestants were competing at AJM by at least 1975).

Like America's Junior Miss, Miss USA was late in crowning its first black winner. Carole Gist, Miss Michigan, won Miss USA 1990. Perhaps because of the Williams scandal six years before, less was made of Gist's achievement. She herself felt it was a bittersweet experience; she was proud to be the first but also looked forward to the day when race would not be an issue.[24] The year that Gist competed, two other black women did as well—Miss District of Columbia and Miss Tennessee. All three made the Top Fifteen, which Gist saw as significant progress in spite of the small number.[25]

Miss Universe actually crowned a black winner before any of the American national pageants—which says a lot about how "ideal" feminine beauty was valued in the United States compared to the rest of the world. Janelle Commissiong, representing Trinidad and Tobago, was crowned Miss Universe 1977. In Miss Universe's first decade, the 1950s, it crowned a Latina (Miss Colombia in 1958), who crowned an Asian woman (Miss Japan in 1959) Miss Universe. The world's definition of beauty clearly included women of color long before America's did.

"VANESSA THE UNDRESSA"

After Vanessa Williams won the title of Miss America 1984 as the first black woman ever in the pageant's sixty-six-year history, black leaders were thrilled. Benjamin L. Hooks, then the executive director of the NAACP, likened Williams's win to Jackie Robinson's integration of professional baseball. Shirley Chisholm, the first black woman elected to Congress, explained, "My first reaction is that the inherent racism in America must be diluting itself. . . . I would say, thank God I have lived long enough that this nation has been able to select the beautiful young woman of color to be Miss America."[26]

Shortly after winning, Williams explained, "It's a jolt. I guess I still haven't been able to realize it yet. It's interesting to know I'm making history."[27] At the 1984 competition, four black women competed at Miss America, and one of them, Miss New Jersey, was named first runner-up to Williams. Right after she won, Williams, who said she entered for the scholarship money and potential media exposure meant to jumpstart an entertainment career, tried to downplay her race: "I was chosen because I was qualified for the position. The fact that I was black was not a factor."[28]

Over the course of her year as Miss America, race *was* a factor. Shortly after the accolades came the criticisms. Some detractors came from within the black community. Williams was panned for looking "white," with lighter skin and green eyes,[29] for growing up in the suburbs, and for having a white boyfriend.[30] Other naysayers were pageant watchers who claimed Miss America was determined to have a black woman win that year because it might help revive waning interest in the pageant.[31]

But the worst attacks came from racists. Williams regularly received death threats (not unlike some of her competitors, like Miss North Carolina, Deneen Graham, who after being crowned the first black Miss North Carolina came home to a burning cross on her front lawn). When Williams was in Selma, Alabama, an armed guard had to be stationed outside her hotel room. Her family also regularly received threats at their home in New York.[32]

Seven months into her reign Williams did an interview with Susan Chira of the New York Times. For the most part, her year had been going well; requests for appearances by Williams were more numerous than they had been for any Miss America in years. But Williams recounted some of the other unexpected difficulties of being the first black Miss America, especially being a young woman held up as a role model with more than the usual expectations and pressure. She explained, "It was like being in a political position overnight. . . . People would say, 'What about black causes?' And I would say: 'What black causes? Be specific.' I would say: 'I'm only 20 years old. What qualifies me to answer?'"[33]

Nonetheless, Williams was very popular, which made it even more shocking when scandal broke three months later. On Friday the thirteenth of July 1984, Williams was doing a phone interview while sitting in a Ramada hotel room in Watertown, New York. She was there for the Miss New York pageant to crown her successor. After answering the usual press questions about her thoughts on the first female vice presidential candidate, Democrat Geraldine Ferraro, and what her year as Miss America had been like, a New York Post reporter slipped in an unexpected final question: "I heard from a very reliable source that there are nude photos of you coming out in September's Penthouse. Is it true?"[34]

Shocked, Williams did not let on that nude photos of her did exist. She reached out to her lawyer, who confirmed that Penthouse had copies of photos she had posed for to help out a photographer (and build her own modeling portfolio) during the summer of 1982 when she was nineteen years old. After getting confirmation that Penthouse did have some nude photos of her, Williams nonetheless continued her travels as Miss America, hoping the story would just go away.

One week later, Williams was in Little Rock, Arkansas. As she re-counts in her memoir, she was signing autographs at a local drugstore "where young black mothers and grandmothers lined up with their daughters and granddaughters to shake my hand and hug me as the first black Miss America. 'My little girls know they can do this because of you. Thank you for being a great role model,' these mothers and grand-mothers said."[35] She cringed inside, wondering how they would feel if, and when, they learned about the nude photographs.

Williams did not need to wait long to find out. After that event her chaperone, appearing confused, raced over to her, saying her lawyer needed to speak with her. News about nude photos of her with another woman was about to break. The morning headlines the next day blared, "Vanessa the Undressa" and "Mess America."[36] The press coverage of the nude photos was intense and wall to wall.

The following morning, July 21, 1984, as Williams traveled back to New York, Albert Marks, still the chairman of Miss America after guid-ing the pageant through the feminist protests of the 1960s and 1970s, called for her to resign as Miss America within seventy-two hours. Ac-cording to Williams, neither Marks nor anyone from the Miss America Pageant ever called her directly—all communications occurred via the media.[37] Marks stated in the *New York Times* that pageant officials were "extremely distressed, terribly distressed," and were meeting to discuss the photographs in light of the contract Williams had signed after win-ning.[38] Unlike Rule 7, the rule in the Miss America contract about "moral turpitude" that Slaughter had added in the 1930s was still in effect, and it would be the source of Williams's unraveling as Miss America 1984.

Nude photos of Miss America on their own would have been dis-tressing. But added to that distress was the fact that Williams was nude with another woman . . . in some very sexual positions. It was a triple whammy during the growing culture wars of the 1980s: full nudity and sex, which definitely appeared to be homosexual.

Marks's stance was clear: "The pageant celebrates the whole woman, and its spirit is intrinsically inconsistent with calculated sexual ex-ploitation."[39] This was of course seen as hypocritical by many; here was an organization largely based on showing women on television walking in bathing suits and high heels. Bob Guccione, *Penthouse*'s publisher, shot back: "If there is anything wrong with her appearing in Penthouse, it is not her, it is the pageant that is wrong. The pageant is out of step with reality."[40]

Nonetheless, during the last hour of the seventy-two-hour ultimatum, Williams decided to resign rather than face a potential lawsuit.[41] She did pursue legal action against *Penthouse*, saying she never signed a release. But when a second set of nude photos emerged in August (complete with a photographer's release), Williams dropped her legal action.

Many in the black community who had lauded Williams continued to defend her and cry foul. Benjamin Hooks of the NAACP declared, "The lifting of her crown not only penalizes the young woman for a bad past error in judgment, but by inference will be used to reflect upon her race."[42] Others cried conspiracy, saying, "Of course—she's black, so they're trying to get rid of her. We should have seen this coming. . . . They planned this all along."[43] The October issue of *Essence* magazine had an open letter to Williams, which stated, "The fact that it took 63 years for a black woman to be named Miss America unmasks a racial bias that we should find more offensive morally than any transgression on your part. Isn't it interesting, Vanessa, that in this country nudity is a disgrace and racism isn't?"[44]

The focus on the intersection of race and gender was very much of the time. In the 1970s, as various rights movements progressed—for African Americans, women, Native Americans, the gay community, and more—they became large-scale political movements. Much of the political organizing had to do with how individuals identified, which was an outgrowth of consciousness-raising. As previously marginalized groups became more engaged politically, this new type of engagement got a name: identity politics.[45]

With an increased focus on identity and political engagement, connections between oppressed groups became clearer. Individuals who identified with more than one minority group faced compounded discrimination. Kimberlé Crenshaw, a lawyer and critical race theorist, articulated this experience and gave it the name *intersectionality* in a 1989 talk at the University of Chicago.[46] Though Crenshaw was initially talking about black women, it became clear that the intersection of double, triple, or even quadruple group identities could combine to form new identities, each subject to (increased) discrimination.[47]

In Vanessa Williams's case, not only was she a *black* woman, a first in her role, she was also being portrayed as a lesbian. Black lesbians face different types of discrimination than white lesbians or than gay men do (regardless of race, ethnicity, or ability status). In some ways it was the issue of her (homo)sexuality that Williams tried to distance herself from the most, as if the addition of lesbian discrimination was the step too far. Six weeks after she resigned, Williams was quoted in the *New York Times*: "I know those pictures are very incriminating. They indicate a life style that is not mine. It's important for me, for my peace of mind, to say that I am not like that. They [the photos] were just a few hours of my life."[48]

That the images of Williams nude with another woman were created for pornographic use (as opposed to personal pleasure) was also a lightning rod for 1980s feminists. While most feminists were antipornography, seeing it as a form of violence against women, a growing schism was emerging between those who identified as "sex-positive feminists" and those who retained more conservative and private views of sexuality. (Ellen Willis, who wrote the 1981 *Village Voice* article that asked if the women's movement was pro-sex, had been a member of New York Radical Women, hinting at the continued divisions within Second Wave feminism.)[49]

That it was a black woman's magazine that came to Williams's defense, especially regarding (homo)sexuality, illuminated the continued racial divides in the women's movement. None of the prominent (white) pro-sex feminists came to Williams's defense, and it is unclear if this was because the content of the nudity was homosexual.[50] That Williams was a very public black woman associated with homosexuality seemed to complicate the situation for many groups and helps explain some of their deafening silence. The Williams Miss America scandal of the early 1980s shows that the growing intersectional movement within feminism was not uncomplicated—though it continued to grow and evolve in the 1990s, and it continues today.

A PLATFORM FOR IDENTITY POLITICS

The now-infamous Vanessa mess did not immediately hurt Miss America. In September 1984 press interest was high, as was spectatorship.

Describing the atmosphere at the Miss America 1985 pageant, Marks said, "There's a festive mood in the air and an aura that I haven't seen in years. I hate to call it perverse recognition, but welcome nonetheless."[51]

Suzette Charles, Williams's first runner-up, wore the Miss America crown only for six weeks. Charles, who had been Miss New Jersey and who also identified as a black woman, crowned Sharlene Wells, Miss Utah, the straightest edge contestant you could imagine. Wells was white, blonde, and a devout Mormon (her father was a high-ranking member of the church's leadership). This meant Wells did not drink (alcohol *or* caffeine), did not have sex, and certainly did not pose for nude photos with anyone—least of all a woman. In the preface to a biography that came out right after her year as Miss America, the author captured many people's views on Wells's win: "By some, she will be remembered as the Miss America who 'saved' the pageant, though she doesn't see herself that way. To others, she will be an irritating recollection of a goody two shoes. But for now, she is a bright moment in a world confused about the role of women."[52]

Wells was basically the anti–Vanessa Williams. Yes, both were beautiful, articulate singers, but where Williams had been liberal (supporting legal abortion and the Equal Rights Amendment), Wells was conservative (she opposed both). In her post-crowning press conference Wells took on reporters' tough questions, declaring that she had a career in mind but that she also supported "traditional values," defined as "no drugs, no profanity, no sex outside of marriage. And the deterioration of the family is one of my greatest concerns."[53]

Wells's views on the Equal Rights Amendment (ERA) were indicative of a major shift in the women's movement in the 1980s, as the Second Wave receded, the culture wars intensified, and feminism became a dirty word. It should come as no surprise that Wells physically resembled the anti-feminist who successfully mobilized against the ERA, Phyllis Schlafly; thin, white, blonde women's rights were not as precarious as those of others. In an interview during her New York City post-crowning tour, Wells told a CBS reporter: "The Fourteenth Amendment already gives women the rights they need. If we were to start giving rights to every minority or special interest group in the country, we'd be in big trouble."[54]

Of course, giving minority and "special interest" groups rights was in fact the goal of many feminists motivated by identity politics, who were trying to fashion themselves as "Third Wave" and not "postfeminism feminists."[55] Meanwhile Miss America was moving more in the direction set by Wells; the rest of the 1980s Miss Americas appeared similar to her in many ways. Wells crowned a Southern, blonde singer, who crowned a Southern, blonde singer.

But then came Miss America 1988, who had light brown hair and a different talent—Tahitian dance—though she hailed from Michigan. What was really different about Kaye Lani Rae Rafko was her focus on promoting a profession about which she felt strongly: nursing. At twenty-four years old, Rafko was a bit older than the traditional Miss America and already had a career. Rafko had tried for six years to make it to Atlantic City, and once she won she was determined to make a change for the cause about which she felt so strongly, caring for all those who needed medical attention regardless of their illness.

In her history of the pageant, Kate Shindle, Miss America 1998, describes Rafko as transformational for merging her year as Miss America with a profession, and especially for talking about cancer, death, and the growing HIV/AIDS crisis. These were not exactly traditional Miss America topics.[56] Because of Rafko's "nursing and hospice crusade," Miss America was getting more positive press attention and many more substantive appearance requests than it had since Williams.[57] The American Nursing Association said Rafko "single-handedly alleviated the national nursing shortage during her reign by speaking out on the need for more nurses."

During Rafko's year, Al Marks decided to retire from his twenty-five-year-long volunteer position with Miss America. His successor, Leonard Horn, like any new leader, wanted to make some organizational changes. Observing Rafko's success, Horn decided to slightly shift the pageant's course by having each contestant advocate for a *platform*, a social cause about which she felt strongly. He viewed the new platform competition as tied to scholastic achievement, thereby elevating the scholarship portion of Miss America.

In her 2015 memoir, *Getting Real*, Miss America 1989, Gretchen Carlson, explains how Horn's changes prompted her to begin competing in the Miss America system in 1988. She recounts the story of her mother calling her in Oxford, England, where she was studying, to convince her to compete at Miss America:

> I'm reading about the new director of the Miss America pageant. His name is Leonard Horn. He says they're changing the direction this year, putting more focus on excellence and less focus on the beauty element, because this is, after all, a *scholarship* pageant. Here, let me read it to you: "Miss America is a relevant, socially responsible achiever whose message to women all over the world is that in American society a woman can do or be anything she wants." Leonard Horn says he wants Ivy League contestants, people who have honed their talents for their whole lives. . . . Because of Leonard Horn, this is the year where the focus on talent and academic achievement will be the greatest. . . . I think this is your year.[58]

Indeed, it was ultimately Carlson's year—despite one of the Miss America preliminary judges being surprised by her victory. In 1990, the Academy Award–winning screenwriter and novelist William Goldman released a nonfiction book, *Hype and Glory*, about his experiences in 1988 judging both the Cannes Film Festival and Miss America (he claimed he was the first person ever to judge both in the same year, or perhaps ever). In his book, Goldman explains that every year his two favorite shows to watch on television were the Academy Awards and the Miss America Pageant.[59] When he mentioned this to his friend and movie director Rob Reiner, Reiner made it his mission to get Goldman on the Miss America judging panel. Reiner succeeded, and Goldman became a preliminary judge for the 1988 pageant to select Miss America 1989.

As Goldman explains, this was Horn's first year at the helm of the pageant, and he made changes to the judging system. Previously the same panel interviewed all the contestants, judged them in preliminary competitions, and then the final night. But this year there would be two separate panels—one to interview all fifty-one and judge them in preliminary competitions, and another for the final, televised night. Goldman, who had a choice, decided he wanted to judge preliminaries to see how things worked. He dubbed himself and his fellow judges the "Grunts" and the final night panel, who were higher profile celebrities, the "Cuties."

Goldman's *Hype and Glory* was the first insider look at judging Miss America. Goldman quickly became persona non grata in Miss America circles for speaking poorly about many contestants, but especially the winner, Carlson. Goldman, and he claims his fellow Grunt judges, were shocked by her victory. He knew she would make Top Ten because she won her talent preliminary playing her violin (and talent was 50 percent of the score). But he assumed she stood no chance to win, because in his opinion she was not attractive enough. He described her as chunky and referred to her as "Miss Piggy." Goldman wrote that his phone rang off the hook after Carlson won; his friends were perplexed by the winner. Goldman blamed the Cuties for Carlson's win, though Carlson went on to be one of the most successful and recognizable Miss Americas (whom you will hear more about in chapter 6).

While Goldman's book came out after she was Miss America, Carlson clearly did not take kindly to his comments. In her 2015 memoir Carlson wrote of Goldman's demeaning words: "It's a good thing I didn't know about the book until later, because it might have shaken my confidence a little to read page after page about my inadequacies, wrapped around the title he gave me, 'Miss Piggy.' . . . His objectification of me and the other women in the pageant was demeaning. Reading it recently, I was surprised to find that it still stung. I was embarrassed, even ashamed. It made me realize that shaming is a potent force."[60]

During her year as Miss America, Carlson often advocated for arts education as she traveled the country. Beginning with the Miss America 1990 pageant each contestant needed to develop a community service initiative that would guide her appearances at the local, state, and national level.[61] Miss America 1990, Debbye Turner, the first black winner since Vanessa Williams, won based on her platform, "Motivating Youth to Excellence." This was also, not coincidentally, the year that the term *year of service* started to be used instead of *reign* for Miss America and state queens. It was another clear attempt to move away from a pretty princess, Hollywood image to one that was more serious and rooted in public advocacy for an issue.

THE RISE OF NICHE PAGEANTS

While the Miss America Pageant certainly received a lot of press coverage in the 1980s, throughout the decade it was in decline in terms of viewers, sponsors, and participants. Vanessa Williams gave it a temporary shot of relevancy, but the reaction to the scandal seemed to take it further away from typical young women of the time, who were now playing sports in record numbers and pursuing other specialized activities both inside and outside of school. Beauty pageants generally were growing, however. Increasingly, specific pageants developed and grew in the era of identity politics.

The September 17, 1984, issue of *Newsweek* captures this sentiment. The cover story, "God and Politics," shares the cover with another headline: "Beauty Contests: An American Love Affair." The subtitle of the pageants story, "Despite Vanessa Williams and Attacks by Feminists, the Love Affair with Beauty Pageants Is Going Strong," represents what was going on with women and pageantry at that time.[62] While Miss America is the hook of the story, the article draws attention to competitions that "span every conceivable religious, ethnic, and physical group and, it seems, every taste." A sampling of those other events includes pageants focused on individuals' religious, ethnic, and physical characteristics: for example, International Jewish Beauty Pageant, Big Beautiful Woman, and Miss Sexy USA. Festival pageant titles sponsored by companies and industries were also included, such as Miss Gum Spirits, Garlic Queen, Miss Rodeo Colorado, Miss Agriculture, Honey Queen, Miss Maryland Dairy Princess, and Miss Peanut.

One thing the *Newsweek* piece does not get quite right is that it claims that this "wide variety of contests serves another function too: consolation prizes for those who haven't a chance at higher levels."[63] As I discovered, while that may be true for some events and contestants, it is far from true for all. For many, winning a title like Miss Chinatown or Miss Navajo or Coal Queen is an end in and of itself, and contestants consider those titles very worthy goals. Other pageants—many motivated by race and ethnicity, all by some sense of group identification—show how the rise of identity politics and intersectionality influenced pageantry during the latter half of Second Wave feminism.

Niche pageants generally insist that their winners be young women who have never been married or pregnant, with the exception of the Senior and Mrs. Pageants and a few others, such as some plus-size contests. This attitude toward sexuality holds true across racial and ethnic boundaries, suggesting that a particular view of conservative femininity prevails throughout the beauty pageant world. Reaction to the Vanessa Williams scandal was reflective not just of Miss America but pageantry more generally.

Though beauty pageants tend to hold similar views about women's sexuality, they differ when it comes to which group of people the winner represents. The existence of niche pageants highlights how exclusive the major national pageants like Miss America and Miss USA are when it comes to their racial or ethnic and bodily ideals. As the following description of many different types of beauty pageants highlights, while there is a diversity *of* pageants, there is not nearly as much diversity *within* pageants. Miss America, Miss USA, Sweetheart, and America's Junior Miss/Distinguished Young Woman *are* the dominant culture, which for much of their histories many would describe as patriarchal (even if the experience for an individual in one of the pageants could be empowering). Subcultures may have a dominant style or preferences for winners, but nonetheless the group's differences are celebrated rather than homogenized, making them more empowering experiences for the minority group represented and not just individual participants. To explore how pageantry operates for specific groups I will describe various racial and ethnic beauty pageants, along with pageants focused on different types and ages of bodies, followed by festival pageants that often celebrate a particular way of life.

African American Pageants

Before Saundra Williams, there were other black beauty queens. In addition to separate photo contests held in the late nineteenth and early twentieth centuries, black institutions held beauty pageants. Historically black colleges and universities often had a variety of campus queens, for events like homecoming and prom or representing fraternities and academic departments. These pageants started in the 1920s but became extremely popular in the period after World War II.[64] Some winners went on to compete for the title of Miss UNCF (United Negro College Fund), which was a well-known contest in the 1940s.[65]

Ballrooms also offered a site for beauty pageants. In 1926, for example, Harlem's Savoy Ballroom hosted a bathing beauty contest.[66] Other contests for black women emerged in the 1940s through the 1960s. The 1940s welcomed Miss Fine Brown Frame,[67] in the 1950s the Chatham

County Colored Agricultural Fair crowned queens in North Carolina,[68] and in the 1960s Miss Bronze Northern California[69] was named in California and Miss Tan America in Texas.

After its first year, 1968, the Miss Black America pageant quickly became a vehicle for ambitious, young black women, including Oprah Winfrey, who won the title of Miss Black Tennessee in 1972. (She previously won the title of Miss Fire Prevention, a contest for girls of any racial background, which she says changed her life. When Winfrey went to the local radio station to pick up her prize, they asked her to read on tape. She was so great that she got her first broadcasting job out of it at age seventeen.)[70]

Miss Black America 1981, Pamela Jenks, saw Miss Black America as a feminist endeavor. Jenks, who was a cheerleader for the New England Patriots, was supported by her cheer friends in her pageant career but not so much by her friends at Boston University, where she was a student. Her classmates refused to see how competing in a pageant helped advance her public relations career. Jenks said she saw the experience as a positive in terms of both skills development, such as public speaking, and exposure, and she explained, "Many of them [her classmates] are ardent feminists. They didn't realize that part of being liberated was being free, choosing what you want to do."[71]

After Vanessa Williams's win as Miss America 1984, some questioned whether Miss Black America was still necessary. But Amina Fakir, Miss Black America 1985, explained why it was after Williams's win: "OK, that's one. [But] in cities all around the country, young ladies get an opportunity to be in a pageant that extols the beauty of black women [because of Miss Black America]."[72] Miss Black America had always been about both protest *and* pride.

Trouble struck in 1991. That year the pageant was held in Indianapolis as part of the Indiana Black Expo. A lot of celebrities came to enjoy the event, and Mike Tyson, a former world champion heavyweight boxer, was one of them. During pageant week, one contestant, Miss Black Rhode Island, caught his eye. The Reverend Jesse Jackson, who was accompanying him, said to Tyson, "Mike, we're not here for that." Nonetheless, Tyson invited eighteen-year-old Desiree Washington up to his room at the Canterbury Hotel.[73] Washington's father was a big fan of Tyson's, so she did not hesitate.[74]

A day later, Washington accused Tyson of rape.

In February 1992 Tyson was convicted and went to jail for nearly three years. He was able to return to boxing, but Washington's life was forever changed, as was the future of Miss Black America. The pageant became tainted by the rape, especially by those who thought the women should have been better chaperoned. In 1996 Miss Black America folded.

In the interim, Miss Black USA became the major pageant for black women. After crowning its first winner in 1987,[75] the pageant system has gone on to start a Miss Black Teen in 2008 and Ms. Black USA, for contestants ages twenty-seven to thirty-five.[76] Other black pageants continued to develop, such as Miss Africa USA (for women of the African diaspora) in 2005 and Miss Black International in 2010.[77]

In 2010 Miss Black America returned, this time led by the founder's daughter, Aleta Anderson.[78] In 2018 the pageant celebrated its fiftieth anniversary, despite the hiatus. Contestants embraced all aspects of the pageant competition, especially the swimsuit competition. Miss Black America 2017, Brittany Lewis (who competed as Miss Delaware 2015 at Miss America), explained to a reporter at the anniversary pageant, "Telling women to cover up is not more feminist. . . . There's nothing wrong with a woman feeling empowered with less on. To suggest so gets into respectability politics."[79]

The year 2019 was notable for black women in beauty pageants, as Miss America, Miss USA, Miss Teen USA, and Miss Universe were all black women for the first time ever, and three won wearing their hair natural.[80] Fifty-plus years after Saundra Williams's crowning, the goal of affirming that "black is beautiful" appears to have been reached in both mainstream pageants and black-specific pageants.

Asian American Pageants

The 1950s saw the development of many Asian American "rainbow pageants," which crowned queens in different ethnic categories, such as Miss Korean, Miss Filipino, and Miss Chinese. These varied pageants helped show that there is not a singular Asian beauty ideal.[81] At the same time, many of these pageants helped preserve traditional culture and femininity—especially regarding language, music, and dance—for Asians in the United States.

Asian pageants, like black pageants, were borne out of exclusion, especially for Japanese Americans. While most Japanese beauty pageants began after internment during World War II, the first was organized in 1934 in Los Angeles as part of the Nisei Week in "Lil Tokyo."[82] The focus on local and festival events is typical of Japanese American beauty pageants, which tend to emphasize community service most of all. Because the audience is primarily other Japanese Americans, these events become places where a community can declare its often hybrid cultural norms, including beauty standards, on a public stage.[83]

Many cities with a sizable Japanese population, primarily on the West Coast, have started their own beauty pageants. For example, Seattle started the Seattle Japanese Community Queen pageant in 1960. This is a scholarship pageant, which takes academic performance into account in the final selection of queen, highlighting a focus of the community.[84] Japanese American leaders in San Francisco's Japantown started the Northern California Cherry Blossom Pageant in 1968, the height of the civil rights movement. This was to celebrate both that "Japanese American is beautiful," similar to the "Black is beautiful" movement, and to bring more people into Japantown's newly renovated commercial area.[85]

Honolulu's Japanese community has a large beauty pageant, also as part of their Cherry Blossom Festival. The Honolulu Japanese Jaycees started this event in 1953. As part of the pageant, contestants perform onstage using traditional Japanese instruments and answer questions (in English) while wearing kimonos.

For decades only "pure" Japanese winners were selected, meaning that contestants had to show that both parents are Japanese. This changed in 1998 to better reflect the Japanese community in Honolulu. While the first queen selected after the rule change was 100 percent Japanese blood, the next year's winner was 75 percent Japanese blood, with a Japanese surname, and the following year's queen was 50 percent Japanese and did not have a Japanese surname.[86]

The increased acceptance of lower blood quantum levels is indicative of changing Asian American communities. In the Chinese American community, the requirement to be "pure" blood has also loosened, most notably at Miss Chinatown USA, which began in 1948 as a bathing beauty contest for Chinese women living in San Francisco. Because of its success (especially after dropping the swimsuit competition in 1952), the Chinese Chamber of Commerce, in 1958, decided to make it a national contest.[87] While it is patterned after Miss America—having an interview and evening gown and talent competitions—many traditional elements of Chinese culture are incorporated in these categories, and contestants are expected to speak a Chinese language onstage.[88] To compete today at Miss Chinatown USA, contestants must sign a contract stating that they are of "Chinese ancestry, meaning your father must be of Chinese descent." While the percentage of the "descent" is not specified, it seems that a contestant with a white or black father and a Chinese mother would not qualify.

Asian pageants, of which there are several types, celebrate a specific notion of femininity, one that was valued in a family member's ancestral nation and which tends to be more conservative, with set expectations about women's roles in the family home, centered on domesticity and the arts. At the same time, the pageants seem to glorify Western beauty ideals, with many contestants choosing to undergo double eyelid surgery. Of course, these pageants exist partly out of exclusion from mainstream, white American culture. While the first Miss USA who was Asian American was crowned in 1962, the next was not crowned until 1984, and there has been only one other winner, in 1997 (that overall percentage of Asian American winners is slightly below the percentage of Asian Americans living in the United States). The first, and only, Miss America who was Asian American was crowned in 2000. Asian American pageants show that there is a diversity of pageants, but sometimes less diversity within all pageants.

Native American Pageants

The focus on blood quantum in Asian American pageants may surprise some, but they are not the only types of racial or ethnic pageants to use amount of ethnic blood to determine contestant eligibility—and implicitly define who can officially be members of a community. Many Native American pageants also rely on blood quantum when deciding who is eligible to compete in pageants meant to select a representative of a particular tribe. Like the early black and Asian pageants, pageants for Native women began because they were often not represented in the major national pageants.

Despite Norma Smallwood's early victory at Miss America, Native American women have not been highly visible in the four national American pageants. A handful of contestants have identified as Native over the years. A few of the more prominent include two Miss Oklahomas. Susan Supernaw, Miss Oklahoma 1971, wrote a book about her experience, *Muscogee Daughter: My Sojourn to the Miss America Pageant.*[89] Triana Browne, a member of Chickasaw Nation, was both Miss Oklahoma 2017 and Miss Oklahoma USA 2019 (holding the latter title, she was second runner-up at Miss USA).[90] Like Browne, Vanessa Short Bull, who is Sioux, represented her home state, South Dakota, at both Miss USA (2000) and Miss America (2002).

More Native women compete in pageants specifically designed to celebrate their culture and not the dominant culture. Miss Indian America (MIA) began in 1953 in Sheridan, Wyoming. Within just a few years it attracted "4000 Indians from sixty tribes."[91] The rules were clear regarding what it meant to be "Indian": "MIA contestants had to be 'at least one-half Indian blood,' and contest rules informed judges that 'facial contour, straight black hair, braids, complexion, stature [and] carriage should be definitely Indian.' Another criterion was 'authentic Indian dress.'"[92]

Miss Indian America often traveled to Atlantic City for the Miss America Pageant in the 1950s and 1960s. As the Red Power movement grew, fighting for civil rights for Native Americans, the MIA pageant's relevance began to decline as participation dropped, with some seeing MIA as too mainstream. In 1984 the event moved to Bismarck, North Dakota, where it crowned its final winner in 1989.[93]

But as MIA was on the wane, a new Native American pageant emerged, showing that many Native women wanted a way to show off their version of what being a well-rounded Native America woman meant. A Miss Indian World winner has been named each year since 1984.[94] The pageant is held in Albuquerque, New Mexico, each year during the largest Native American powwow in North America. To win, a contestant must be a Native language speaker and demonstrate tribal knowledge, have traditional dance skills, and display a traditional talent representing her tribe onstage. While the criteria are slightly different from national beauty pageants, winners of this contest also receive a sash and crown but with a Native touch, usually beading.

Many individual tribes have their own pageants, and rodeos and powwows often have their own princess or queen competitions.[95] Miss Navajo Nation is one of the most prominent, and it was the subject of the 2006 documentary *Miss Navajo.*[96] The first Navajo beauty pageants began in the 1950s, but it was not until the 1980s that the Navajo Nation created the Office of Miss Navajo Nation to run the pageant and schedule the winner's appearances.[97] To win, a contestant must be able to answer questions in Navajo and demonstrate skills essential in daily tribal life, like sheep butchering, food preparation, and rug weaving. These different elements of the competition show what the community values.

Miss Navajo, while celebrating a culture that is often overlooked by mainstream society, nonetheless promotes a conservative type of femininity. Like nearly every other niche pageant, as mentioned, Miss Navajo specifies that only those who have been born female and who have never been married or pregnant can participate. But Miss Navajo goes further. In the 2019 pageant paperwork, the rules state that "as a Miss Navajo Nation contestant, it would not be acceptable to cohabitate with an intimate companion." The application also is clear that any "intimate displays of affection" are not tolerated. While the wording is inclusive of both boyfriends and girlfriends, this policing of sexuality goes further than many other pageants. This may be because the Navajo are a matriarchal society, so expectations for women are even more stringent—and helps explains why cooking is a pageant category not seen in other niche pageants. While Miss Navajo Nation and other Native pageants embrace a beauty and feminine ideal different from the dominant, mainly white, culture, they embrace their own brand of conservative femininity.

Other Ethnic Pageants

Despite the massive popularity of pageants in South America[98] (including girls as young as four years old in Venezuela attending beauty schools to learn how to walk in high heels[99]), Latinas have neither historically participated in national pageants in the US in great numbers nor been very successful. As of 2019, a Latina has not won the title of Miss America, and the title of Miss Puerto Rico has been awarded only sporadically.[100] Latinas have been more successful at Miss USA, and certainly at Miss Universe, though not in numbers you might expect, given both the size of their population and the culture's focus on a hyperfeminine appearance.

This may help explain why, starting in the 1980s, several different Latina pageants developed in the United States. Miss U.S. Latina began crowning winners in 1986 as a "celebration of Latina beauty and culture in the USA."[101] Miss Latina USA crowned its first winner in 1998,[102] followed by Miss Munda Latina USA in 2005.[103] Both Miss Latina USA and Miss Munda Latina USA have a teen contest, a Miss contest, and a Mrs. division.

As is the case with black and Asian American pageants, so long as Latinas do not feel integrated into national pageants, they will organize their own. This is a culture, broadly defined, that embraces celebrating heightened femininity from a young age—for example, elaborate quinceañera dresses, and bodily preparation more generally, are common in the Latinx community. The celebration for a girl's fifteenth birthday often includes many pageant or debutante elements, including a ball gown, a crown, and a court. Some even compare the quinceañera experience to Miss America.[104]

Another group that still continues to organize its own events may surprise some—the Irish. The Irish as a group tend to have pale skin, but in the United States, for much of the nineteenth century, they were thought of as not white.[105] The Rose of Tralee pageant began as a festival in Ireland in the 1960s to welcome Irish immigrants home for a time and to recognize the large Irish diaspora. Different cities and states send contestants to Ireland for the Rose of Tralee pageant, some from long-standing festivals, like Boston, which began in 1960,[106] or Arizona, which started in 1983,[107] or South Carolina, which began only in 2015.[108] The second winner ever was an American woman, representing Chicago, a city that continues to send a "Rose" each year. The annual event is televised in Ireland and continues to draw hundreds of thousands of viewers, probably because it retains a nostalgic tone of femininity, while changing with the times regarding contestant appearance, crowning winners of mixed Irish descent, including women of color (from Africa, the Philippines, and India).[109] Like other racially or ethnically based pageants, including those for Italian Americans,[110] the Rose of Tralee tends to focus on the positives of a community by showcasing traditional forms of dance, music, food, or other aspects of a culture.[111]

Pageants for Different Bodies

Different pageants exist to celebrate different beauty ideals, but in most of the specifically racial and ethnic pageants the participants' and winners' bodies look similar—young, slim, and able-bodied. Other niche pageants have developed to celebrate a range of bodies that do not look like the beauty pageant ideal that tends to prevail even within racially or ethnically diverse pageants. The development and growth of many of these pageants coincided with the rise of intersectionality at the tail end of Second Wave feminism.

The first differently abled Miss America did not have a physical disability. Despite facing significant challenges, it was not immediately clear when you looked at Miss Alabama, Heather Whitestone, that she had a disability. Whitestone, Miss America 1995, was profoundly deaf when she won.[112] Whitestone wrote in her 1998 memoir that she was "like a pioneer, navigating [her] way through situations and circumstances no other Miss America had ever explored. There was really no one to ask for advice."[113]

Whitestone came to the Miss America pageant system after previously competing in one America's Junior Miss preliminary and in the Miss Deaf Alabama pageant.[114] The first Miss Deaf America pageant was held in 1972 and run by the National Association of the Deaf. The main components of the competition were similar to Miss America's, with an emphasis on interview and talent (though no swimsuit). However, Whitestone—who primarily communicated using speech and lip reading rather than sign language—discovered that Miss Deaf America emphasized sign language as a judging criterion. Talent was also a bit different, given that the vast majority of contestants did not sing or play a musical instrument. Whitestone danced, by counting and feeling the vibration of her music through the floor, but she was an outlier.

When Miss Deaf America was rebranded as the Miss Deaf America Ambassador Competition in 2012, to be more inclusive and welcome contestants of older ages, it dropped the talent portion.[115] For deaf pageant contestants who want to compete in an event with a talent portion there is Miss Deaf USA, which began in 2005. The winner of that pageant goes on to compete at Miss and Mister Deaf International.[116] Intersectionality is also apparent in deaf pageants; Miss Black Deaf America began in 1983.[117]

Four years after Whitestone won Miss America, Miss Virginia, Nicole Johnson, was crowned Miss America 1999. Johnson also had a body that was differently abled, as she has type 1 diabetes and competed while wearing her insulin pump.[118] Other contestants have since competed on the Miss America national stage wearing their pumps. In 2017 Miss America had its first state winner with a major physical difference—Miss Iowa, Nicole Kelly, was born with only one arm. No contestant has ever been on the Miss America stage who needed assistance walking.

Miss USA was the first (and so far only) national pageant in which a contestant with a mobility-related disability competed. Abbey Curran, also representing Iowa, won her state title in 2008. Curran, who was born with cerebral palsy, explained what winning a crown meant to her: "That crown meant that people remembered me for something other than being disabled."[119]

Curran walks with a pronounced limp; as she describes it, she drags her left leg behind her.[120] While in everyday life she walks without assistance, walking in heels and walking on stairs can be difficult without a handrail or something else to help her keep her balance. But Curran never let this stop her from entering pageants. She grew up in the small town of Kewanee, Illinois, the county seat, and each year Curran would attend the Miss Henry County Fair Queen pageant at the county fair.[121] As a little girl she dreamed of entering, and when she was sixteen years old she threw her hat in the ring, despite naysayers who thought she could not physically compete with able-bodied contestants. The first year Curran competed she made Top Ten and her pageant career began.

At the same time as she started competing, Curran started her own pageant. In 2004, inspired by one of her classmates with cerebral palsy who used a walker, Curran organized the first Miss You Can Do It pageant in her hometown. She wanted all girls, regardless of ability, to feel beautiful and valued. While the first Miss You Can Do It, designed for girls with physical or mental differences, had only ten contestants, Curran was motivated to make her pageant bigger and better after she saw how happy and excited each of those contestants were to appear onstage.

Curran continued to grow Miss You Can Do It throughout the rest of her time in high school and when she went away to college in Iowa. It was while she was living in Iowa that she received a flyer to compete in the Miss Iowa USA pageant. Inspired by her own contestants from Miss You Can Do It, Curran entered the 2008 pageant. She was one of fifty-four contestants, and the only one with an onstage escort.

Curran was thrilled to make it to the Top Ten and compete in swimsuit and evening gown. Her onstage question was "Why did you decide to compete in this pageant?" Curran had a unique answer: "Every accomplishment, small or great, begins with two words . . . 'I'll try.' We never know unless we try. . . . I am not here tonight just for myself, but for everyone else with a challenge who is afraid to try."[122]

Curran was shocked to win—a win that not only opened up many opportunities for her but also brought her a lot of negativity. Immediately after she won, people started posting nasty comments online, especially suggesting that she won only because of her disability. The question of whether she would be able to compete at Miss USA came up as well, because the rules supposedly stated that a contestant is required to walk onstage alone. However, officials at the Miss USA Pageant quickly arranged for Curran to have an escort, not just onto the stage but also for the entire three-week Miss USA experience.[123]

Though she did not place at Miss USA, the title allowed Curran to grow Miss You Can Do It. Since 2008 the number of contestants has increased, and the types of activities contestants do at the pageant has expanded as well (like eating with Disney princesses and getting their hair done). In 2013, HBO released the documentary *Miss You Can Do It*, which also increased the visibility of the pageant while spreading Curran's message that pageantry can be about what is right with a contestant rather than about what is wrong.

Many girls at Miss You Can Do It compete in wheelchairs, and they are also able to compete in wheelchair pageants targeted at teens and women. Ms. Wheelchair America started in 1972. Since then, another wheelchair pageant system emerged in the 1990s.[124] Of course, there is also a "USA" competitor: Ms. Wheelchair USA.

Just as bodies can do different things, they also look different from each other. The Ms. Full-Figured USA pageant celebrated its thirtieth anniversary in 2019.[125] Miss Plus America is more recent, starting in 2003 (and it has a Christian faith component as well[126]).[127] American Beauties Plus is the youngest of the major plus-sized pageants, starting in 2005, but it received quite a bit of attention as it was the subject of the 2013 short documentary *There She Is*, which follows the competitive journey of two women.[128]

Shorter women have their own pageant as well. In petite pageants, contestants can be no taller than 5'6" without heels on. A few options for competitors include USA Petite and Petite America pageants, which aim to celebrate short women by offering them special opportunities. Though short women have won Miss America before (for example, my mother at 5'4"), the assumption is that being tall is a necessary condition for being successful at Miss America and especially at Miss USA. So, having a separate pageant for petite women allows a different and specific type of body an opportunity to shine.

At another point on the body spectrum are body building contests, which display a high level of routine, dedication, and, at times, restraint. The first Miss Muscle Beach beauty pageant was held in the summer of 1947, but not many female muscles were on display, as having too many was not considered feminine.[129] That changed in the late 1970s when the first women's physique competition was held in Ohio, which specifically judged muscularity.[130] Shortly thereafter, in 1980, the first Ms. Olympia bodybuilding contest was held, which evaluated the presentation of muscles onstage.[131]

It is not a stretch to say that a pageant exists for every body, though no pageants have as big an influence on American culture as Miss America and Miss USA. Together, however, they show that diversity can exist in pageants and that mainstream standards of beauty are expanding.

Senior Pageants

Pageants for older bodies, mainly defined as over age sixty, exist as well. Ms. Senior America, which began in the 1930s, was still going strong in the 1980s and 1990s. Eventually additional competitors arrived on the scene. Like Miss America, Ms. Senior America soon was vying for contestants with rival Ms. Senior USA, which began in 1986 in Las Vegas.[132] Ms. Senior USA, which is connected to a Universe title as well, awards a few different titles based on the age of competitors. For instance, each year a woman between the ages of fifty and fifty-nine is crowned Ms. Senior United States, whereas Ms. Grande Dame has to be over ninety.[133] Nursing home pageants have also become more common as baby boomers age. Missouri has had a Ms. Missouri Nursing Home winner since 1980.[134]

Feminists started embracing senior pageants in this era of identity politics. A cookbook published by NOW in 1998 featured Cindy Judd Hill. Hill was crowned Ms. National Senior Citizen in 1993 while representing Pennsylvania. She was one of the earliest members of NOW, joining in 1966 after she was fired from her teaching job for being pregnant.

NOW helped her get her job back, along with back pay, setting a precedent that a woman could not be fired from her job due to pregnancy. Hill was an active NOW member in the Pittsburgh area for decades and a national feminist leader.[135]

So it came as a surprise to some that "nearly 30 years later, the same woman who was a favorite speaker at feminist conventions and who once brandished a protest sign that read 'My Uterus Is Not Government Property' did the unexpected and won a pageant for older women, saying that sometimes she'd 'rather dance than fight.'"[136] But at sixty-seven years old, Hill was ready to pursue the dreams of her youth—to be a singer and a dancer—which she had abandoned when she married at nineteen. After raising four children, teaching music, and traveling around the country fighting for women's rights, Hill said she just wanted to do what she loved: entertain. Senior pageants offered her a path to do that later in life, like singing the national anthem at sporting events and touring retirement homes while sporting her four-inch tap heels.

The 1980s and 1990s saw the continued growth of pageants for nearly every group at nearly every age level. A 1995 how-to book on competing in pageants declared that, given the multitude of choices, a competitor could now take a "cradle-to-death" approach to pageants.[137] In chapter 5, I will focus on child beauty pageants and how their rise fit into changing views on childhood, especially girlhood, as the Third Wave of feminism began to crest.

Festival Pageants

Festival pageants are what they sound like—pageants associated with a festival. Often these are small town events, often they are rural, and often they are majority white. These festival queens can have unusual names, perhaps representing community experiences or products, such as Blueberry Queen, Apple or Cotton Princess, Rhododendron Queen, Miss Traffic Safety, Livestock Queen, or Miss American Legion.[138] These events are important to communities, and some people attach an outsize importance on winning them as an end in itself, as opposed to moving on to another larger competition.

While the 1999 mockumentary *Drop Dead Gorgeous* is roughly based on an America's Junior Miss/Distinguished Young Woman preliminary in Minnesota, it also gives a sense of what many festival pageants are like.[139] As the dark cult classic comedy shows, the annual local pageant in a small town is a center of social life. It can connect generations—especially mothers and daughters—in ways both positive and negative. It can suggest a path to another kind of life for ambitious young women interested in pursuing higher education and professional careers. And it can be an occasion that town residents become overly and unhealthily invested in.

Local festival pageants endure because they preserve a core part of a community's experience or interests, hopefully in ways more positive than negative. This is true for rodeo queens, which are common in the American West, where cattle herding has long been a part of local economies and identities. Where you find rodeos at the town, county, and state levels, you will find a rodeo queen contest to help lead the celebration and festivities.[140]

This is also true in small communities on the East Coast, like on the Eastern Shore of Maryland, which use a festival to celebrate a way of life. For seventy-five years a Miss Outdoors has been crowned as part of the National Outdoor Show, which features competitions involving muskrats (skinning and eating them).[141] On occasion, Miss Outdoors contestants have competed in the muskrat-skinning contest or skinned one as a pageant talent entry "in full makeup and sparkly earrings."[142] While most of the time muskrat skinning—a necessary skill to eat the animal—is separate from the pageant, when a young woman combined the two, she was celebrated as bridging two parts of her region's culture. On her third try at the title, Tiffany Brittingham was crowned Miss Outdoors.

Coal-themed pageants, mainly held in Appalachia, also use festivals to celebrate a way of life that some perceive as in decline. A 2005 documentary, *The Bituminous Coal Queens of Pennsylvania*, with the subtitle *A Heartfelt Homage to Small Town America*, captures what an event like this means for the high school girls who are competing and for former queens.[143] The latter group are featured celebrating their experience as Coal Queens, a pageant that has endured for over sixty years. The contestants, from different schools and states across the region, are shown hoping to use the title of Coal Queen as a springboard to a different way of life. Coal pageants are surprisingly common and include children's versions at the West Virginia Coal Festival, industry versions in Alabama at the Miss Coal Miner's Daughter pageant, and protest versions such as the Miss Coal Hearted pageant in Virginia, which donates money to the families of coal miners affected by layoffs.[144]

While many of the festival pageants mentioned here are not part of the American South, there is a strong and enduring perception that beauty pageants, at all levels, are dominated by Southern participants. Beauty pageants undoubtedly are a part of Southern culture. In the fourth volume of the *Encyclopedia of Southern Culture*, a University of Mississippi professor writes, "Southerners tend to take their beauty queens seriously and to see them as models"—so it is not surprising that beauty queen Mary Ann Mobley of Mississippi, Miss America 1959, was featured on the cover of the book.[145]

It is true that in the 1950s and 1960s Miss America winners were predominantly Southern queens; from 1950 to 1963 seven Southerners were crowned, with Miss Mississippi earning back-to-back victories in 1958 and 1959. Historian Blain Roberts argues that the rise of winners like Mobley had an uncomfortable, racially tinged underbelly: "Other whites, many of them pro-segregation themselves but fearful of the national reaction brought on by anti–civil rights violence, understood that Southern beauty queens could serve as persuasive public relations agents, a genteel veneer to cover up the region's unsavory behavior."[146]

But Southern winners, and even white winners, started to wane at the same time as all the rights movements grew. A 1989 *New York Times* editorial about the crowning of Debbye Turner, the first black winner since Vanessa Williams, remarked on the fact that the first runner-up was an Asian American from Maryland (who had just graduated from Princeton University). Additionally, for "the first time in living memory, none of the top five finishers was a Southerner. Once, not so long ago, it seemed that the South had a lock on the Miss America title."[147]

While the South may not always win at Miss America—no Southern state tops the list of most winners per state—they do indeed tend to do well, with many Top Ten placements. This suggests strong state and local programs in the South, with a lot of participants who are consistently well prepared to compete. For Miss USA, a large Southern state does take the top spot—Texas, with nine winners—but none of the other most-winning states are Southern (California comes in second, with six, and Hawaii, Illinois, New York, and District of Columbia are tied at four apiece). America's Junior Miss/Distinguished Young Woman is the only major national pageant that began in the South, and it is still held there. Perhaps not surprisingly then, they have more Southern winners. Southern beauty pageant culture is indeed a very real thing, with more pageants at every level and participants, even if that does not always translate into more national crowns.

Overall, individual pageant contestants' diverse characteristics became something to celebrate at a variety of pageants, and in some cases the locales contestants hailed from became something to celebrate as well. Even as mainstream pageants were becoming more diverse during the last decades of the twentieth century, a growing diversity of pageants also made different women feel represented and applauded. As identity politics grew during this time, so too did the types of pageants available to those who identified as female, and greater attention was paid to increasing diversity of all types, even within niche pageants.

IDENTITY PAGEANTS AS A THIRD WAVE?

Many historians and scholars consider the identity politics of the 1980s and 1990s as the Third Wave of feminism. I disagree, and a documentary called *Miss . . . or Myth?* about protests outside the annual Miss California pageant in Santa Cruz helps explain why.[148] In 1979 a group of radical feminists started an annual protest called Myth California. The concept was not new—it was clearly modeled after the New York Radical Women's protest outside the 1968 Miss America Pageant. The 1987 documentary featured the 1985 Miss California pageant and the counter pageant, juxtaposing images from both. In the film, Debra Johnson, a black contestant at Miss California from Compton, discusses how she felt her race hindered her success at the state pageant. This open discussion of race shows how the rise of identity politics played out more explicitly during the latter half of the Second Wave, but it also was not something entirely new.

In 1988 there was another feminist protest at Miss California, this one onstage. During the crowning of another contestant, Michelle Anderson, representing Santa Cruz, pulled a banner out of her dress that read "Pageants Hurt All Women."[149] At the same time Anderson yelled that the night's winner, Marlise Ricardos, was anorexic and that her body was covered in bruises.[150] Ricardos, the first Latina to ever win the Miss California crown, was upset about the accusations and that her crowning moment was so marred after she had tried to win the state title for years. Despite the accusations and drama, Ricardos went on to be named third runner-up to Gretchen Carlson at Miss America.[151]

Even though national pageants were beginning to embrace identity politics in the 1980s, there was still a need and demand for identity-specific pageants. Often, there were competing demands. You may have noticed a pattern: one type of pageant will develop and then a competitor follows: Miss Black America and then Miss Black USA; Ms. Senior America and then Ms. Senior USA; Miss U.S. Latina and then Miss Latina USA. Because of how charged some of these identities can be due to historical marginalization that continues today, people often have very specific ideas about how those pageants should be run, what they should reward, and what the prizes should be. Because groups do not always agree internally, rival competitions frequently emerge. The ways in which different marginalized identities combine to form new identities, which competing racial and ethnic pageants reflect, was exactly what Kimberlé Crenshaw wanted to shed a light on in her legal work that helped articulate intersectionality and the rise of identity politics.

In 1991 Crenshaw was part of the legal team supporting Anita Hill in her testimony during the Senate Judiciary Committee hearings for Supreme Court justice nominee Clarence Thomas. Many credit the Thomas confirmation hearings as reinvigorating the women's movement.[152] They helped define and spotlight sexual harassment in the workplace (a concept that was not even articulated until the 1970s as part of the Second Wave) and energized women to run for national office, many successfully, in 1992. Looking for a large-scale public event on which to anchor Third Wave feminism, some scholars have pointed to the Thomas hearings as a possible site—although if you have to look for a public event, it probably was not defining enough. Instead, the Thomas hearings set the stage for Third Wave feminists two decades later.

Sexuality was certainly a component of the Thomas hearings, and it was also the subject of a lot of activism in the 1980s and 1990s, especially regarding the HIV/AIDS crisis. Notice that when I discussed niche pageants, nearly every group represented in those niches has also managed to find major success in mainstream pageants, with the exception of lesbians. Not one "out" contestant has yet been successful at a major national pageant (though at least one, Miss America 2005, Deidre Downs, has come out after her year of service, in 2018, when *People* magazine ran a story about her marrying another woman). Drag pageants, like Miss Gay America, started in 1972, which I discuss in the next chapter.

While pageants for more types and groups of people were expanding into the 1990s, it was not until the mid-1990s that Miss America attempted to respond to the changing landscape of beauty pageants in American women's culture. In 1995 Miss America announced that it was going to allow the public to vote on whether it should keep swimsuit as part of the competition. Given that the vote was live during the show, and callers had to pay fifty cents for each call, it is not surprising that the vote was to keep bathing suits, with nearly 80 percent giving the thumbs up.[153] Pageant fans generally like tradition, especially those willing to pay money to uphold it.

There *was* one change related to swimsuit, though, two years after the vote. After five decades, contestants were finally again allowed to wear two-piece swimsuits in competition.[154] The shift was rapid. By 1998 nearly every contestant competed in a bikini, and not a one-piece, to better show off their physiques. The reintroduction of bikinis was one change the pageant faithful embraced.

As the second phase of Second Wave feminism was pulled back by the tides of evolving history, it is interesting to reflect that Miss America 1984, a black woman, was excoriated for appearing nude with another woman. Twenty years later, in 2004, Miss America was a black woman, who won the title wearing a swimsuit that bared her midriff and who crowned a woman who would ultimately marry another woman. The identity politics movement that characterized the latter half of Second Wave feminism clearly had a major impact on both society at large and beauty pageant culture. It influenced women's continued fight to gain access in education and the professions—but the fight to make those spaces truly safe and open for women would not come until the twenty-first century with the establishment of Third Wave feminism.

PART III

Tabloids, Trump, Tits

CHAPTER 5

Tabloids and Tiaras

The JonBenét Ramsey Murder and "Reality" TV

JONBENÉT PATRICIA RAMSEY participated in her first beauty pageant when she was four years old. It was a small event in the resort town of Charlevoix, Michigan, where the Ramsey family had a summer home. Only two other girls were in her age category, and after the on-stage competitions for modeling and talent (a patriotic song-and-dance routine), JonBenét was crowned Little Miss Charlevoix.[1]

In many ways it was not surprising that JonBenét was a beauty queen. Both her mother, Patricia (Patsy), and aunt, Pamela (Pam), had competed in pageants as young women. They are only the third pair of sisters to be state queens in the Miss America system, representing their home state of West Virginia.[2] When Patsy competed in Atlantic City, as Miss West Virginia 1977, she performed an original monologue, which won her a non-finalist talent award. One of the judges that year was Frank Deford, five years after the release of his book about Miss America, *There She Is*.[3] Three years later, in 1980, Pam Paugh sang her way onto the Convention Hall stage. JonBenét used to watch the videos of her mom and aunt competing, mimicking their movements.[4]

In June of 1994 the Ramseys traveled from their main Colorado residence to West Virginia for the fiftieth anniversary of the Miss West Virginia pageant. Patsy was recovering from her first bout with ovarian cancer, so taking her only daughter to the pageant meant a lot to her. After seeing the pageant, and her mom onstage, JonBenét became obsessed with pageants, playing pretend with her friends and her mom.[5] So, when

Patsy saw an advertisement in the local Michigan newspaper during the family's summer vacation, she decided to enroll JonBenét in the Little Miss Charlevoix pageant.[6]

Patsy was delighted. She had loved her experiences in pageantry and always felt that if she had started participating in pageants when she was younger, she could have made the Top Ten at Miss America, or maybe have won the whole shebang. Back in Colorado she asked around and learned from her hairdresser about other child pageant options. Over the next two years, with the help of Pam, Patsy enrolled JonBenét in a total of nine child beauty pageants.[7]

In late 1996 JonBenét competed in a Christmas pageant in Colorado, where she won the title Colorado's Little Miss Christmas.[8] It would be her last pageant.

After waking up on December 26, 1996, Patsy discovered that Jon-Benét was missing. A few hours later John, Patsy's husband and JonBenét's father, found her body in the basement of their home. Needless to say, the Ramseys' lives would never be the same.

But neither would the world of pageantry.

In the days following JonBenét's murder the media descended upon Boulder, Colorado. Two years after the O. J. Simpson murder trial, tabloid television was primed for another blockbuster case. The Ramsey murder was irresistible due to a confluence of factors: a slow news cycle right after Christmas, a wealthy family, and a beautiful, blonde little girl.

And then there were the pageants. Five days after the murder, NBC and CBS started showing videos and photos from JonBenét's pageants. ABC and CNN soon followed, along with local television stations throughout the country. The major networks bought the images from those who shot them at pageants; the Ramseys had no control over the footage because they did not own the rights. Patsy's Miss West Virginia title was completely overshadowed by JonBenét's child pageant experiences. In one journalist's opinion, "Child beauty pageant photos and video became the criminal record the Ramseys didn't have."[9] Those child pageant images would go on to dominate the airwaves for years.

The coverage of the Ramsey murder occurred during a time when Miss America was in decline, reality television was in ascent, and Take Back the Night events (focused on ending domestic and sexual violence in all forms) were becoming more common. The first decade of

Image from motion picture of the 1904 Asbury Park baby parade recorded by Thomas Edison.

Women wearing sashes that display their beliefs while marching in Washington, DC, during the 1913 suffrage parade.

The 1921 Miss America contestants in dresses and sashes on the Atlantic City Boardwalk. The winner, Miss Washington DC, Margaret Gorman, is second from the right in the front row.

Miss Pittsburgh 1921, Thelma Matthews, in the Rolling Chair Parade.

Lenora Slaughter with three contestants at the 1946 Miss America Pageant. She is quite literally holding the rule book.

THEY ARE ALL POTENTIAL WINNERS

"MISS NEW YORK CITY"
Bess Myerson

"MISS BIRMINGHAM"
Frances Dorn

"MISS TEXAS"
Polly Below

"MISS NORTH CAROLINA"
Dorothy Louise Johnson

Bess Myerson, Miss America 1945, is pictured as a contestant in the official Miss America competition book. She is the only contestant to wear graduation robes and be fully covered up.

Miss New York, Jacqueline Loughery, was crowned the first Miss USA in 1952. The swimsuit company Catalina split from Miss America after it was decided the winner would no longer appear in a bathing suit, which explains Loughery's attire.

An iconic image from the 1968 protest outside the Miss America Pageant, organized by New York Radical Women, shows protesters being confronted by a male opponent.

The first Miss Black America, Saundra Williams of Philadelphia, after being crowned in Atlantic City in September 1968, as part of an NAACP positive protest pageant.

Mom in utter shock after being announced Miss America 1970. Next to her is Miss Ohio, the first runner-up.

Miss America 1984, Vanessa Williams, was the first black Miss America and also the only Miss America thus far to resign her crown. Here she is pictured with the first runner-up, Miss New Jersey, Suzette St. Charles, also a woman of color.

Marla Maples standing onstage as Alicia Machado of Venezuela is crowned Miss Universe 1996. Twenty years later Machado would speak out against Maples's ex-husband, Donald Trump, in the 2016 presidential election.

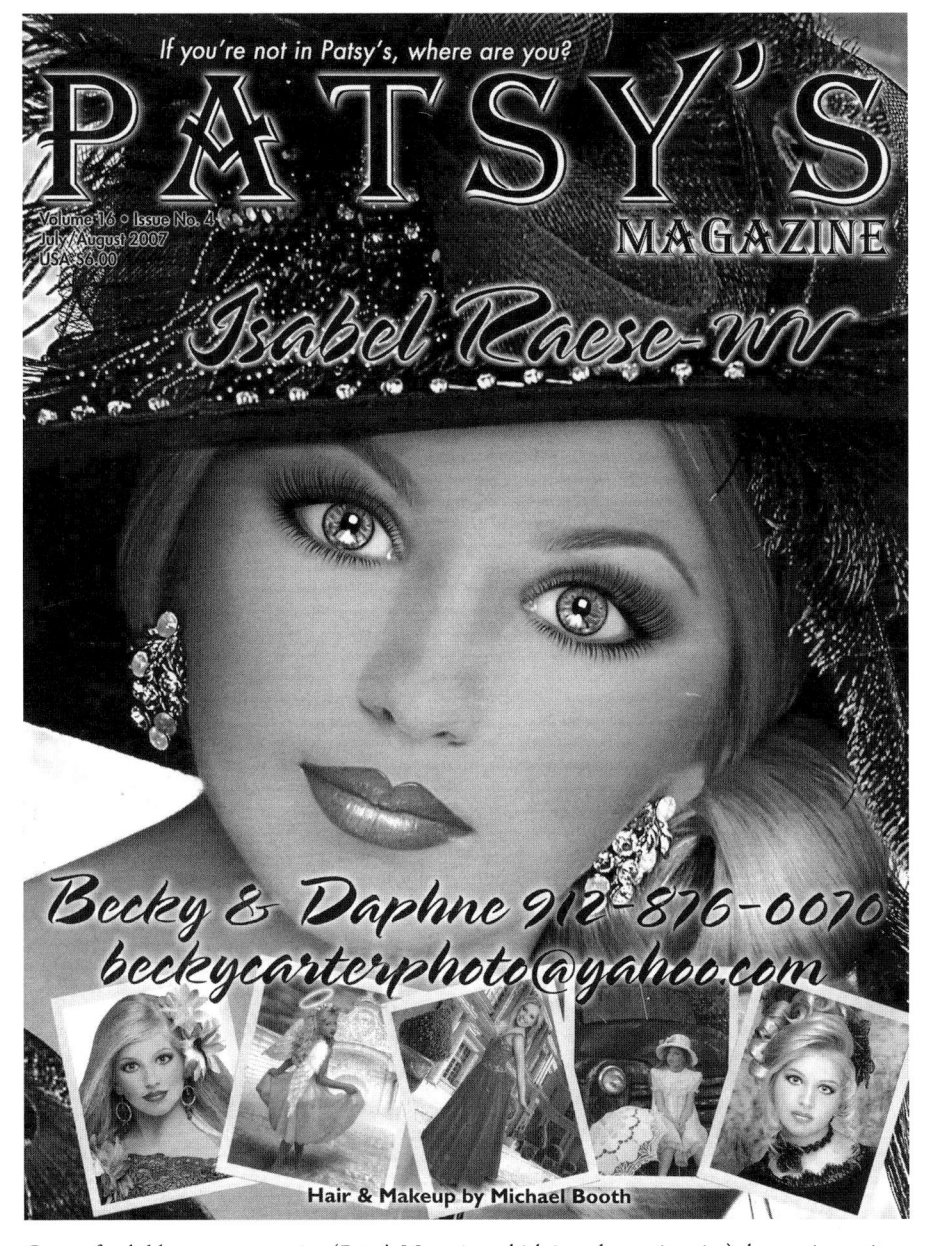

If you're not in Patsy's, where are you?

PATSY'S
MAGAZINE

Volume 16 • Issue No. 4
July/August 2007
USA $6.00

Isabel Raese-WV

Becky & Daphne 912-876-0070
beckycarterphoto@yahoo.com

Hair & Makeup by Michael Booth

Cover of a child pageant magazine (*Patsy's Magazine*, which is no longer in print) showcasing a nine-year-old pageant participant.

Leandra Thomas crowned
Miss Navajo Nation 2012–13.
Notice the use of the sash and
crown but with a culturally
specific twist.

Donald Trump and Olivia Culpo, Miss Universe 2012.

the twenty-first century saw not only growing concern about the early sexualization of young girls but also the fight against "slut-shaming," or condemning healthy sexuality, especially among young women. All this concern about younger girls and popular culture was helping to grow the rising Third Wave of feminism.

While researching this book, I attended over twenty child beauty pageants—and interviewed dozens of mothers with daughters six and under, former contestants, coaches, and pageant owners.[10] In the wake of intersectionality and concerns about what pop culture teaches young girls, I discovered a more complete, nuanced, and "within world" per-spective on the child beauty pageant community than what you may have seen on your "reality" television screen. I have found that, like most parents, child beauty pageant moms seem to have the best intentions for their daughters' long-term success in life. But those intentions come with a high price tag and lasting implications.

BEFORE *TODDLERS & TIARAS*

The media coverage of JonBenét's murder, and subsequent television shows like *Toddlers & Tiaras*, often make it seem like child beauty pag-eants are a new phenomenon. They are not. As I pointed out in part I, baby parades and contests were popular during the nineteenth century through the mid-twentieth century, until polio concerns (among others) put large groups of children from congregating on hold, especially in the summer months.

By the 1960s, with a safe and effective polio vaccine and interest in pageants at an all-time high given the massive television success of Miss America and Miss USA, the time was right for the return of children's events. But this time, they were called child beauty pageants. In 1962 Our Little Miss, the oldest continuously running child beauty pageant in the United States, was founded in Louisiana. This pageant patterned itself after the Miss America system, even awarding "scholarships"[11] to winners, meant to be saved for college tuition, beginning in 1964.[12]

Child beauty pageants grew exponentially throughout the 1960s as people wanted to become pageant directors to cash in on the growing popularity of kid pageants.[13] These were often one-off pageants, mean-ing that the title was an end in itself. There was little or no pyramidal hierarchy (like local, state, national), and the events were not necessarily associated with a festival. Rather, these were for-profit competitions for young girls.

Soon the media began to notice, and in July 1977 the *Chicago Tribune* ran a story entitled "Pageants: Little Misses, Big Dreams (for Their Mommies)." The reporter noted that "youngsters who travel the circuit learn how to fill the bill wherever they are, acting naïve and spontaneous here and knocking them dead with vampiness there."[14] Clearly, the child beauty pageant circuit was alive and well by the late 1970s.

A September 1984 *Newsweek* article on the Little Miss Pink Tomato pageant, held in Utah, further highlighted the proliferation of events run by those looking to make a quick buck.[15] The authors noted that these events "have sprung up across the country as profitmaking ventures, playing on the ambitions and vanities of parents to extort large entry fees—frequently in the hundreds of dollars—and offering token or worthless prizes."[16] Ten years later, in April 1994, a *Life* photo spread featured an eleven-year-old competitor with the whimsical name of Blaire Pancake.[17] Even with surprising revelations at the time—like the fact that Blaire had competed in over one hundred pageants, that she wore glue-on nails, that she had been accused of wearing hair extensions and having plastic surgery performed by her father—there was little outcry among the public about this American subculture.

Put another way, child pageants were hidden in plain sight in the United States. They were thought to be little more than a subcultural footnote in Southern culture. Other parts of the world, however, were interested in learning more about American child beauty pageants. In 1996 the BBC aired the documentary *Painted Babies*, which followed two five-year-old competitors, Asia Mansur and Brooke Breedwell, as they tried to win the biggest crown at the Southern Charm beauty pageant in Atlanta, Georgia, in 1995.[18] Both Asia and Brooke were Southern blondes; Asia grew up in Louisiana and Brooke in Tennessee. Both sang for their talent performances; Asia warbled out country star Brenda Lee's 1959 "Sweet Nothings" and Brooke tried to belt out another 1959 song, "Everything's Coming Up Roses" from the Broadway musical *Gypsy* (sung by the ultimate stage-mother character, Momma Rose). Both girls' families were focused on money; Asia's family was focused on acquiring it and Brooke's on how much they spent to help acquire more of it.

Instead of negatively focusing on issues of appearance (though the use of a dental flipper to cover missing teeth is presented without commentary), the documentary producers were most critical when they highlighted the related issues of money and pushing children to practice. They include a quote from Asia: "We like to go where the money and the cars are. I like to win money and cars because my grandma really wants a car and we really want money, money, money, money."[19]

Brooke's family also wanted to win big—whether that meant cash prizes between $6,000 and $10,000, a car, a cruise, or a new bedroom set. Consequently, they were willing (and apparently able) to invest more money to help secure a big victory. Brooke's mother Pam explained that each year she invested about $3,500 in her daughter's pageant wardrobe (just under $6,000 in today's money), including a beauty dress, talent costume, vogue modeling, and Western wear outfits. When a producer asked Pam what her husband thought of all the money, she replied, "Oh, he doesn't like me to spend a lot of money on it. He'd rather see me put it in the bank and let it draw interest for her education. But I feel like that this is an investment in her education because she's learning to sing and get up in front of people and have skills that will go with her the rest of her life."

In one scene where Brooke, Pam, and Pam's mother, Bunny, are practicing, Brooke complains that her feet hurt. The producer asks Pam, "Do you ever have to push her?" Pam replies, "Sure I do. I encourage her. But I have to say just like myself, sometimes I had to push myself to get up and go to work. But it's a fact of life, living in America or anywhere. We have to do some things, you know, that we don't like, just like getting up and going to work."

The producers negatively highlighted the work-like aspects of pageants for five-year-old girls more than issues of appearance and sexuality. The only reference to sexuality in *Painted Babies* was when Brooke's mother, Pam, criticized Asia's Western wear outfit, which had diamond cutouts up the pant legs on each side. She said, "Well, it's a no-no. You never go to a pageant with cutouts down the leg. It looks like something you'd see at a nudie joint or something. It's not classy."

Major public criticisms of sexuality and adultification in child beauty pageants did not begin until after JonBenét Ramsey was murdered, in

1996. Reporters converged on child pageants, and media interest exploded. It was not just network news showing clips of JonBenét's old pageants. Mainstay entertainment shows like *Entertainment Tonight* and *The Insider* did segments on child beauty pageants, as did daytime talk shows like *Dr. Phil*. Parents and directors were quickly on the defensive, especially bristling at the suggestion that JonBenét's participation in pageants had anything to do with her murder. Still, people stopped competing in child pageants in droves, because the activity now seemed tainted by death. All the attention essentially destroyed the child pageant circuit in Colorado, where the Ramseys lived, and in parts of the South.[20]

But only for a time. In the end, JonBenét Ramsey became a reverse ambassador for child beauty pageants, much like Vanessa Williams did for Miss America after her scandal.

While many were turned off by what they saw of child beauty pageants, others were intrigued. And in the early years of the twenty-first century, several documentaries, and then TV series, exposed child beauty pageants to a much bigger national and international audience, apart from the now-tainted images of Ramsey competing. For example, HBO produced a critically acclaimed documentary in 2001, *Living Dolls*. The special focused on Robin Brooner, a drill-sergeant-like pageant mom, and her blonde, waifish daughter Swan. Robin mused, "If I had a dollar for every time someone told me she looks like JonBenét . . ."[21] Other child pageant insiders confessed that parents seemed to be using JonBenét's wardrobe as a model for how to dress their children at child pageants.[22]

One of the earliest series on the pop culture–focused cable channel Bravo was *Showbiz Moms and Dads*. The 2004 show followed five families as they tried to guide their children into successful performing careers. Four of the five families featured aspiring child actors, but the fifth family was a pageant mom, Debbie Tye, and her four-year-old daughter, Emily. Like Brooke's mom a decade earlier, the producers highlighted how much Debbie spent on Emily's pageant participation (she estimated she spent $20,000 per year, which is about $27,000 today). There was also a big focus on how much Debbie forced Emily to practice her on-stage modeling routines; she estimated ten hours per week, which at over an hour per day is a lot for any four-year-old. While oversexualization was not a focus in the series, *Showbiz Moms and Dads* highlighted other questionable parenting decisions on Debbie's part related to Emily's pageant participation. This show was the first to highlight the "pageant breakfast" of Pixy Stix, which contain fifteen grams of sugar in a small tube (the entire daily recommended amount of sugar for kids is twenty-five grams). Debbie would pour multiple sticks into Emily's lipsticked mouth to give her a jolt so that she would be energetic onstage.

The early Bravo series, and people's (online) fascination with the Tyes on growing message boards, helped inspire what would become the child beauty pageant series juggernaut *Toddlers & Tiaras*. The show premiered in 2008 on the cable network TLC. Each episode followed three girls and their families as they prepared to compete in the same pageant. By the fourth season about two million people watched each weekly episode, and some of the pint-size princesses from the show were featured in *People* magazine, even earning the cover.[23] *People* also did a "*Toddlers & Tiaras* Celebrity Edition," highlighting stars like Britney Spears, Katy Perry, and Demi Lovato, who had once competed in child pageants.[24] *Toddlers & Tiaras* produced several child pageant spinoff shows like *Here Comes Honey Boo Boo*, *Eden's World*, and *Little Miss Atlanta*, along with *Cheer Perfection* (about youth cheer competitions).

But when you watch these documentaries and television series you get a somewhat skewed version of the world of child beauty pageants. Most of them focus on the most extreme version, because that is what is most fascinating and "other" to viewers. Based on my years of research, I have identified four types of child beauty pageants for girls ages six and under: natural, hobby glitz, national, and circuit.[25]

Most pageants featured on TV series are circuit pageants. Oftentimes they focus on a *hobby* or *national*-level competitor who is now "going glitz" (*circuit*) for the first time. Because circuit pageants are so extreme in terms of altering a girl's daily appearance, it makes sense that there is more media interest in them (a common tactic employed on *Toddlers & Tiaras* was a split screen showing the before-pageant girl and the made-up pageant girl).

The four pageant types are similar in that they have the beauty, or formalwear, competition. Because the child beauty pageant industry is not centralized or regulated, this is the only event that one expects at every pageant. A 2011 article in *People* magazine concluded that there are "more than 5,000 pageants a year today (*Pageantry* magazine CEO Carl

Dunn estimates that 250,000 children below age 14 compete annually),"
but it is impossible to know the true figure because there is no organization overseeing child pageants or collecting numbers on participants.[26]

While scoring standards vary from event to event, the main categories usually include facial beauty, poise, personality, and overall impres-
sion (which takes into account wardrobe issues like fit and color, even
though a judge is supposed to assess only the girl and not her clothing).
In the beauty portion of the competition, a panel of judges evaluates
contestants as they move across a T-shaped stage to a slow-paced song
while wearing a child pageant dress. Turns and poses are worked into the
beauty walk, which is supposed to glide, as the contestant maintains eye
contact with the judges and wider audience.

Many child pageants also have a modeling category. *Pro-am modeling*, or simply *pro-am*, was invented in the early 1990s by modeling
coaches to distinguish between the "professionals," that is the seasoned
pageant kids, and the "amateurs," or the pageant newbies. Today the
term is used to characterize the almost dance-like routines that you see
at child pageants but nowhere else. The routines usually last one minute
and are high energy.

To do well in pro-am it is not enough just to have a pretty face and
the right moves. You also need the right outfit if you want to become a
Supreme, a big winner at child pageants. In her 2009 coffee table book
of images of child beauty pageant contestants, *High Glitz: The Extravagant World of Child Beauty Pageants*, Susan Anderson describes pro-am
outfits as "the most inventive and outrageous in pageantry. This is the
full-on peacock moments! Costumes are covered in layers of ruffles,
fringe, mesh, fur, feathers, beading, sequins, stones, and other decorations of all kinds."[27] Certain terms associated with child pageant modeling—like a "prissy walk"—today sound like drag terms, such as RuPaul's
exhortation to "sissy that walk" or "sashay away" on the show *RuPaul's
Drag Race*.

In her 2012 book *Cinderella Ate My Daughter*, Peggy Orenstein includes a chapter on child beauty pageants. She does not focus on pro-am
per se but on the total-package contestant. To win, these contestants had
to perform "pageant conventions—the walk, the stage presence, the non-
stop smile, the nymphet moves—and, of course, the flashy outfits and
gaudy makeup."[28] Orenstein was surprised how total this transformation

could be for the young contestants: "Surprisingly, few were classically pretty and several were on the chunky side—stripped of their glitz, I would never have pegged them for pageant queens."[29]

Unlike at most Miss pageants, in child pageants it is not necessary to start at the first level and progress upward. Rather, a girl can start competing at a hobby glitz or national level and still be successful, as participation at previous levels is not a prerequisite to competing in the next level up. The ability to pay to enter is the main requirement, which many (stage) moms are willing to do.

STAGE MOTHERS: THE POSSIBILITY OF A DIFFERENT LIFE

"Those moms are just living through their kids." I cannot tell you how many times I heard this sentence when people found out I studied child beauty pageant moms, first for my senior honors thesis, which was completed in 2002, and fifteen years later to see how the mothers and daughters felt participation in child pageants had affected them longer term.

The stereotype of a stage mother is certainly rooted in reality. At Jon-Benét Ramsey's funeral (where she was buried in a pageant gown complete with a crown on her head[30]), the song "Together (Wherever We Go)" from the musical *Gypsy* was played. *Gypsy* is about the relationship between vaudeville child performer and burlesque striptease legend Gypsy Rose Lee and her prototypical stage mother, Rose.

Stage mothers have existed since children first appeared onstage. The numbers of stage moms, like Momma Rose, expanded during vaudeville days and continued to intensify as mass media developed. The advent of movies and television produced a whole new level of child star.[31]

Some of the hallmarks of stage mothers include living vicariously through a child to fulfill personally unfulfilled dreams, placing pressure on a child to succeed even if they are not very interested in the activity, being obnoxious and demanding of others to place the child on a pedestal, and putting other children down (either directly or indirectly) to raise their own child up. Not all the pageant moms I met would be considered stage mothers, though many most definitely would.

Within the group of pageant moms whom I interviewed, I found three different tracks of involvement in their young daughters' pageant pursuits. The first, and most common, was mothers who did *not* get to do pageants, or similar activities, growing up. As a consequence, they wanted to provide an opportunity for their own children that they had not experienced. The second included moms who had done pageants (or a similar activity like cheerleading, figure skating, baton twirling, or competitive dance) themselves. This group, just under 40 percent of the moms I met, were pretty happy with how their lives turned out and wanted to share similar experiences with their own daughters. The third was the smallest group—women like Patsy Ramsey who did pageants but who felt that with greater attention and investment they could have been more successful, so they were starting their daughters earlier than they had started. On some level, all these groups of women were living through their children, but that does not always result in negative consequences.

While their motivations may differ, as a group the pageant moms I interviewed were demographically similar. Most were white, with close to 90 percent identifying as such (though several of them identified their children as biracial). Most were married, at a higher percentage compared to the general population, with over 80 percent married at the time we spoke. In terms of social class, the pageant moms I talked to were more heterogeneous. Slightly more than half could be categorized as working class and the rest middle class (no very wealthy families were among those I interviewed).[32]

The class background of pageant moms helped shape choices made for their daughters. Many focus on entertainment careers for their children, which are assumed to bring financial rewards. Imagine if having a child succeed in Hollywood seems more likely, from your vantage point, than having a child go to an Ivy League school—or any college or university, for that matter. In that case, enrolling your daughter in child pageants when young to acquire skills you think will help her succeed in the entertainment industry seems like a more rational choice. In this sense, child pageants can be seen as a training ground for hoped-for financial success, rather than simply playing the lottery.

One pageant mom explained this idea, saying, "I want to see my daughters go somewhere in life. I didn't. I ended up having kids right away. I'm stuck at home now. I'm doing this for them." She thought her four daughters—ages nine, seven, four, and two at the time—could be models or entertainers and make a lot of money using what they have learned from their pageant experiences.

Moms emphasized potential future entertainment careers, not just in my interviews with them but also during pageants. At ten of the child beauty pageants I attended, when a competitor appeared onstage, the emcee read her stated life ambition. Of course, given the age of the competitors, it is highly doubtful that they actually chose these goals themselves. When I asked a mom about this, she confessed, "It is mainly the parents." She laughed. "I mean, obviously, especially when they are really young, usually a kid does not come up and say what they want to do."

I recorded all these ambitions—there were over one hundred—and then classified them into four categories. Of the girls ages six and under competing at these pageants, 56 percent had specific goals announced, more than half of which were related to the entertainment industry. Other specific career ambitions included nurse, doctor, teacher, and astronaut. The rest of the girls announced age-appropriate goals—such as learning to use the potty or how to read—or identified hopes for a future characterized by intangible values like "bringing happiness to the world" and "being the best [I] can be."

Even mothers who do not envision a career in entertainment for their daughters see child pageants as teaching their daughters how to best use their appearance for financial gain. At one pageant I attended I noticed a six-year-old girl whose read-aloud ambition was to become a dentist and a doctor. Later, in an interview, I asked her mother her opinion on how child pageants fit into the goal of becoming a doctor, a dentist, or both. She replied, "Obviously, if the child looks like Barbie, and my daughter does, I mean there are some obvious attributes, I tell her to exploit it. I tell her you're gorgeous, exploit it. Use it everywhere you can. Use it in your life."

Not all pageant moms saw physical appearance as something to exploit, especially if their daughter was differently abled in some way. I met one mother, Dorothy,[33] whose daughter Matilda was born with a cleft lip. Dorothy's niece also was born with a cleft lip, two years before Matilda. Dorothy and her sister had never done pageants, but they decided that it would be a good idea to enroll their daughters in pageants. They said they wanted to "build their self-esteem," so that they would know that they were beautiful no matter how others might react to them.

One day when Matilda was younger, before her lip was "fixed," Dorothy took her grocery shopping. She said that a child came up and said,

"Ewww, look at that girl!" Dorothy explains what happened next: "I went over to the girl's mother and to the little girl and I bent over and said, 'She's got a boo-boo, honey, and it's going to be fixed, but it's a boo-boo.' But the mother should have done that! I was very upset." When Dorothy took Matilda to her first pageant, after this incident but still before she had surgery on her lip, she said that the crowd was totally behind them, that "they were like 'Yes!' for Matilda," though Matilda did not win. Dorothy went on to reflect about Matilda's pageant experiences as a child with a cleft lip: "I've had more positive experiences at pageants than I have out in public."

Using pageants to teach a child to exploit her Barbie-like looks and using pageants to celebrate what some might see as a physical flaw seem so different that it may be hard for people to think of them hanging together. But these moms show the diversity of perspectives that exists within the world of child beauty pageants. In fact the "Barbie-looks" mom and Dorothy had their daughters competing in the same pageants. Both are types of stage moms—they have fought for their daughters and complained when they thought the girls should have won (in the process, sometimes putting other children and their mothers down)—even if their personal goals for their daughters differ.

Other pageant moms told me that they go out of their way to remind themselves that pageants are, at root, for their children. One mom—with five- and seven-year-old daughters—told me, "I asked myself a question. Was I looking at it in terms of my pastime or theirs? I realized that, and I asked them. I said if they didn't want to do it, to tell Mommy." Of course, if a five-year-old can really say she does or does not want to do pageants anymore is debatable. When pageants are all a young girl has known, it is difficult to imagine her requesting to stop, especially when combined with the possibility of disappointing her mother.

A small minority of mothers told me that their daughters, who are all six years of age and younger, actually control their own participation in pageants. Whether or not a young girl asks to do pageants, in the end it is the mother who provides the funds to pay entry fees, buys clothes, and transports the children to the pageant. Ultimately, it is the mother's decision to say yes to pageant participation. In saying yes, mothers are telling their daughters that pageants are a worthwhile activity. So how do they explain their decision?

GOING GLITZ: WHY MOMS SAY THEIR
DAUGHTERS DO CHILD PAGEANTS

Marta, a Puerto Rican woman, participated in her first beauty pageant when she was sixteen. She explained, "I don't know what made me decide to do it. It was my idea to do it, and I did it. From then on it was just like I learned how to speak. Before pageants I was a very quiet, very introverted kind of person." By the time she was twenty-five she had competed in over twenty pageants. But she hung up her pageant heels when she got married and settled in New Hampshire, where Marta started teaching elementary school. Shortly after, Jacinta, was born.

Jacinta was born with cerebral palsy. After Jacinta's arrival Marta's house turned into "Grand Central Station, between the therapists and everything that have to come through here each day." Even with all the visitors, Marta and Jacinta became isolated in their home, especially because Marta had a hard time being around children who were younger than Jacinta and able to do more.

Because of her positive experiences with pageants, Marta decided to try one with Jacinta. She explained, "I wanted to do something that was like what anybody else would do with their daughters. I just wanted to get away and do something that I would normally do. If she didn't have these problems I would probably put her in, so why shouldn't I do it now too? It was a fun mother and daughter thing to do."

Jacinta was six months old when she did her first pageant. Like the other girls her age, she was carried onstage. Jacinta actually slept through the whole pageant, while Marta held her, and she won. Marta was thrilled, but her husband was not. He did not like pageants when Marta did them, and he certainly did not like them when Jacinta did them, complaining that they were too expensive. After her win, Marta and Jacinta did not do any other pageants for over a year.

When Jacinta was two, her grandmother thought they should do another pageant as a way for the three generations of women to do something fun together. Since Marta's mom was paying, her husband acquiesced. Privately, Marta worried because she knew that at two years old, little girls walked onstage—but she would have to carry Jacinta. Her fears were confirmed when Jacinta did not win or even get a runner-up trophy at that pageant. Still, Marta felt it was a bonding experience for the family.

If most of what you know about child beauty pageant participants comes from what you have seen on TV, you might not be sure what to make of Marta and Jacinta. The family is not wealthy like the Ramseys. The family is not in pursuit of fame like many on *Toddlers & Tiaras.* They are an intact family *not* from the American South, like Alana Thompson's family, of *Here Comes Honey Boo Boo* notoriety.

While each mother I interviewed entered her daughter(s) in pageants for their own combination of reasons, like Marta, I found that many of them focused on skill development for their daughters. In this section I present the mothers' views, largely in their own words, before interrogating some of their views in the following section.

One woman, with a five-year-old and a seven-year-old in pageants, captured the seemingly rosy view of why many pageant moms enroll their young daughters in child pageants: "If the parents use pageants to teach their children how to win graciously, lose with dignity, practice hard, set goals, and make plans on how to achieve them, pageants can be a very useful tool in teaching children how to deal with life." The idea that pageants can teach children specific skills that will help them be successful was brought up literally hundreds of times in interviews with pageant mothers. The women's explanations of these benefits tend to fall into four major categories: that pageants teach confidence and poise in front of others; that pageants teach other skills like practicing and listening; that pageants teach life lessons about success and failure especially in competitions; and that pageants teach sociability and provide a setting where friendships flourish. Of course, these are lessons and skills the moms *want* their children to learn, but which their children may not actually be learning over time.

The number-one skill that moms believe pageants can teach their very young daughters, named by over 80 percent of the women I spoke with, was confidence—also referred to as poise. One woman asserted that the confidence her five-year-old daughter gained from pageants helped her be more successful in school: "On the first day of school, when all of the children were hiding behind their moms crying, my baby had the confidence to start school. She is at the top of her class academically, socially, and in personal conduct. I feel that her participation in pageants is responsible for this."

With pageants, according to moms, girls not only learned to be poised and confident in front of an audience, but they also learned to be confident when people are watching and judging them. One woman said that because of pageants her three-year-old daughter had: "Learned how to project herself in front of people. She's aware that the judges are watching her. She's okay with that."

Another mom of a five-year-old competitor further explained how pageants offered her daughter long-term benefits, explaining, "No matter what profession or role my child chooses she will more than likely, at some point, need to be able to speak and conduct herself confidently in front of others—whether it be on the PTA, as a stay-at-home mom, or in front of a board of directors of a large corporation—and pageants help with that."

A majority of moms I interviewed also focused on a second benefit— that pageants teach other specific life skills, like learning how to practice and not give up. These moms say that pageants teach their daughters that to succeed in life, you must work hard. For the girls, this means practicing their beauty walks, modeling routines, and talent numbers if they compete in that category. One woman with a three-year-old daughter said, "I've seen pageants have a very positive influence on her, because I've seen her lose, and then she's like, 'Why did I lose?' And I say, 'Because you need to practice more.' And it's taught her that. Even in school, if she's going to succeed, she has to know she has to work at it."

According to several other mothers, pageants also teach more general life lessons, the third category of reasons offered by moms. These lessons again focus on success—how someone becomes successful, and how you should not give up if you are not at first successful. Mothers again said that these life lessons are important to understand at a young age, since their children will need to deal with competition and loss in many other areas of life.

This woman's comments about her five-year-old captured the sentiment of other moms: "She's got to learn that life is not always going to be easy. It's not always going to be going her way. It's the same thing when you enter school. As you get older, there's going to be competition to get good grades. There's going to be competitive sports as she gets into that. She's got to understand that she's not going to be the only winner all the time."

Another mother emphasized that it is not just how you perform but how you react to your performance that matters. She commented on why it is important to her that her four-year-old daughter learns how to win and to lose: "I think it teaches children how to win graciously and lose graciously. They realize sometimes it's just not their day and it depends on how they behave and how they perform, just like in life. How you perform is what becomes of your life."

But pageants are not just about teaching girls serious and difficult life lessons. A sizeable number of mothers whom I spoke with emphasized that through pageants their daughters have learned how to be sociable and make friends, the final category of explanations offered by pageant moms. Close to half of the women said that pageants enabled their little girls to make friends, and that is why they stayed involved.

For example, one mother said about her three-year-old daughter, "She's an only child and she's not in day care or anything, so really her pageant friends are the ones she sees." In this case, the social event of a pageant is a child's first opportunity to forge friendships and play with girls their age. Continued involvement in pageants solidifies bonds and provides continuity of friendship for the girls. Mothers said that their daughters asked about pageants and were excited when an event is approaching because they want to see their friends. Their enthusiasm helped drive continued pageant participation.

At least a quarter of pageant mothers reported that because of their daughters' participation in pageants they also developed friendships. Just as their daughters forge relationships, mothers also had the opportunity to do so while socializing around the hotel swimming pool, at pageant parties, in hair and makeup rooms, and in the ballroom. One woman explained why this socializing appealed to her at a pageant: "My girlfriends and I sit down and have dinner and breakfast together with our kids. I myself found that pleasant because you get to talk to other mothers, especially those with kids your [child's] age, and get different outlooks from them."

These friendships contributed to mothers' sustained involvement with pageants, because they helped create excitement about upcoming pageants. One woman told me, "We're competing this weekend and I can't wait, because I'm rooming with two other women and their daughters and we're just going to have so much fun!" Another described how "there are a couple of moms from Massachusetts and we email each other. It's just over the internet, and not in person or on the phone, but it's good to know that they'll be at this one, and I can tell my daughter when her friend is going to be at the same pageant as her."

Cliques develop at child pageants, often around a coaching group or hair and makeup artist, and are evident in person and online. As often happens with cliques, they can quickly become a negative. People can turn on one another, with mothers exhibiting the worst type of stage-mother behavior if their child, or their friend's child, does not win. Name-calling, including racist terms, is not uncommon online, and loud, verbal altercations that sometimes become physical are also not unusual at child pageants. That is just the start of some of the more negative experiences associated with child beauty pageants.

CHILD PAGEANT BANKRUPTCY

Some pageant mom statements undoubtedly cause people to bristle, and there are legitimate reasons for critics' concern. Despite moms' uplifting intentions and authentic concern for their children's futures, involvement in pageants can come at a high economic and social price.

The most problematic observation I made in my years studying child pageants may surprise some people, but it came up in the BBC documentary *Painted Babies:* money. The money involved in child beauty pageants is concerning. Perhaps because the Ramseys were wealthy, press coverage didn't present money as a central issue after JonBenét's murder. But obviously all the costumes, fees, and costs for travel and accommodations add up, oftentimes to an exorbitant amount.

For most pageant families I met, who are working class, the costs of child pageants were a burden. Every pageant mom I spoke with mentioned how expensive pageants are and how it can be a hardship to do them. Some women called pageants a "rich man's sport," much like horse racing. Many mothers talked about going without things for themselves or for other children in the family in order to pay for items related to child beauty pageants. When I asked moms how much they spent on average per year, for many following their answer was the request to "not tell my husband!"

There were two common strategies for trying to allay pageant costs. The first was to become a pageant vendor. Many moms I met have picked up a pageant side job to subsidize their daughter's participation. Some have started spray-tan businesses, others make pageant clothes; a few started doing pageant hair and makeup for others, or graphic design to help others sell their pageant businesses. This illustrates how small and insular the child pageant community can be, with participants running associated businesses as well. It also complicates the web of relationships that lead many to suggest that pageants are rigged or that people paid off pageant directors to make sure their clients or even their own children would win. Online, this is often referred to as COI, conflict of interest.

The second way moms try to cover the cost of pageants is for their daughters to compete for cash prizes, which they then roll back into participating. However, the vast majority of pageant contestants never win back as much money as their parents spend for them to compete. The few exceptions tend to be pageant kids who have a parent who has a pageant business as well; so a lot of overall family time is devoted to pageantry, and most weekends include a pageant (further highlighting conflicts of interest). Moms often hope for a big title win to fund the attempt at the next big one.

This is a common strategy for families, I found, though some child pageants never actually give out their advertised prizes. Many pageants try to get out of fully awarding the advertised prizes, citing fine print about how many contestants they would have needed for that to happen (often a high number). Other pageant directors simply disappear—of course with the money brought in from entry fees.

In some sense this seems like gambling on the part of the moms, and in fact the language of addiction is frequently used when participants talk about child beauty pageants. Likening child pageants to drug addiction is common in the child pageant world, as people talk about the "high" of the first win, the experience "getting in your blood," and the need to get a "pageant fix." One pageant mom (turned director, manager, and reality television personality) wrote, "It takes just one hit of the Pageant Bong for these highly competitive personalities to become instantly addicted to the thrill of victory when their child beats another for a title based in beauty."[34]

Some families went into debt and even bankruptcy because of their child beauty pageant addiction. One pageant mom told me "There are parents down here [in the South] that are losing their trailers over pageants. They're like addicted; they're crazy." She went on: "I personally had a friend who literally lost her trailer. It was pretty much because they were doing too many pageants." That the home was a trailer further highlighted the precarious financial position of the family.[35]

When it comes to the high monetary cost of child pageants, for most families the real issue is what they are *not* spending all that pageant money on. For some, it may be activities for other children in the family. For others, it may be rent or medical costs. For nearly all, it is at the expense of fully investing in educational funds for their daughters. While families can justify the expense of registration fees because of skill acquisition or rebrand travel costs as family vacations, the reality is that spending over $1,000 on a dress for a four-year-old, which she will grow out of, is hard to justify.

The notion that some people might be so into child beauty pageants that they lead their families into financial ruin is especially galling to those who already find child beauty pageants appalling because they teach girls that their appearance is a valid criterion on which to be judged. Concern over girls believing their self-worth is related to how they look is a common criticism of beauty pageants, and particularly child beauty pageants. Some pageant moms seem to accept that the game of life may be stacked in favor of "pretty people," and they want to prepare their daughters to succeed in that system rather than fight against it. Of course, another way to fight that system is to focus on achievement in other areas like school, sports, music, languages, or fine arts (which, again, is why spending so much money on child beauty pageants may not be the best choice).

Another negative dimension of the overemphasis on physical appearance at child beauty pageants is that much of the ideal beauty is fake. Makeup and spray tanning begin at the hobby glitz level and are everywhere at the circuit level. As you move up in pageant levels, add in flippers to cover teeth, false eyelashes, hair falls or dye, and more.

We know from psychological studies, referred to as rouge and mirror tests, that by eighteen months, half of all children recognize their reflection in the mirror as themselves. Sixty-five percent of children at twenty to twenty-four months try to wipe off rouge or other makeup on their faces when they see them in the mirror, because they know that those marks are not "them."[36] While we do not know what happens when one sees a version of oneself who appears much older, it presumably elicits a similar response.

When mothers pay others to help their children look different through hair and makeup or spray tanning, they may be putting their children at risk in another way. One concern raised about children using makeup and spray-tan solution is whether the materials are toxic or formulated specifically for children.[37] Additionally, unlike cosmetologists, who must be licensed in each state—which helps ensure hygienic standards are maintained—many people who are paid to perform these services at child pageants are either not licensed cosmetologists in any state or not licensed in the state where they are performing the services. At many pageants I have attended, the lack of hygiene in pageant beauty services has led to the spread of sicknesses like pink eye. At child pageants these services are often rendered in hotel rooms, a practice that may also be illegal given statutes about running businesses out of hotel rooms (usually meant to prevent prostitution, but applicable here as well).

Most of the fake enhancements mothers pay for at child pageants are tied to sexuality. False eyelashes make the eyes appear wider—which, according to evolutionary psychologists, people consider to be attractive, because the eyes widen at the time of sexual climax. Similarly, cheeks are rouged and lips darkened because both occur due to heightened blood flow during arousal. Having lots of hair on the head is related to fertility, which explains why long hair extensions are often used. (The two sexual exceptions are having white teeth and tan skin, which are now more associated with class status than sexuality.)

This is especially true in child pageant photos, which are in a category by themselves. The usual photo is a close-up of a child's face, punctuated by bright colors and accessories. The faces are then retouched in a way that makes all the photos look similar. The cumulative effect of retouching makes the girls look almost double their age and highlights sexual features. The process adds eyelashes and a glint to the eyes, and often reshapes facial features (like more almond-shaped eyes or rosebud-shaped lips). Retouching also often smooths out the skin, but in a way that is not natural. When you see a retouched glitz pageant photo, you will likely be startled by how much the child looks like a doll.

Undoubtedly, young girls in pageants are being sexualized. Based on my research, this may not be intentional on the parts of the mothers, and the girls likely do not understand what it means, but nonetheless prepubescent girls are being sexualized when they get done up to compete at a child beauty pageant.

With some girls this sexualization can also happen through their outfits. This may be intentional, like one mom on *Toddlers & Tiaras* who dressed up her three-year-old as the prostitute version of Julia Roberts's character in *Pretty Woman*, or unintentional, like the cutouts in Asia's Western wear, from *Painted Babies*, that drew criticism from mother of rival Brooke.

Then there are the routines that girls perform while wearing those outfits. Some child pageant modeling routines showcase skill, like pro-am routines with multiple heel and fashion modeling turns. But those that incorporate lots of winking and blowing kisses at the judges and audience raise concern. Typically, a wink is meant to show affection or be flirty. While this may not be how it is intended in the context of a child pageant, it has that meaning outside a hotel ballroom. Similarly, when a girl shakes her hips and shimmies onstage, mothers may not think they are teaching their girls to be sexual, but the movement itself is sexual regardless of the intention.

As some moms told me, anyone who "twists" what a three-year-old does onstage at a child beauty pageant into something sexual is the sick one. On the one hand, I understand where they are coming from. At child pageants the environment is pretty tightly controlled. More often than not, someone at the door checks to be sure that anyone entering the ballroom has bought a ticket because of being connected to someone competing at the pageant. Also, far from being a male environment, child beauty pageants are remarkably female dominated. Yes, some of the more successful hair and makeup artists, photographers, and coaches have been men—but they are usually men who are openly gay. Most of the time the judges are also female.

While in the context of a child beauty pageant a four-year-old may blow kisses and bat her *fake* eyelashes because that is what other winners have done in their onstage routines, the reality is that outside a pageant ballroom those same actions would have a very different meaning. From my observations, mothers do not do a good job of explaining to their daughters what might be pageant appropriate and what that means outside pageants.

But I would be remiss not to point out that some of the same fake aspects of child beauty pageants are common in other children's competitive activities. This is especially true at dance competitions, including ballroom. In the competitive versions of those activities, girls sometimes go a step beyond the child beauty pageant, using highlighter to paint on abdominal muscles and biceps or to darken the space on their chest that could indicate a bust.

In 2010, a video of a group of five seven-year-olds dancing to the Beyoncé song "Single Ladies" went viral. Yes, the dancers were cute and talented, but the performance went viral because they wore costumes that suggested lingerie and thigh-high boots. Also at times the choreography was extremely suggestive, which made viewers liken the routine to child pornography.

One might also say the same about cheer, gymnastics, figure skating, and even synchronized swimming—all activities where sequins and rhinestones are often embraced along with makeup, hair falls, and false eyelashes. One thing that unites these activities is that the female body is being subjectively assessed, which partly explains the emphasized femininity that is displayed. At the same time, it is fair to say that in these activities there is a much bigger focus on what that feminine body can *do*, rather than mainly focusing on how it *appears*. In fact, many child pageant girls go on to do at least one of these other activities as they get older. Until their girls are old enough to cheer or compete in gymnastics, these moms choose pageants as a way to jumpstart their daughters' performative skill-based acquisition.

But what if a child does not happen to be physically talented or strong enough to do those other activities? If a mom wants to teach her daughter that physical appearance is likely to be assessed in our society, she could turn to child modeling or child acting. Of course, both have also been the subject of criticism, but they still have not been as marginalized as child beauty pageants. Interestingly, among child performers, enhancing appearance with alterations such as flippers is also common.[38] But, because in these instances children make money as opposed to parents spending it, child actors and models are often seen as more socially acceptable than child pageant queens (though still problematic). The stories about what happens to child performers as they age prompted me to explore what happened to some of the child pageant contestants I met when they reached young adulthood.

"GIT IT GURL!": BUT FOR HOW LONG AND AT WHAT COST?

One of the biggest issues raised by child pageant critics is what the long-term impacts are on the young participants in child beauty pageants. Most assume that the effects will be profoundly negative, and that they will undoubtedly include eating disorders or body dysmorphia, low self-esteem, and an intense focus on appearance (likely at the expense of educational achievement). With few exceptions, no one has been able to follow a group of child beauty pageant participants into adulthood. But because I began studying child beauty pageants in 1999, most of the young girls I saw compete are now young women. I located many of them via social media and was able to interview them, along with their mothers again, in some cases.

In 2008 the BBC did something similar when it aired *Painted Babies at 17*.[39] The director of the 1996 documentary *Painted Babies*, returned to the American South a little over a decade later to find out what happened to Asia Mansur and Brooke Breedwell. Recall that the initial *Painted Babies* featured the two five-year-old girls as they prepared to face off in a Georgia pageant. When the filmmakers returned to find the girls in high school, Asia was still competing in pageants, even after her father left the family, which plunged them into financial uncertainty. Brooke no longer competed, instead focusing on her studies at a boarding school in Tennessee.

After the release of the BBC follow-up, Brooke spoke out against child beauty pageants, saying they caused her anxiety and complicated her relationship with her mother. Brooke is now married and works as a speech-language pathologist. Asia has worked as a pageant coach and as a Hooters waitress. She has two children, including a girl who has competed in pageants.

The divergent paths shown in the *Painted Babies* documentaries are similar to divergent paths I found when I interviewed young women whom I saw compete as very young girls at child beauty pageants. Some are in college, playing sports on college scholarships, while others became teen moms. Some own their own businesses, while others have unfortunately passed away (one from long-standing health problems and another from an apparent accidental drug overdose). In reflecting on their child beauty pageant days, all the young women I spoke with focused on the pivotal role that their mothers played in their participation in child pageant. But, as a group, they had mixed reactions to the lasting impact of their pageant participation.

Sally Anne[40] began competing in pageants when she was two years old. She did at least one per month until she finally stopped around age eleven. While she had a lot of fun playing with kids at pageants, she longed to be a "normal" kid, like her friends at school. Sally Anne hated missing school to get to and from a pageant, feeling like she was missing out on key aspects of childhood friendship with her peers.

Now, at twenty-one, she is pursuing a bachelor of science degree and dreams of becoming a physician assistant. With the benefit of distance Sally Anne now wishes she had not stopped participating in pageants. She explains, "I think that being different is completely okay. When you're at pageants everybody is the same and pretty much has the same goal. But when I was younger at school, pretty much no one did pageants; they were doing sports or dance. Now I realize that being the same as all the other kids at school isn't great. . . . Now I *want* to be a little bit different."

Sally Anne also feels that pageants gave her a great deal of confidence. For instance, because she started competing so young, she never got nervous onstage, and she never wondered what the judges thought, because she knew there would always be another chance at a pageant around the corner. She contrasts that to how her friends today act: "Going onstage, or in front of a classroom, or in front of a bunch of people, compared to friends who are so nervous to do something like that, I know that it just doesn't matter. I get that confidence because I did pageants as a kid."

Audriana, who often competed against Sally Anne, shares similar feelings about missing out on "normal" childhood due to her pageant participation when she was younger. But for Audriana, distance has brought less of a rosy view of her childhood pageant experiences. Audriana's mom put her in her first pageant before she was a year old, and she estimates she must have done one hundred pageants before stopping at age nine. Audriana hated practicing with her mom, and she hated that pageants took up so much time. She felt like she was always getting ready for a pageant rather than having time to sing or play the piano or be with friends.

Audriana also hated that mothers fought with one another and that the environment was so stressful. When she was younger she was much more of an extrovert, but now she reports that she is very shy because she wants to avoid "drama." While Audriana admits that she did learn good interview skills from child pageants (interviews can begin at the types of pageants she did at age four or five), she qualifies that by saying she learned how to "talk to people, get them to be interested [in you], hear more about you, and like you." She sees this as more about artifice than reality. Now a student at a major state university, Audriana has no interest in watching a pageant of any type and is rarely in touch with kids she met from her pageant days.

Other girls have remained involved with pageants, gearing up for participation in Miss pageants, like Sommer. Sommer plays basketball on a partial scholarship at a Division II school. She competed in national level teen pageants and is now competing in both the Miss America and Miss USA systems. Karen, Sommer's mom, says that they "wouldn't change anything they did, even though we don't know if Sommer's success is only from pageant participation."

Sommer did about one hundred child pageants before taking a break after an injury that damaged skin on her body. Somewhat counterintuitively, Sommer feels that child pageants taught her that how you look is not the only thing that matters. She continued to succeed in pageants even after the injury that altered her physical appearance, and being in pageants allowed her to do charity outreach for kids with similar challenges, like burn victims. For Sommer, pageants give her a platform to promote and display service.

As I found with moms, some former child pageant contestants plan to do child pageants with their own children someday. Sommer counts herself in that category, explaining, "I feel it would be unfair if I didn't share those experiences with my children. I loved pageantry as a child, and still love it to this day. I feel my mother did a wonderful job of always making sure I was having fun (even if there were moments where I became grumpy)."

Others disagree. Neveah, who is already a mom, says, "I will never have them [her kids] participate in something like pageants. . . . It teaches girls at an early age that you will always be objectified, like a doll." Neveah and her sisters stopped doing pageants when they were much younger than Sommer, Audriana, and Sally Anne. Neveah was five when her pageant career ended because "we didn't have the money to continue to travel."

When I asked many former pageant contestants how they felt about all the money their parents invested in pageants over the years, I was surprised that there was not much resentment expressed over "lost" funds. Of those who did not attend college later in life, like Neveah, that was more of a personal choice than a financial one. Nonetheless, the financial cost of child beauty pageants was the most cited explanation by this group of former contestants as to why more girls do *not* participate in child beauty pageants, followed by the negative stigma associated with them due to media coverage.

Though no one told me they were angry with their parents over the cost of pageant participation, many of the young women reported having strained relationships with their mothers today. Feeling pushed to succeed was a continued source of tension for some. But most of them, along with their moms, felt that in the years they were doing pageants it helped them become closer, because they were "united behind the same goal." Usually this meant winning and being a Supreme or pageant name. Even mothers and daughters who no longer are close concurred that participating in child beauty pageants helped give the young women confidence in front of crowds, which has followed them to the present. This is the one skill that mothers most wanted their daughters to learn from pageant participation, and the good news is that it seems to have stuck long term.

Another skill had more mixed results longer term: learning to lose gracefully. Former child pageant contestants definitely report that they learned about winners and losers from pageants. However, the *gracefully* part did not always happen.

Mary, who competed between the ages of five and thirteen, certainly learned that not everyone is a good sport in pageants—this lesson came from watching her mom. Mary's mom, Tiffany, was the one who told her daughter that she should exploit looking like Barbie throughout her life, so perhaps it is not surprising that Tiffany was not exactly a graceful loser. While Mary won a lot, Tiffany was never happy when Mary lost. She spent a lot of time of time gossiping and attacking other families on internet message boards (commonly known in pageants as the Voy boards).

Despite Tiffany's (over)investment in Mary's pageant career, one thing Mary and Tiffany agree upon is that in Mary's case, she absolutely was the initial impetus for getting involved in child beauty pageants, and that she was also the reason she stopped. Three-year-old Mary saw a poster one day in an elevator for a pageant and begged her parents to let her participate. The only child eventually wore her parents down, and as soon as she participated in the first one, the whole family was invested. Once Mary said she was no longer interested, just before she turned thirteen, her parents were supportive. Mary decided child pageants were no longer for her, because she wanted to spend more time with her school friends.

Mary thought of pageants as an elaborate form of dress-up, which is still basically how she thinks of child beauty pageants today. "What little girl doesn't want to play dress-up?" Mary mused. Although, as she discovered, the dress-up can be a façade and "uncomfortable at times." She specifically mentioned wearing a flipper and having hot curlers rolled tightly in her hair as moments she does not remember fondly and that caused physical discomfort.

Mary is now married and a successful small business owner. While not all her memories of the nearly one hundred pageants she competed in are fond, overall she thinks that "people make it more dramatic—both worse than it is in real life and more of a fantasy. It's just like a sport, no different than soccer, football, or cheer." While she does not currently have children, she said if she did she would direct them toward sports like dance, soccer, or basketball, which she thinks carry the same socialization tools but at a better price. Though she is critical of the need at pageants to be "perfect" in terms of outward appearance ("tan, teeth, muscle, outfit"), in the end it is the cost that would keep her away in the future.

One of the few studies to look at the impact of young girls' participation in pageants was published in 2005 in the academic journal *Eating Disorders*. The study looked at responses from eleven college-age girls—a very small sample size—who reported ever having done a pageant along with responses from similar girls who did not. The hypothesis was that the pageant girls would be more likely to have an eating disorder. But the authors found that on measures of bulimia, body perception, depression, and self-esteem those who participated in pageants did not differ significantly from those who did not. However, "childhood pageant participants scored higher on body dissatisfaction, interpersonal distrust, and impulse dysregulation than non-participants."[41]

This appears consistent with what I found: pageants have a lasting impact, but not always as deeply negative as what you might predict. None of the young women I interviewed reported any issues with disordered eating (though those that may have eating issues could be less likely to have a public presence on the internet, making it harder for me to find them now, or for them to respond to my inquiry). Some of them did have issues regarding interpersonal trust, though, especially with their mothers. In both the study and my sample, all the past child pageant participants were young women when they replied (no one was older than early twenties), so it is possible that more negative outcomes could surface later in life.

But Blaire Pancake, a woman in her thirties, suggests that also may not be the case. Recall that Blaire was the eleven-year-old pageant contestant featured in a major *Life* article in 1994, which insinuated that her father performed plastic surgery on her. At the time, she said she wanted to be Miss America, but after her father's early and untimely death, Blaire stopped doing beauty pageants.

In 2006, just before she aged out of the Miss America system, Blaire decided to compete for the title of Miss Tennessee. Her pageant training kicked in and she won on her first try. Notably, Blaire became one of the few women with MBAs to compete at Miss America. While she did not place at Miss America, she has remained involved with pageantry, running a local Miss America preliminary in Texas.

With the benefit of time and reflection she now likens her pageant experiences to being a competitive athlete. Her younger sister, Brooke, is a professional golfer on the LPGA tour, so Blaire does have a good frame of reference. Now married with three young children, one of whom is a girl, her pageant story ended on a positive note, despite an early negative media experience. When I asked Blaire if she would ever put her daughter in pageants, she replied, "I want to introduce her to a lot of different things—sports, the arts, etc.—and find something she excels at and is passionate about. I have no idea what that will be yet—she's eight months and has two big brothers. If she wants to try a pageant at some point in her life, I will definitely support her, and if she never wants to compete in a pageant, I will absolutely support that too. I want her to be confident in herself whether she chooses to compete in something with a helmet or with heels."[42]

Not all the stories of former child beauty pageant contestants have happy endings. A few months after I re-interviewed one pageant mom, her then nineteen-year-old daughter died of an apparent accidental drug overdose. Similarly, when I located Marta, I was saddened to learn that Jacinta, who would have been nineteen, passed away in her sleep when she was three-and-a-half years old.

Marta's daughter Kenya was four months old at the time of Jacinta's passing. By that age, Kenya had already competed in her first beauty pageant. When Kenya was two and a half, the family relocated to South Carolina, where they had a third daughter, Selena. Marta said that Selena looked just like Jacinta as a baby, proof that "God gave her back to me." Selena has also competed in child pageants sporadically, and Marta would love for her to be able to do more, because she has a "big personality."

Marta still enjoys doing pageants with her daughters, but the cost means they do only a few per year. Living in the South now also means that the pageants are bigger, which means more preparation is needed. But because they do it only once in a while, she said, "they have more fun with it." For Kenya and Selena, it is exciting, a time for family bonding, and offers an environment where they can learn to have no fear onstage.

As Marta reflects on what pageants meant to Jacinta, she emphasizes that "it helped her to be around people and feel like one of the other kids, not feeling different." Marta feels that it "was also important for other people to see that we are different from each other, but we need to celebrate that." While pageants, including child pageants, celebrate an ideal, there is also space for others, even if those differences are not reflected on a television screen.

THE "REALITY" OF PAGEANTRY AND TELEVISION

It is not a stretch to say that the Miss America Pageant, when it first aired on national television in 1954, was the first reality television show. It created a celebrity overnight, a no-name girl who suddenly was elevated to the status of royalty by virtue of being the ideal American woman. In the

1950s and 1960s Miss America was joined by a range of games shows, including *Queen for a Day*, all a different form of reality television.

An American Family, which ran on PBS in the early 1970s, is recognized as the first reality television series.[43] The series had more of a documentary, amateur videographer quality, but it was both popular and powerful as it tackled controversial issues at the time, like divorce and homosexuality. It would take two more decades for a similar series to come out—this time on the cable network MTV. In 1992 *The Real World* premiered as an unscripted soap opera detailing what happened when young strangers—all very different—moved into a house together.[44]

The year 2000 marked the opening of the floodgates for American-based reality television. That is when *Survivor* and *Big Brother* premiered on national network television in the United States. Both were competitive shows in which a single winner walked away with a big prize, which further increased viewer interest. Since then, non-scripted television has taken over both network and cable airwaves.[45]

Two of the biggest reality television juggernauts were born in 2002—both with beauty pageant links. *The Bachelor* was created by producer Mike Fleiss, who shot to television stardom with his 2000 one-off special on Fox, *Who Wants to Marry a Multi-Millionaire?* The show pretty much sounds exactly like it was . . . except that the multimillionaire was not a multimillionaire. While pitching the idea, Fleiss "won over the Fox executive after he said he envisioned the special as a version of a Miss America pageant."[46] Twenty-three million people watched, making it a huge success and paving the way for *The Bachelor*, the series, to premiere on ABC in March 2002.[47]

If you were to watch that first season, or even the most recent, at times you might be confused, thinking you are watching Miss America. For two hours fifteen women wear evening gowns, don bathing suits, and attempt to show off a talent. The male host, Chris Harrison—who hosted the Miss America Pageant from 2004 to 2017—asks questions, teases the audience, and moves the show along. Millions watch to see who the eventual, singular winner will be.

While the Miss America Pageant—and other pageants like Miss USA and Miss Universe—have been decried as out of touch, misogynistic, and retrograde, *The Bachelor/Bachelorette* franchise has swooped in not only to lay claim to these same criticisms but also to claim a larger market share. All episodes in the *Bachelor* franchise had higher ratings than any pageant aired in the same year.

Note that in a true Miss America–*Bachelor* crossover, Mike Fleiss judged the 2012 Miss America Pageant. That year's winner, Miss Wisconsin, Laura Kaeppeler, married Fleiss in 2014. And, yes, in case you were wondering, Chris Harrison performed the wedding ceremony.

When *American Idol* premiered on Fox a few months after the first *Bachelor*, it started to make the talent portion of Miss America obsolete. If you were a singer from a small town, why use Miss America as a springboard? Former Miss America contestants did much better on *American Idol* than they did in state pageants. For example, season 3 winner Carrie Underwood did not even make it to the Miss Oklahoma state pageant after competing at a preliminary; season 1 runner-up Tamyra Gray won Miss Atlanta but did not make a strong showing at Miss Georgia.

As more competitive reality television shows continued to develop, the cultural relevance of beauty pageants on television continued to decline. Simon Cowell on *American Idol* often lobbed the "too pageant-y" criticism, which meant a contestant was being too robotic or trying to be perfect and not natural. Tyra Banks did the same on *America's Next Top Model.*

While *America's Next Top Model*, which premiered in 2003, has not succeeded in creating high fashion editorial models, it has changed the mindset of many who had previously thought of modeling as a mindless job for those lucky enough to win the genetics lottery (or discipline their bodies in sometimes extreme ways). Tyra Banks took it upon herself to try to convince viewers that modeling is hard work—about knowing one's angles, understanding lighting, and approaching the enterprise as a business with the skill to brand oneself. Models, especially those who do runway and editorial work, generally have higher status than pageant contestants do. But both groups face similar critiques—especially about oppressive beauty standards and objectification of women's bodies by a patriarchal system for monetary gain.[48] Tyra Banks has become a high-profile defender of modeling, but pageantry does not have an analogous figure.

Two other competitive reality shows with pageant implications—*So You Think You Can Dance* and *Dallas Cowboys Cheerleaders: Making the Team*—premiered in 2005 and 2006 respectively. Both brought into relief how, well, *untalented* the Miss America talent portion could be at times. *Making the Team* has had many former pageant contestants and winners compete over the years. In 2018 Rachel Wyatt, who was a first runner-up at Miss America and had been Miss America's Outstanding Teen from South Carolina, tried out for the Dallas Cowboys Cheerleaders (DCC). The coaches often said when Wyatt was in training camp that they wanted her to look less perfect, similar to how Banks and Cowell would chastise pageant contestants.

Wyatt made positive comparisons between pageants and the DCC. She explained in an on-camera interview on *Making the Team* that both look for "total package" women (borrowing a phrase common in child beauty pageants), which means a woman who is beautiful, talented, intelligent, and well spoken. To Wyatt this means that she has to do it all and be more than just a pretty face. Though, of course, to be an NFL cheerleader, or a model, you do need that pretty face as well as a particular type of body; namely, thin and toned. The level of criticism the coaches on *DCC: Making the Team* make about these women's bodies is in fact much more extreme than what is done at a pageant. On the show the competitors are regularly weighed in (which no longer happens at pageants). They also can be cut, sometimes solely because their bodies do not look good in the team uniform.

Not surprisingly, as competitive reality shows with a focus on appearance and talent continued to develop, Miss USA and Miss America continued to lose viewers. Competitive reality shows were not the only unscripted shows to affect pageants on TV; makeover shows have as well. Many makeover shows draw inspiration from beauty pageants. Take the controversial show *The Swan*, which premiered in 2004. On that Fox show, "ugly" women were given plastic surgery extreme makeovers, and they then competed in a pageant-like format to see who would be named "the swan." Other well-known makeover shows include *Bridalplasty*, *Queer Eye [for the Straight Guy]*, and *What Not to Wear*.[49] Many of these shows, like *The Biggest Loser* and *Extreme Makeover*, promoted hypergendered forms of femininity (and masculinity), as they made over participants.[50]

As these shows developed, Miss America was pushed off network television for the first time since 1954.[51] The Miss America 2006 pageant was different from the previous year in three ways. First, it moved from network to cable television, airing on CMT (Country Music Television). Second, for the first time since 1921, Miss America was not held in Atlantic City, New Jersey, but rather in Las Vegas, Nevada.[52] While Miss USA had started in Long Beach and then found a more stable home in Miami for over a decade, after the 1970s it moved around to a different location nearly every year. Not so for Miss America, which was almost synonymous with the Boardwalk in the Jersey Shore town. Related to this move to Vegas was the third change, a new date. No longer was Miss America related to extending the summer season on the shore past Labor Day—it was now held in January.

While many factors contributed to the decline in interest in Miss America over the years (from increased concerns about objectification of women to more opportunities, like sports, being open to young women), the reasons it moved off network television in 2005 can almost all be attributed to the popularity of the reality TV show format, especially competitive reality TV. Owen Edwards wrote in *Smithsonian Magazine*, "Before 'Survivor,' 'The Apprentice,' and 'Fear Factor,' only two elimination contests mattered to America. One gave us a president, and the other gave us Miss America."[53] This quote also suggests how males and females were generally sorted and evaluated in America during the twentieth century.

A *New York Times* headline in 2005 captures this sentiment: "'Fear Factor' Era Poses a Challenge for Miss America."[54] *Fear Factor* was a show in which people performed stunts (like eating sheep's eyes or letting rats crawl all over them in a tunnel); being dignified was not exactly what was getting ratings.[55] The article argues that a "multinight elimination, complete with appeals for audience sympathy and votes, something like 'America Idol'" could work to "save" Miss America on network TV, along with "behind-the-scenes segments and, perhaps, some of the plotting that has made shows like 'The Apprentice' on NBC so popular." Before shows like *American Idol* and *The Apprentice*, it was usual that the viewing audience would not know the pageant contestants, especially over an extended period of time, but that changed with the rise of reality television, as viewers wanted to invest in individuals and their stories.[56]

By 2008, CMT had dropped Miss America as well. TLC picked it up, a few months before it started airing *Toddlers & Tiaras*, and tried to give it a reality TV makeover in keeping with other programming on the network. Over the two years it was on the cable network it was preceded by a four-week series in which the Miss America contestants had to do obstacle courses and take trivia quizzes to try to earn a public vote for a spot in the Top Sixteen. One problem was that the two winners of those years—Miss Michigan, Kirsten Haglund, and Miss Indiana, Katie Stam—were barely featured (the latter more than the former). Winning seemed like a separate skill from being a television personality, although there were later many pageant contestant crossovers to competitive reality shows, like *The Amazing Race.*[57]

But in 2012 Miss America moved back to network TV, airing on ABC. It was a huge victory for then Miss America CEO Sam Haskell, who worked his previous Hollywood connections as a top agent to facilitate the new contract. Despite cable channel attempts to make the broadcast more reality TV friendly, the two-hour network telecast stuck to its long-standing format. Two years later Miss America also returned to Atlantic City and its traditional September broadcast date—although the future remained unclear, especially as the one hundredth anniversary approached. In 2019, after being picked up by NBC, Miss America was held for the first time ever in December, and in Connecticut.

In 2009, one of the years that Miss America was on TLC, a game-changing competitive reality television show premiered on Logo, a network at the time aimed at LGBT viewers: *RuPaul's Drag Race. Drag Race* combines many genres—it is like a pageant, talent competition, modeling demonstration, and challenge show all in one. Each week a drag queen contestant gets eliminated after two challenges: a runway performance and a lip sync competition. The series proved so popular that in 2017 it switched to a more watched cable network, VH1.

Pageant contestants are often disparaged on *RuPaul's Drag Race*, the same way they are on other competitive reality TV shows. In this case the pageant contestants come from the world of drag pageants. Miss Gay America is the oldest and largest of the drag pageant systems, but like other niche pageants, there are many rival pageant systems. One of the most popular is Miss'd America, which is held in Atlantic City as a spoof of Miss America. Some of the other top drag pageants include Miss Gay USofA and Entertainer of the Year. Both include divisions for gay men to compete (not in drag).

Separate pageants for lesbians and drag kings also occur, though not on the national scale of drag pageants like Miss Gay America. Many major cities host Pride pageants, where multiple winners are crowned for the year. For example, in 2019 I judged the Rhode Island pride pageant, which crowned Miss Gay Rhode Island (those who identify as men in drag), Mr. Gay Rhode Island, Miss Lesbian Rhode Island, Mx Trans Rhode Island, and Mx Bisexual Rhode Island.

Before *RuPaul's Drag Race*, pageants were the primary way for a drag queen to make a name for herself and book top performance venues. With the rise of the television show, that has shifted (in fact, many drag queens now report that it is harder to book gigs if they have not been on the show, and those who have not been on *Drag Race* often get paid less at appearances[58]). As a consequence, many drag pageants, especially Miss Gay America, are making changes to stay relevant, much like Miss America has tried to do. Whereas Miss America has cut one competition category—swimsuit—Miss Gay America has talked of adding new categories or at least winnowing down the extensive rules it has, including prohibitions on surgical enhancements and hormones.[59]

Of note is that within the past few years both Miss USA/Miss Universe and Miss America have welcomed trans women to compete in their pageants. While none of the American pageants have had trans women compete at the national level,[60] Miss Spain 2018, Angela Ponce, competed at Miss Universe, and Jenna Talackova competed at Miss Canada in 2012. Talackova fought for the right to compete at Miss Canada, changing the rules for Miss Universe and paving the way for Ponce to compete.

Toddlers & Tiaras and *RuPaul's Drag Race* began airing within a few weeks of one another, with the latter preceding the former. Though comparing drag pageants to Miss pageants seems obvious, there are also a remarkable number of similarities between child pageants and drag. Both are at heart about the art of female illusion, as the little girls are dressing up to look like women—a form of exaggerated femininity that relies on makeup and costumes to complete the transformation. In fact, in several *Toddlers & Tiaras* episodes, drag queens are featured. In season 4 one family looks to drag for inspiration on how to be fierce. In season 5 one child pageant contestant is coached by a drag queen (recall that some of the modeling terms seem similar), and in season 6 a full drag-queen panel judges a child pageant in Las Vegas.

Gay men in general have a big role in pageantry, but especially in child pageantry. (Within Miss pageantry, where gay men are often coaches and fans, there is sometimes a cultural divide with more conservative pageant boosters like the Jaycees.)[61] Many of the child pageant circuit-level coaches, hair and makeup artists, and photographers have been gay men. In HBO's *Living Dolls*, what I consider to be the best child beauty pageant documentary, the gay couple featured are successful coaches, photographers, hair and makeup artists, and fathers to their own child beauty pageant–winning legend. One of the coaches, Mr. Shane, would energetically yell at all his clients to "Git it, gurl!" Other men associated with child beauty pageants, like pageant emcees, are presumed to be gay—which, again, somewhat uncomplicates the ways in which the pageant transformation of a four-year-old girl can have sexual overtones.

Another group linked to child beauty pageantry—though the connection is rarely made—are Irish Travellers. Irish Travellers are an ethnic group in both the United Kingdom and the United States (mainly in the South). In recent years, thanks to—you guessed it—reality television, this marginalized group of largely itinerant families has been in the spotlight. In the UK a series called *Big Fat Gypsy Weddings* started airing in 2010. Many gypsy women, another name for many Irish Travellers, marry young in elaborate weddings. Their attire at weddings and community dances, where the purpose is finding a mate, is very sexual, despite the fact that brides are expected to be virgins. TLC ran the British series and then developed a spin-off focused on Travellers in the United States, *My Big Fat American Gypsy Wedding*. The similarities in wardrobe to child beauty pageants is remarkable. In one episode an eight-year-old Traveller girl is shown competing at a child beauty pageant.[62]

Irish dancing competitions, which have historical links to Traveller culture, also have similarities to child beauty pageants, though they are rarely discussed. Irish dancing competition dresses not only share a similar shape to the "cupcake" dresses of child beauty pageants, but they both also have a lot of embellishments, like rhinestones and glitter, which some describe as "gaudy." The top Irish dancing girls, usually all under eighteen, compete wearing wigs full of sausage ringlet curls, often with crowns (or hair decorations that resemble crowns). Tans are also expected at these competitions. As one insider put it, "If you don't have tanned legs, if you go up there with white legs, you can forget it."[63] Irish dancers wear heavy stage makeup, often including false eyelashes and bright red lips. It should not surprise you to learn that TLC ran a special on Irish dancing in 2012 (based on a 2011 documentary, *Jig*, about children competing in the Irish Dancing World Championships[64]).

It is not a stretch to think of the cable network TLC as the modern version of P. T. Barnum's museum, which was filled with "odd" people on display alongside adorable children competing in baby shows or photos of beautiful women. In the twenty-first century, TLC transformed itself from The Learning Channel into a station featuring stories of unusual families and rare people. Often children have been involved. Examples, beyond the ones mentioned, include the Gosselin children (first on *Jon and Kate Plus Ei8ht* and later on *Kate Plus 8*) and the Duggars (of *17 Kids and Counting*, then *18 Kids and Counting*, then *19 Kids and Counting*, until finally *Counting On* as the kids starting have their own).[65]

Unlike child performers on television, whose earnings are somewhat protected (from stage moms and other relatives) through the Coogan Law,[66] which requires that a certain percentage be put in a trust for only the children to access when they come of age, reality television kids are not granted the same protections. That also means that for any *Toddlers & Tiaras* girls, and those who got their own spinoffs, like Honey Boo Boo Alana Thompson or Eden Wood, the money their families earned by doing the shows does not legally have to trickle down to them, even though they were the stars.[67] It is unclear how being on reality television might affect these children long term, as we just do not have many cases yet.[68]

SLUT-SHAMING PAGEANT PARTICIPANTS

Almost a quarter century after JonBenét's murder the pageant industry has perversely profited because of the attention. Without JonBenét there would be no *Toddlers & Tiaras*—and there probably would not have been a fictional *Little Miss Sunshine* either.[69] In the end, child beauty pageants are a bigger business than before, thanks in large part to all the post-JonBenét publicity, which exposed a relatively small and unknown American subculture to a broader audience.

The growth in mass media coverage of child beauty pageants occurred at the same time as the interest in pink princess culture grew among girls in the United States. The first American Girl store opened in Chicago in 1998. The Disney Princesses line of marketing started in the early 2000s. Justice clothing stores for girls opened in 2004. But as successful as these brands have been, they have also faced critiques, including from those who say that girls are being taught too early to be consumers and, in some cases, to be too sexy too young.[70]

The American Psychological Association Task Force on the Sexualization of Girls released a report in 2007. All the companies named in the previous paragraph were mentioned in the report, along with specific activities, including child beauty pageants. The report delineates four ways in which sexualization can occur:

> a person's value comes only from his or her sexual appeal or behavior, to the exclusion of other characteristics; a person is held to a standard that equates physical attractiveness (narrowly defined) with being sexy; a person is sexually objectified—that is, made into a thing for others' sexual use, rather than seen as a person with the capacity for independent action and decision making; and/or sexuality is inappropriately imposed upon a person.[71]

The last of these most applies to child beauty pageants. Having been to so many child beauty pageants, I can say with certainty that in context there is nothing sexual about them. Outside a hotel ballroom would some of the moves be considered sexual? Absolutely, but that meaning is nearly completely absent in the room, and certainly to the children I watched. The same can be said for the makeup they wear and some of their clothing. But as communications professor Gigi Durham writes in her book *The Lolita Effect*, "Clothing and makeup aren't problematic. It's the corollary assumption—that youth is sexy, that little girls are sexy, and that because of that they can be seen as having the same sexual awareness as adults—that's of real concern."[72]

The first time I taught my seminar on beauty pageants at Brown University, in 2015, my students had a strong reaction to the readings and documentaries on child beauty pageants, including one that surprised me. Many of them almost took offense to criticisms of the child pageant girls, especially when it came to issues of sexuality. It was not that they were condoning all aspects of child pageants, but rather, they were challenging the criticisms based on what contestants wore. My students made a connection that I had not—they likened those criticisms to a form of slut-shaming.

Slut-shaming is when someone who usually identifies as female (sometimes also a gay man) is criticized for wearing clothing or behaving in such a way that seems to transgress social norms about sexuality. That may mean having multiple sexual partners, kissing in public, or walking around in a short skirt or a midriff-bearing top. While slut-shaming has been around for centuries, the term came to life in the 2010s, especially with the rise of social media, as people online would comment on images with statements like "She's asking for it."

To reclaim the word *slut* and to take some of the power away from detractors, the first SlutWalk was held in Toronto in 2011. The key message was that no one deserves to be a victim of sexual assault or violence. The SlutWalks soon spread to the United States and became "the most successful feminist action of the past 20 years."[73]

My students, who were very much women who might attend a Slut-Walk, did not want to see any woman or girl criticized for how she chose to dress. This perspective is a key part of Third Wave feminism, which focuses on choice. Unlike Second Wave feminists who pooh-poohed pornography and criticized prostitutes, budding Third Wave feminists have embraced sex work as being about bodily autonomy. If a woman wants to strip, so be it. If a woman wants to be Miss America, she has that right. And if a girl enjoys the accoutrements of competing in a child beauty pageant, why impose outside societal norms on her?

It *is* fair to criticize the mothers' decisions to enroll their young daughters in pageants, given the girls' lack of agency in the vast majority of cases, but to today's young feminists, criticizing the girls themselves should be off limits. This is in keeping with criticizing institutionalized systems of oppression, especially patriarchy, but not individuals who may be constrained by it.

A great example of how young women today are comfortable with this dichotomy was the final paper a student wrote for my pageants course. She compared the ways in which many of her peers assiduously prepare their bodies and, shall we say, small wardrobes to be ready to wear a bikini on spring break each year to how pageant contestants prepare for the swimsuit competition. Exercise and strict dieting were key to both

groups. While she did not judge her peers, she did judge a society, dominated by social media, for promoting thin and fit bodies that many could
achieve only through severe deprivation and dedication. The women she
knew punished their bodies to attract a sexual partner, yes, but also for
the perfect image to put on Instagram.[74]

JonBenét did not ask for the sexual assault she appeared to suffer
when she was murdered either. Regardless of whether her murder is ever
solved, under no circumstances should we see her participation in child
beauty pageants as an excuse for the violent way in which her life ended.
Just as baby shows helped bring women's bodies into the public sphere,
allowing them to compete and be judged, debates about child beauty
pageants continue to challenge us to think about female-presenting bodies in public—and the ways in which we can keep them safe. This became a major rallying cry as American feminism's Third Wave crested in
2017—with ties to Miss USA/Miss Universe through Donald J. Trump.

CHAPTER 6

The Pageantry of Politics

Campaigns during the #MeToo Era

"ONE OF THE WORST THINGS he said was about a woman in a beauty contest—he loves beauty contests, supporting them and hanging around them—and he called this woman 'Miss Piggy,' then he called her 'Miss Housekeeping' because she was Latina."[1]

The "he" was Donald J. Trump. "This woman" was Alicia Machado, Miss Venezuela 1995 and then Miss Universe 1996. The speaker was Hillary Clinton in the waning minutes of the first presidential debate of the 2016 presidential cycle, on September 25, 2016, at Hofstra University. The most watched debate in American history, with eighty-four million viewers, ended by connecting pageants and politics.

Donald Trump is a central figure linking pageantry, politics, and feminism. Until the twenty-first century, pageants and politics mainly mingled through marriage.[2]

The Machado-Trump story was not the first time that pageants and politics had come into play during an American presidential campaign (or for a Clinton). During the 1992 campaign, Miss America 1982, Elizabeth Ward, originally Miss Arkansas, was romantically linked to Bill Clinton in 1983—when both were married.[3] Ward denied the allegations throughout most of the 1990s.[4] During the US House impeachment inquiries led by Ken Starr, she avoided directly answering the questions, leaving it open-ended as to whether they had ever had an affair. It was not until April 1998 that Ward publicly admitted to a one-night stand with Bill Clinton back in 1983. After reports surfaced that Clinton forced himself upon her, she came forward to vehemently deny those allegations and finally go public with the truth.[5]

Clearly, pageants and politics have a complicated past. During the twenty-first century the relationship continued to evolve as more Miss America contestants decided that they did not want to marry (or sleep with) the politician. Rather, they wanted to *be* the politician. At the same time, more and more Miss America contestants begin attending elite colleges and universities as the Third Wave of feminism continued to swell.

Miss USA/Miss Universe changed as well. This chapter begins with Donald Trump, and his 1996 acquisition of the Miss Universe Organization (which also owns Miss USA and Miss Teen USA), when Alicia Machado was crowned Miss Universe. Trump's opponents emphasized his behavior with and toward women—both at his pageants and beyond—during the 2016 US presidential campaign. Partly fueled by the now infamous 2005 taped conversation with Billy Bush on *Access Hollywood* in which Trump bragged that he could "grab [women] by the pussy," anger over misogyny snowballed into the Women's March, a massive public event on January 21, 2017, marking the start of Third Wave feminism. The march inspired more women to run for political office. It was followed soon after by the #MeToo movement, one of the first major actions of Third Wave feminists and which would become tied to Miss America.

TRUMP'S (MISS) USA AND UNIVERSE

Donald Trump bought the Miss Universe Organization in 1996, but the origin story starts earlier, in 1990, somewhat ironically in Atlantic City. That was the year Trump's massive casino and hotel the Taj Mahal, dubbed the eighth wonder of the world, opened on the Boardwalk. It is also where and when Marla Maples finally went public about her affair with Donald Trump.[6] Speaking from the Atlantic City home of Trump friends, Maples declared to Diane Sawyer (America's Junior Miss 1963, lest you forget), "I do love him."[7]

Marla Maples grew up in a small town in Georgia about two hours north of Atlanta near the Tennessee state line. The only child of a homemaker and a small-scale real estate developer, who moonlighted as an Elvis impersonator, her childhood seemed idyllic. In high school she played varsity basketball and was named homecoming queen.[8]

After graduation in 1981 Maples headed to the University of Georgia. But she was more interested in fame than academics, and she soon dropped out to pursue modeling work in Atlanta. Maples identified a path she believed could help her attain her goal of celebrity: beauty pageants. In 1983 Maples won the first-ever Miss Resaca Beach pageant. The title was a joke—there was no beach near the Georgia town where the contest was held. It was also a throwback to the early iterations of contests like Miss America, promotional gimmicks dreamed up by businessmen. The main responsibility of the winner was to host carpet shows, the major industry in the Dalton, Georgia, metropolitan area.[9]

After her victory as Miss Resaca Beach, Maples competed in the 1984 Miss Georgia USA pageant, where she finished as first runner-up. The following year she entered, and won, the Miss Hawaiian Tropic International beauty pageant, a bikini contest to select a spokesmodel for suntan lotion. The then twenty-one-year-old wrote on her entry form under "long term goal": "I hope to become successful as a screen actress and some day do Broadway."[10]

Some have suggested that Maples and Trump met in Daytona Beach when she was Miss Hawaiian Tropic 1985.[11] It is not implausible that Maples and Trump met at a bikini beauty contest. Ron Rice, the businessman who founded Hawaiian Tropic and its company pageant, explained that Trump would "come to our pageants because he enjoys being around the girls. . . . He was kind of a regular with us."[12] Wherever Trump and Maples met, there is no question that in the late 1980s they started an affair that would redefine tabloid culture and rock New York society.

After Trump's divorce and subsequent remarriage to Maples, in 1993, he needed a way to bring her into the "Trump brand" and business. Since both had been around beauty pageants, it seemed that pageantry could be a natural fit. Jim Gibson, a musician and producer who was a longtime friend of Trump (and who, coincidentally, had dated Maples in Georgia), suggested Trump purchase his own pageant.

Shortly after Gibson's suggestion the Miss Universe Organization was put up for sale.[13] According to Gibson, "I went to Donald as I would if I had a property to renovate and modernize and make it profitable enough to sell. . . . Donald, as he always does, brought in CPAs and did financial reviews and he came to the conclusion that the valuation was low and there were things he could do to bring the valuation up."[14] In the end,

Trump's plan to up the value was pretty basic: make the heels higher and the bikinis smaller.

Trump also decided to sell half of the Miss Universe Organization to CBS. In his 2004 book *How to Get Rich*, Trump explains that he wanted CBS to be both owner and broadcaster in order to cut out the licensing fee and maximize promotional opportunities.[15] He also saved money, and promoted the family brand, by having Marla Maples host. In 1996 and 1997 she cohosted Miss USA and Miss Universe.[16] Some whispered behind the scenes that it was a way to keep Maples busy and away from her husband as the marriage crumbled. By 1999 Maples and Trump were divorced. Even with Maples gone, Trump stuck with the Miss Universe Organization. He simply loved being around beautiful women . . . while making money off them.

His takeover was not without controversy of course. Trump's first Miss Universe, Miss Venezuela Alicia Machado (crowned with Marla Maples standing to her right), created headlines long before the 2016 presidential campaign. Machado was crowned in mid-May 1996. By August, press reports surfaced about her weight gain, including quotes from Trump about her being fat. When she appeared at the 1996 Miss Teen USA pageant, Machado had just been given an ultimatum: lose a significant amount of weight or lose the crown.[17] The issue of the nineteen-year-old's weight would continue throughout her entire reign. Trump would call the press (whom he would castigate as well: "A lot of you folks have weight problems. I hate to tell you."[18]) to watch her work out in New York and Palm Beach. In February 1997 he flew Machado to Mar-a-Lago so she would be in shape for the May 1997 Miss Universe Pageant in Miami, Florida. Trump said he put Machado on a diet because "'it is obviously not healthy to be overweight,' . . . adding that his office has been 'besieged' with calls about Machado's weight."[19] Despite all the criticisms, Machado completed her year as Miss Universe and crowned her successor, Brook Lee of the United States (Hawaii), in February 1997.

Machado was not the only problematic Miss Universe in Trump's early years of ownership. In May 2002 Miss Russia, Oxana Federova, was crowned Miss Universe. Four months later she was dethroned—the first Miss Universe ever to lose her title. The true reasons have never been made clear (pregnancy? marriage? an alleged affair with Vladimir Putin?).[20] But, after the 2002 Miss Universe debacle, Trump was able, through a bidding war, to make a more lucrative television deal with NBC to air his pageants.[21]

Two years later, Trump struck a different deal with NBC, this time for his own television show. *The Apprentice*, a competitive reality show, premiered in January 2004. That April over twenty-eight million people watched the finale. With the showman Trump at the helm, *The Apprentice* was a hit. Not surprisingly, there were pageant contestants on the show. For example, season 4's Marshawn Evans came from the "other" pageant—she was second runner-up at the 2002 Miss America Pageant.[22] Trump was always on the lookout for a (pageant) crossover. He says he convinced NBC to do the *Fear Factor* episode featuring Miss USA contestants.[23]

Trump turned a different Miss USA Pageant scandal into another reality television series, *Pageant Place*. Miss USA 2006, twenty-year-old Tara Conner, almost lost her title after news stories came out about wild partying, including underage alcohol consumption and cocaine use. There were also photos of her kissing Miss Teen USA, Katie Blair, while they danced on tables.[24] But Trump, "a believer in second chances," sent Conner to rehab instead of taking her crown away, calling her a small-town Kentucky girl who got caught up in the whirlwind of the Big Apple.[25]

In 2007 Trump was the executive producer of the MTV series *Pageant Place*. Meant to star the three queens he "owned" who were living in their Trump Tower apartment during their reigns, the series featured Conner, as a fourth addition, who moved back into the apartment. Part of the series focused on the arrival of Miss Teen USA 2007, Hilary Cruz, whose win was overshadowed by the cringe-worthy final answer by Caitlin Upton, Miss South Carolina Teen USA 2007.

Upton's viral question and answer was "Recent polls have shown a fifth of Americans can't locate the US on a world map. Why do you think this is?" To which Upton replied, "I personally believe that U.S. Americans are unable to do so because, uh, some, uh, people out there in our nation don't have maps and, uh, I believe that our education like such as in South Africa and, uh, the Iraq, everywhere like such as, and, I believe that they should, our education over here in the U.S. should help the U.S., uh, or, uh, should help South Africa and should help the Iraq and the Asian countries, so we will be able to build up our future. For our children."[26] Trump definitely embraced any type of press—positive or negative—so it was a surprise when 2007 became the last year Miss Teen USA was shown on television.

Miss USA 2009 brought a new scandal, one in which Trump directly inserted himself. During the final questions, Miss California USA, Carrie Prejean, was called over by host Billy Bush (yes, *that* Billy Bush, of the "grab them by the pussy" recording). Prejean selected a judge at random, and her questioner was celebrity blogger Perez Hilton. Hilton asked, "Vermont recently became the fourth state to legalize same-sex marriage. Do you think every state should follow suit? Why or why not?"[27]

Prejean's answer roiled the gay-friendly pageant world: "Well, I think it's great that Americans are able to choose one or the other. We live in a land that you can choose same-sex marriage or opposite marriage. And you know what, in my country, in my family, I think that I believe that marriage should be between a man and a woman, no offense to anybody out there. But that's how I was raised, and that's how I believe it should be—between a man and a woman."[28]

After that answer there was no way Hilton, who himself is gay, would allow Prejean to win. He gave her the lowest score possible, and she finished as first runner-up. Prejean, conservative in both her religion and her politics, lost her Miss California crown a few months later over contract violations (showing up late to appearances or not at all), though her answer, and subsequent notoriety, seemed to be the real reason.[29] The winning Miss USA 2009 was also an evangelical blonde—Kristen Dalton from North Carolina—so it was not as if Prejean's views on same-sex marriage were so far out of the realm of what many pageant contestants may have believed.[30]

In her 2009 book about her brief time as Miss California USA, Prejean recalls what happened when Trump visited the contestants during Miss USA's pageant week. "Donald Trump walked out with his entourage and inspected us closer than any general ever inspected a platoon. He would stop in front of a girl, look her up and down, and say, 'Hmmm.' Then he would go on and do the same thing to the next girl. He took notes in a little pad as he went along."[31] After the "inspection," girls were separated into two groups, what Prejean dubbed the "hot from the not." While she made the "hot" group, she confessed, "Even those of us who were among the chosen couldn't feel very good about it—it was as though we had been stripped bare."[32]

Prejean's report, seven years before the presidential election, lends credence to accounts of other former contestants who spoke out during the 2016 presidential campaign in the wake of the Machado story. Prejean's story is even more damning to Trump, because Prejean is one of his supporters, often wearing a MAGA (Make America Great Again) hat on her social media. Contestants from the Miss Teen USA 1997 pageant provided similar accounts, but go further than Prejean did, saying Trump went backstage and saw them naked while they were changing (and, of course, they were all underage).[33] The story was the same at the Miss USA 2001 pageant,[34] along with Miss USA 2006.[35]

Trump himself admitted to this behavior in an interview on *The Howard Stern Show* in 2005, the same year he got married for the third time, to Slovenian model Melania Knauss. "I'll go backstage before a show, and everyone's getting dressed and ready and everything else," he said. "And you know, no men are anywhere. And I'm allowed to go in because I'm the owner of the pageant. And therefore I'm inspecting it."[36]

But these accusations and admissions were *not* why Trump was forced to sell the Miss Universe Organization in September 2015. The main reason Trump lost control of the pageant he ran for almost two decades was because on the day he descended the escalator at Trump Tower to declare his candidacy for president, June 16, 2015, one of the many things he said was "when Mexico sends its people, they're not sending their best. They're not sending you. . . . They're sending people that have lots of problems, and they're bringing those problems with us. They're bringing drugs. They're bringing crime. They're rapists. And some, I assume, are good people."[37]

The outcry was swift, especially at Univision, an American Spanish language television network. Univision said it "could not remain in business with a presidential candidate who had offended many Hispanics."[38] Both Univision and NBC canceled the upcoming Miss USA telecast on July 12. The hosts and judges pulled out as well. But the show went on, broadcast on the cable channel Reelz.[39] After Trump sold the pageant at the end of 2015—first he bought back NBC's share and a few days later he sold it to WME/IMG (William Morris Endeavor and International

Management Group, now known as Endeavor)[40]—Fox picked up the annual broadcast. Trump had dropped *The Apprentice* from his portfolio earlier in 2015 after announcing his presidential bid, as it was too big a conflict for a candidate to be on network television.

As was later revealed, the pageant roots of Trump's presidential campaign ran even deeper. In November 2013 the Miss Universe Pageant was held in Moscow. It was an unusual choice for a bikini-based pageant, given the weather. But Trump wanted to do more business there. The previous June, just after Trump announced that the Miss Universe Pageant would take place in Russia, he tweeted, "Do you think Putin will be going to The Miss Universe Pageant in November in Moscow—if so, will he become my new best friend?"[41]

Jeffrey Toobin wrote in a February 2018 *New Yorker* article detailing the links between Moscow, Miss Universe, and the 2016 presidential election, "Today, the Miss Universe pageant in Moscow looks like a harbinger of the Trump campaign and Presidency, featuring some of the same themes and characters."[42] This is not only the supposed date and location of the alleged compromising material related to "golden showers," it is also where the Trump family spent a lot of time with the Agalarov family, Russian billionaires with dreams of celebrity. On June 3, 2016, Emin Agalarov's publicist (Emin performed at the 2013 Miss Universe Pageant) emailed Donald Trump Jr. "offering damaging information about Hillary Clinton as 'part of Russia and its government's support for Mr. Trump.' Donald Jr. replied, 'If it's what you say I love it.'"[43]

Many people, especially women, were less than thrilled with Trump's election over Hillary Clinton. The apotheosis of this upset was the Women's March held across the United States and around the world on January 21, 2017, the day after Trump's inauguration. The marches have been declared the largest single-day demonstration in American history.[44] Millions, likely over four, marched because they were outraged, disturbed, and scared by Trump's unexpected victory.

Janaye Ingram, one of the main organizers for the Women's March, competed as Miss New Jersey at Miss USA 2004, under the gaze of Donald Trump.[45] One of Trump's beauty queens turned on him, helping organize what would be the definitive founding event of Third Wave feminism. Soon many women, including former beauty queens, were significantly more politically engaged, fighting for safer environments for women.

FROM REIGNING TO CAMPAIGNING

To put it simply, the way Donald Trump treated (pageant) women objectified them. He fulfilled the worst stereotypes about how men regard women in beauty pageants. Yet, many women who have competed in beauty pageants see their participation as a way to advance themselves, particularly when it comes to politics. On the surface level, pageants and politics are similar because they both are about one person winning a title that represents a specific locale. Digging deeper, pageants, and especially Miss America, seem to help women cultivate some of the skills of a successful politician. Those skills include developing a public narrative, being verbally quick on your feet, advocating for an issue, raising funds in order to compete, and having the stamina to do multiple events in one day (especially when it comes to giving the same stump speech over and over while gripping and grinning before and after). Local and state pageant winners also often attend the same functions and parades as elected leaders; they eat the same chicken dinners and wave at the same crowds as they engage civically.

A few Miss Americas were politically active prior to Trump's election. Before 2016, however, only three had run for an elected, public office, including Bess Myerson, Miss America 1945, who ran for US Senate in the New York state Democratic primary in 1980.[46] After Trump's election that number doubled as more recent Miss Americas ran for offices at the local, state, and federal levels. In 2017 Ericka Dunlap, Miss America 2004, ran for the Orlando City Commission to represent District 5. In 2018 Mallory Hagan, Miss America 2013, ran as the Democratic nominee in Alabama's 3rd Congressional District. In 2019 Heather French Henry, Miss America 2000, ran for secretary of state in Kentucky as the Democratic nominee. As of yet, no Miss America (or Miss USA) has won elected office.

Miss America state queens have been successful in running for, and winning, public office. Teresa Benitez-Thompson, Miss Nevada 2002, is one of the most important currently in office.[47] Benitez-Thompson, a Democrat, was elected to the Nevada Assembly in 2010 and in 2017 became the majority floor leader. This is noteworthy because in 2019 that body became majority female—the first time in American history that a state legislature was made up of a majority of people who identify as women.[48] Benitez-Thompson frequently fights for women's issues. In

2019 she was a leader in passing the Trust Nevada Women Act, which lifted restrictions on abortion and made contraception more accessible. She also has led on issues related to maternal health and economic justice, especially for women and children living in or near poverty.

Miss America local title holders have also risen to political prominence—with Sarah Palin being the most well known. Palin, the former governor of Alaska and 2008 Republican vice-presidential nominee, was second runner-up at the 1984 Miss Alaska pageant. Palin, who identifies herself as a feminist (in the "women and men should have equal opportunities to succeed" sense, not the "change structural forms of patriarchy" sense), has never supported women's issues as Benitez-Thompson has. For example, while Palin was pro-contraception, she was anti-choice and anti–gay rights.[49]

Notably, the woman who beat Palin to become Miss Alaska 1984 (and the first African American winner, to boot), Maryline Blackburn, is now an elected official. In 2017 Blackburn won a spot on the Smyrna, Georgia, city council representing Ward 5. She was reelected in 2019, fighting for issues of economic justice, diversity and inclusion, and environmental stewardship.[50]

Miss America is not the only pageant system to see their former queens elected to office, though it does appear to have the highest concentration. Of the other three national pageants I have discussed, all have former competitors who have run for public office. Republican US senator Marsha Blackburn of Tennessee competed for Mississippi's America's Junior Miss title in 1969 while representing Laurel. Miss District of Columbia 1994, Angela McGlowan, a Miss USA contestant, ran for US Congress out of Mississippi's 1st Congressional District as a Republican. Lauren Cheape Matsumoto, Miss Hawaii Sweetheart 2010 (and Miss Hawaii 2011), also a Republican, was elected to Hawaii's House of Representatives in 2013.

Festival pageants are also popular among voters, which makes sense, given their strong local and community ties. Melanie Stambaugh, the 2009 queen of another well-known festival pageant, Miss Daffodil in Washington State, and a Republican, became the youngest member of the Washington House of Representatives in 2014.[51] The current governor of South Dakota, Republican Kristi Noem, was South Dakota's Miss Snow Queen 1990. Former Michigan governor Jennifer Granholm, a

Democrat, won San Mateo County Dream Girl of 1977 as Miss San Carlos at the San Mateo County Fair, in California.[52]

Most of America's beauty queen politicians started their campaigning after 1990. The introduction of the platform competition at Miss America likely played a role. The term *platform* itself has political implications, as political parties and candidates put together platforms detailing their goals and stances on major policy issues. Language matters; the same year that platform was added, 1990, the Miss America Organization (no longer called a *pageant*) stopped referring to a Miss America's *reign*, instead calling it a *year of service*. Since the introduction of platform, it has become much more common for contestants to say that they are "running for Miss Oregon" or "running for Miss America."

When Caroline Bright "ran for" Miss America as Miss Vermont 2010, her platform issue was "Rock the World—Run for Office." She committed to run for office before age twenty-five, which she did just two years out of the pageant system. At age twenty-two she was thrilled that more than seven thousand people voted for her to represent Franklin County as a Democrat in the Vermont state senate. About the results of the election she said, "The margin was so small. We came 390 votes from electing the youngest female senator to any state senate in the U.S.' history, so that's pretty cool."[53] In 2016 Bright again ran, this time for Vermont's House of Representatives, but also came up short.

Bright believes that Miss America contestants have great potential as political candidates and politicians because "we're trained for it. We spent all year getting ready to do this job [of Miss America], which has the same qualifications you need to run for public office."[54] Bright identified those qualifications as intelligence, a commitment to public service, being media savvy, having the ability to handle a rigorous travel schedule and attend countless civic events, and the knack for listening and speaking to a group of people at a moment's notice.[55]

One Miss America turned politician highlighted the ways in which being directly engaged with the legislative process, as part of her platform, solidified her decision to run for office someday. Heather French Henry, Miss America 2000, ran for secretary of state of Kentucky as the Democratic nominee in 2019. As Miss America her platform was advocating for homeless veterans, an issue that was very personal to her because her father is a disabled Vietnam War veteran. Henry's advocacy took her to Capitol Hill multiple times to testify before Congress as Miss America, particularly on the Homeless Veterans Assistance Act.

Henry told me that she learned during her year as Miss America that "if you want to make a profound change in the area you care about, you must do legislative work."[56] While she first turned to policy and administrative jobs, even serving as commissioner of the Kentucky Department of Veterans Affairs, eventually she turned to electoral politics. This is not surprising, according to Jennifer Lawless, a political scientist who studies women running for office, who found that many eventual candidates identify the political proximity they acquired on a job to be a motivating factor in their decision to run for public office.[57]

For a time, Henry also served as Second Lady of Kentucky, after marrying the then lieutenant governor of the state, from 2000 to 2003. She told me she was shocked at the time to discover that, because of her time as Miss America, she had better media training than any other political person around her. Not only that, Henry was one of the few who had direct experience being thrown into meetings in the White House, with cabinet members, or doing a lot of spontaneous public speaking. Regarding the latter she said she got used to giving her "platform speech and translating it differently to different audiences. . . . Everything I did during my Miss America year was sharpening skills that are vital for being a public servant."

Henry's choice to highlight media training is telling. As Miss America evolved in the 1990s, so too did politics and the way it was covered. The rise of twenty-four-hour cable news from across the political spectrum has made politics look more like entertainment at times, and it helped turn some politicians into TV personalities. Candidates and pols are expected to "always be on," sound bites win the day, and politicians are expected to look the part—qualities Miss America contestants actually strive to develop while still in their twenties. This means that beauty queens are often prepared for a higher level of media scrutiny.[58]

Erika Harold, Miss America 2003, who has thrice run for office as a Republican in her home state of Illinois (for Congress in 2012 and 2014 and for attorney general in 2018), remembers watching Miss America and political conventions on television as a child. The ritual and, yes, pageantry, of both appealed to her: constituents waving signs, wearing buttons, and cheering wildly for their state rep. The fact that politics and pageantry have converged more generally in American society does not surprise her: "Reporters ask [celebrities] their opinions about political events a lot more. Decades ago you could be a public figure without being forced to engage on other issues. Now in order to be relevant you have to be able to give your opinions."[59]

Miss America 2018, Cara Mund of North Dakota, who herself has political ambitions, concurs with Harold. The final questions the night she won were extremely political. Fellow finalists were asked about allegations that Trump's 2016 presidential campaign colluded with Russia (though Miss Universe was not mentioned), if Charlottesville protestors were really "very fine people," as President Trump had characterized them, and if Confederate statues should be taken down. After the pageant, when asked if she thought it was fair for the judges to ask contestants about political issues, Mund was adamant: "Miss America needs to have an opinion, and she needs to know what's happening in the current climate."[60]

Another way in which politics has become more like entertainment is evident in the rise of celebrity culture, particularly with television and movie stars running for office. Ronald Reagan, a former Hollywood actor and president of the Screen Actors Guild, has been the most prominent example.[61] But the election of Donald Trump showed that reality television stars were now included as well.

Another person who directly links pageantry, politics, celebrity culture, and reality television is Arnold Schwarzenegger. Schwarzenegger first rose to prominence by winning the titles of Mr. Olympia and Mr. Universe multiple times and being featured in the documentary *Pumping Iron*.[62] In these bodybuilding competitions he showed much more skin than any beauty pageant contestant. Bodybuilding helped him become a Hollywood actor and, in turn, become governor of California in 2003. In 2015 Schwarzenegger took over for Donald Trump on *The Apprentice* after Trump announced his presidential campaign.

Schwarzenegger's career highlights that former professional athletes are part of celebrity culture as well. Other professional athletes who have been successful in national politics include Bill Bradley (NBA), Jim Bunning (MLB), and Jack Kemp (NFL). No women have made this list— yet—given unequal professional opportunities. But it is precisely the lack of similar athletic opportunities for women to date that illuminates how beauty pageants, in lieu of sports, can be an effective path to power for women.

Celebrities in general, whether athletes or actors or beauty queens, have become increasingly politically active as individuals want to use their personal platforms to promote issues they care about. Social media has made this easier. Some media scholars argue that the mingling of entertainment and politics makes for a more inclusive democratic process. Celebrities can attract more people and subsequently help politicians engage with a larger audience.[63]

Why might a past as a celebrity be helpful in *being* a politician? Celebrities are used to performing in front of large crowds, especially when it comes to public speaking. Similarly, they are used to dealing with the media—being interviewed and being observed. As political candidates, celebrities are able to leverage their popularity, which provides built-in name recognition at the ballot box. They also often have greater financial resources to buy more advertising and hire field staff to canvass door to door, which also increase name recognition.

Also, looks matter in politics. Recall the reaction in 2010 to photos of President Obama on the beach in Hawaii. He was ogled and dissected, even though how a president looks in a bathing suit has no bearing on his leadership abilities. Politicians know that ideally they need to be fit, healthy, and attractive to be successful at the ballot box. Jeb Bush practically starved himself to get thin for the GOP 2016 presidential primary race, and Chris Christie's larger swimsuit body came in for intense criticism in 2017 after a photo of him on the beach circulated. Most celebrities (especially actors) tend to be considered especially attractive, and former professional athletes are apt to take excellent care of their bodies, looking extremely fit.

For male politicians, being attractive is seen as an overwhelming positive; it is a bit more complicated for females. Being *too* attractive can backfire on a woman if it leads others to dismiss her as ditzy or just a pretty face. In her 2016 book *Breakthrough: The Making of America's First Woman President*, Nancy Cohen writes about the balance of appearance when it comes to women in politics: "You don't have to be an amazing beauty to run for office . . . you just have to look like you are pulled together."[64]

This may also be because a focus on being beautiful, especially for women, tends to be associated with more traditional notions of femininity, which many see as tied to a more conservative outlook. This has led some to assume that beauty pageant contestants must lean right. Sue Lowden—a former Miss America board member, Miss New Jersey 1973, and second runner-up at Miss America when she competed as Susan Plummer[65]—confirms that "many of our gals are conservative."[66] Lowden would know. She was a Nevada state senator and chairwoman of the Nevada Republican Party, and ran for Harry Reid's seat in the US Senate in 2010 and for lieutenant governor of Nevada in 2014.

However, many of the pageant campaigners I have mentioned ran and won as Democrats, who generally have much more liberal platforms. Overall, pageant politicians are bipartisan. Regardless of political party or ideological leanings, competing in the Miss America program seems to help women prepare to compete in the public arena, a rare opportunity for them relative to their male counterparts.

By virtue of representing a locality, a state, or a nation on a large stage, pageants provide an opportunity for women to learn what it is like to be in a symbolic but representative role and speak for others. This symbolic representation can translate into one with legislative import and political power. Far from being inconsequential, participating in beauty pageants can almost uniquely help women access a public path to power.[67]

IVY+ BEAUTY QUEENS

Not all Miss Americas, or pageant contestants more generally, are well suited to electoral politics. Many have been successful in other realms. Just as their participation in politics has heated up in recent years, so has their pursuit of an elite education and advanced, professional degrees.

When Angela Perez Baraquio was part of the Top Three at Miss America 2001 she found it "extremely humbling." As she wrote in her 2014 memoir, "[First runner-up] Faith Jenkins, Miss Louisiana, had an incredible voice, a commanding presence, and was studying to be a lawyer. . . . [Second runner-up] Rita Ng, Miss California, a Stanford valedictorian, was a concert pianist who won the Preliminary Talent Award, and was a pre-med student aspiring to become a pediatrician. I stood five-foot-four-inches tall, was a Hawai'i-born Filipina physical education teacher and athletic director, Swimsuit Preliminary Winner, and graduate of the University of Hawai'i at Manoa—not the most obvious stats for a Miss America finalist, but, hey, I made it into the Top Three!"[68]

Baraquio went on to win the title of Miss America, and she is currently the principal of an N–8 Catholic school in California. Ng did become a doctor, though she is now a cardiologist and not a pediatrician, after graduating from University of California at San Francisco Medical School, one of the most prestigious medical schools in the country. Jenkins went on to graduate first in her law school class; you may have seen her on TV from 2014 to 2018 as *Judge Faith* or in 2020 as the judge on *Divorce Court*. Note that this was a Top Three as diverse as it was accomplished. Ng was the first-ever Asian American Miss California, Jenkins was the second-ever black Miss Louisiana, and Baraquio was the first-ever Asian American Miss America.

Clearly, beauty and brains mingle, and according to pageant numbers they do so even more often than pageants and politics. In my coding of the Miss America program books, one thing that stands out is the increase over time in the number of the contestants who attended elite universities, which I'll refer to here as Ivy+. They include the eight schools that are part of the Ivy League (Brown, Columbia, Cornell, Dartmouth, Harvard, Princeton, the University of Pennsylvania, and Yale) and the seven schools that typically round out the fifteen most highly ranked colleges and universities in the US (the California Institute of Technology, Duke, Johns Hopkins, the Massachusetts Institute of Technology, Northwestern, Stanford, and the University of Chicago).

Based on my analysis of the official Miss America program books, from 1972 to 2016 forty-one contestants have undergraduate degrees from an Ivy+. They account for about 2 percent of all those who competed on the Miss America stage. To put this in perspective, in 1985 female students from those fifteen schools made up about .01 percent of all females attending college in the US. By 2000 the percentage was 1.3 percent, and the three contestants from these schools—Harvard, Northwestern, and Stanford—made up 6 percent of Miss America contestants. So Miss America contestants from Ivy+ schools are over-represented relative to all college-going women in the United States.[69] However, only two Ivy+ queens in my sample won the title of Miss America (Gretchen Carlson, Miss America 1989, graduated from Stanford in 1990, and Kate Shindle, Miss America 1998, graduated from Northwestern in 1999).[70] Forty-nine percent of all Ivy+ queens have been crowned in the twenty-first century. This shows increased success and interest in Miss America among women who perform highly academically.

The Ivy+ queens are also a diverse group racially and ethnically. Thirty-two percent are women of color. Nearly half of the women of color are Asian, five are black, and two, Latina. This is much more diverse than a typical year at Miss America (the year that had the most diversity ever, 2003, had 24 percent state queens who were women of color).

This Ivy+ subgroup also differs from the general population of Miss America contestants in terms of talent. As you may recall from chapter 3, the majority of state winners have been singers, followed by dancers, and then instrumentalists. Among the Ivy+ queens the majority played an instrument for their talent (sixteen played piano, four played violin, and one played cello). Only five were dancers, one recited a monologue, and the rest sang.

Clearly, there is something different about being an Ivy+ beauty queen. To find out more about them, I interviewed the majority of the women who graduated from an Ivy+ college and competed on the Miss America stage. Perhaps not surprisingly, I found that the majority competed at Miss America because they were drawn to the scholarship money. Because of the emphasis on academic achievement and the potential for college scholarships, there is a strong America's Junior Miss/Distinguished Young Woman link among this group, with AJM/DYW functioning as a pathway and feeder to the Miss America program. Two of the Ivy+ Miss America state queens won the title of America's Junior Miss (during the time it was called Distinguished Young Woman of the Year, but for clarity I will refer to it as AJM).

Chuti Tiu was the first woman of color to win the AJM title. Both of her parents were born in the Philippines, though her dad identifies as Chinese and her mom as Latina and Filipina. She represented Wisconsin and played the piano to help her secure the title in 1987. Winning AJM paid for her first three years at Northwestern University, and winning the title of Miss Illinois in 1994 helped pay for her last year, along with some graduate studies.[71]

Sara Martin also used her AJM winnings to pay for her first three years at Northwestern. Martin won AJM in 1990 while representing Illinois. She got involved "for the scholarships after seeing an ad in the local newspaper. It 100% never would have occurred to me to compete if not for the scholarships."[72] Martin, one of three children raised by a single mother who taught kindergarten, depended on scholarships to finance her higher education. During her sophomore year at Northwestern, Martin mentioned to her voice teacher that she was getting concerned about how she would finance the remainder of her college education after her AJM money ran out. Her teacher was the one who suggested she consider competing for the title of Miss Illinois. At age twenty Martin won Miss Illinois and crowned her AJM sister queen Chuti Tiu as Miss Illinois the following year.

Crystal Lee, who was first runner-up to Miss America 2014, had a different but related path to the Miss America stage.[73] Her first foray into pageants was through a Miss Chinatown Teen pageant when she was fifteen years old. The pageant had a link to Lions Clubs, which in turn had a charitable link to combating vision problems around the world. Lee's father, who made eyeglasses, loved celebrating his family's Chinese heritage, so participating in the pageant felt like a way for her to honor her family's work and legacy.

At that first pageant Lee was recruited to take part in Miss America's Outstanding Teen pageant, which crowned its first winner in 2006 (the year before the last Miss Teen USA was crowned on television). Like its big sister pageant Miss America, Miss America's Outstanding Teen (MAOT) awards college scholarships to participants. The winner usually receives $30,000 to attend any college or university, and there are many other scholarship and in-kind tuition opportunities for all the competitors. MAOT is modeled after the phases of competition at Miss America—private interview, talent, evening gown and onstage question, and fitness—with the latter being an important exception. Unlike at Miss America, at MAOT contestants must do a fitness routine onstage (including planks, jumping jacks, and lunges) while wearing tight fitness clothes. There is no bathing suit competition. At MAOT in 2008, while representing California, Lee won a preliminary award for her fitness and made the Top Ten. After that she was hooked on competing in beauty pageants.

Lee wrote about her pageant experiences in her college application essay. After she was admitted to Stanford, she competed in the Miss Chinatown pageant system again as a Miss contestant, ultimately winning the national title of Miss Chinatown USA in 2010. Lee had just graduated from Stanford with a degree in human biology when she was one of the final two standing in Atlantic City.

Clearly, these Ivy+ Miss America state queens are all high-achieving women. Nonetheless, the majority of them that I interviewed were surprised by how mentally and emotionally challenging they found competing in a beauty pageant to be. Jennifer Caudle graduated from Princeton University in 1999, right before being crowned Miss Iowa 1999. Now a family physician and television personality, Caudle told me that while getting into Princeton and winning Miss Iowa were both challenging (especially as an African American woman), she found competing for Miss Iowa to be more difficult from a self-identity standpoint.[74] Admission to Princeton was more "by the numbers," an instance where she just had to be who she was based on what she had already done. If she had the right test scores and GPA and could explain her accomplishments in an essay, she was in. To compete at Miss America, however, Caudle had to "learn a new version of herself." She had to learn how to present herself in interview and onstage as herself, but an *enhanced* version. Caudle credits the Miss America Organization with helping her feel more confident about her appearance. Though she had previously performed onstage many times as a cellist, she had never given much thought to her looks. Learning how to wear false eyelashes and a weave was an overall positive experience for her, helping her develop beautifying techniques that she now uses every week as an on-air health expert on *Dr. Oz, The Rachael Ray Show, The Steve Harvey Show*, and other TV programs.

Like Caudle, most of the Ivy+ queens I interviewed went on to earn an advanced degree. Sara Martin was named a Marshall Scholar in 1995, and she completed a master's degree at the University of Warwick in England. Martin recognizes that participating in Miss America helped her do well in her high-stakes interview for the prestigious British fellowship. Her answers were crisp and clear, thanks to pageant interview prep. Miss America 2005, Deidre Downs, who was a Rhodes Scholar finalist, adds, "People are shocked when I tell them that my pageant interviews were much more difficult than any medical school I ever interviewed at. And I interviewed at Duke and Dartmouth and Georgetown."[75]

Downs did not attend one of these private medical schools, instead graduating from the University of Alabama School of Medicine in Birmingham, part of her home state's public university system. The $50,000 scholarship she was awarded when she won Miss America covered her four-year medical school tuition, which was $12,766 in the 2006 school year for in-state students ($35,396 for out-of-state students).[76] Downs shows that winning Miss America can in fact pay for advanced degrees, but how true is this for other contestants? Is it still possible to use the Miss America program to fulfill Slaughter's vision of helping young women access higher education?

The cost—both real and inflation adjusted—of a four-year college degree at a public school has gone up over time, whereas the inflation-adjusted value of a Miss America scholarship has declined. Since 1972 the real value of Miss America prize money has decreased by 11.82 percent. The combined impact of rising college costs and decline in current value of the scholarship makes it harder, but not impossible, to use Miss America scholarships to cover the cost of an undergraduate degree (all contestants also earn scholarships at the local and state levels). But note this covers only tuition and fees and not room and board.

Also, this calculation is based on tuition costs at public institutions, which are more affordable than private ones. Scholarship monies certainly helped Ivy+ queens offset the costs of tuition, but they could not come close to covering the final bill. Nonetheless, winnings did matter to Ivy+ queens like Marcia Turner. Turner, Miss Massachusetts 1995, recalls that the week before she won the Miss Massachusetts crown she was cleaning toilets as part of a Harvard work-study program referred to as Dorm Crew.[77] The following year, thanks to her win, she had enough money to pay her tuition without doing Dorm Crew. Several other Ivy+ queens were able to use the money they won to pay off undergraduate loans.

Since the 1940s Miss America has been the largest private provider of scholarship money to American women. This has remained true even after the organization had to walk back a figure they liked to tout—that they made available $45 million in scholarships every year—following an investigation by TV host John Oliver in September 2014.[78] Oliver exposed the organization's practice of including in their calculations all potential in-kind scholarships for every single contestant. A year later, Miss America clarified its figures in a press release: "In 2014, the Miss America Organization and its 52 state organizations awarded nearly $6 million in combined cash and in-kind tuition waiver scholarships to women across the country."[79] To put this in context, one of the most prestigious college scholarship competitions is the Coca-Cola Scholars. They award 150 scholarships of $20,000 each year. In 2018, 56 percent of those awards went to women, which is $1.68 million.[80]

One Ivy+ queen never got the chance to use her scholarship money. Cara McCollum, originally from Arkansas, was in her junior year at Princeton University when she won the title of Miss New Jersey 2013. I was one of her judges at Miss New Jersey that year, and I was in Atlantic City to see her compete, as that was the year Miss America returned to Convention Hall (the same year Crystal Lee was named first runner-up).

After her year as Miss New Jersey, McCollum returned to graduate from Princeton in 2015. At Princeton all undergraduates are required to write a senior thesis, and she drew inspiration from her brief but successful foray into beauty pageants. On April 7, 2015, she submitted her thesis "All That Glitters: The Pretty, the Plastic, and the Problematic of the Miss America Pageant." In it she tackled complex issues, including diversity in pageants, ethnic beauty standards, pressure on young women, the plastic surgery industry, reality television trends, and the psychological effects of various types of competition. The thesis showcases a sharp observer with a clear voice, and she earned an A.

Unfortunately, Cara McCollum's voice was silenced on an icy night in February 2016 when she lost control of her car while driving home from work, which was anchoring the local television show *SNJ [Southern New Jersey] Today*. Her death makes her observations in her thesis all the more poignant. She wrote, "The Miss America pageant is not just some beauty pageant, or some reality TV show, and the role of Miss State is not just a hand-shaking, baby-kissing bimbo—it's a real competition, and a real job, with real-life implications for both the girls and the definition of the American female ideal."[81]

McCollum knew that many people have preconceived ideas about—take your pick—blonde girls, Southern girls, pageant girls, smart girls, Princeton girls. But McCollum was the living embodiment of each of these "girls." She fully understood the complexities, the contradictions, and the commonalities of these identities.

At the time of her death, however, she was cynical about pageantry. McCollum was still sorting out her feelings about balancing an appearance-based experience (including the profession of journalism) with being a role model to young girls. In her thesis she explained,

> Throughout my reign, I traveled to dozens of classrooms and talked to thousands of young girls and told them about the importance of being self-confident. But I almost always followed it up by saying that I was currently wearing fake eyelashes, and lots of makeup, and hair extensions, and sometimes my hair extensions were wrapped around a sock I had cut a hole in to make a bun. . . . I didn't tell girls those things so that they'd emulate them, I told them so that they'd know that I didn't "wake up like this."[82]

McCollum was also frustrated that the Miss America Organization itself seemed to promote stereotypes instead of nuance. She wrote, "Instead of national article headlines reading,

> "Miss America Contestants Raise $x for Charity" or "Ivy League Student Competes in Miss America," they read, "Miss America Beauty Secrets: Butt Glue and Lots of Tape." Show a Miss America contestant being smart, studious, philanthropic, eloquent, poised, and talented, and maybe people will start taking these pageant girls more seriously. . . . But until then, she's just going to be viewed as a silly and irrelevant beauty queen.[83]

McCollum herself was all the words she wrote: smart, studious, philanthropic, eloquent, poised, and talented. She was far more than a stereotype—much like all her Ivy+ sister beauty queens.[84]

MISS AMERICA, #METOO

The 2018 Miss America Pageant, held September 10, 2017, was the first since Donald Trump was elected president. Not surprisingly, Trump's actions were fodder for the final questions. When Miss Texas was asked about Trump's response to the August 2017 riots in Charlottesville, she labeled them acts of white supremacist terrorism.

The eventual winner, my former student and Brown University graduate, Cara Mund, representing North Dakota, was also asked about Trump. Her question came from judge Maria Menounos (an entertainment reporter who was Miss Massachusetts Teen USA 1996, the year before Trump bought that program as part of the suite of Miss USA/Miss Universe pageants): "One-hundred-ninety-two countries signed the Paris agreement, in which each country sets nonbinding goals to reduce man-made climate change. The U.S. is withdrawing from the agreement, citing negligible environmental effects and negative economic impact. Good decision? Bad decision? Which is it and why?"

Cara replied, "I do believe it's a bad decision. Once we reject that, we take ourselves out of the negotiation table. And that's something that we really need to keep in mind. There is evidence that climate change is existing. Whether you believe it or not, we need to be at that table, and I think it's just a bad decision on behalf of the United States."[85]

The press focused on three things in the wake of Cara's victory and in a time of women's massive public engagement. First, that she was the first winner from the state of North Dakota. Second, that she was a graduate of Brown University who had already been admitted to law school. Third, that her ultimate goal was to be the first female governor of North Dakota. Cara's win was so of the moment—a small-town girl who graduated from an Ivy League school with political aspirations. She was the embodiment of the direction Miss America had been moving in since the 1968 protests.

But the good feelings lasted only three months. In December 2017 scandal struck. Four days before Christmas the *Huffington Post* broke a story that the executive chairman and CEO of the Miss America Organization, Sam Haskell, "regularly maligned, fat-shamed and slut-shamed the former Miss Americas, calling them shocking names and in one case laughing at the suggestion that one of the women should die."[86] The article shared examples from three years of internal emails.

Sam Haskell officially joined the Miss America board of directors in 2005, but he had been involved with the pageant for decades. He attended his first Miss Mississippi pageant when he was fifteen, and while in college at the University of Mississippi he directed the Miss University pageant for three years. In his last year, the winner, Mary Donnelly, went on to win the title of Miss Mississippi.[87] A few years later she would become his wife.

The Haskell family moved to Los Angeles so Sam could pursue his dream of working in Hollywood. In 1978 he started in the mailroom at the (then) William Morris Talent Agency. In 1980 he became an agent. By 1999 he was the agency's worldwide head of television. Throughout a very successful career, Haskell continued to love the Miss America Pageant. In his memoir he recounts a story of calling then Miss America chairman Albert Marks in the early 1980s and offering his assistance—which resulted in Haskell not only helping to book hosts and judges but also helping Vanessa Williams secure a Diet Coke commercial before she was dethroned.[88]

After the Williams scandal, Marks invited Haskell to judge the national pageant himself. Haskell was part of the judging panel that selected Sharlene Hawkes as the Miss America to "save" the program. Over the next two decades, Haskell would judge many times for Miss America, especially at the state level.[89]

It was another time of uncertainty, two decades later, that escalated Haskell's involvement with Miss America. When ABC dropped Miss America in 2005, several board members reached out to Haskell for assistance in getting the pageant a new TV deal. This was something Haskell was well positioned to do, and which he had the time to do, as he had left William Morris the previous year.

Here is how Haskell describes the way in which he became chairman of the Miss America Pageant:

> First, I helped sell the pageant telecast to Country Music Television (CMT) for the 2006 and 2007 contests. Then, in February 2006, the Miss America board decided to toss out the sitting chairman and nominate me from the floor. I said, 'No, no, I don't have time! I have to get back to what I'm doing! I've already helped with CMT! I can't do this!' I won the election 15 to 1. You know who voted against me? Me![90]

According to Haskell, the organization was almost bankrupt when he took over. He fired staff who were not securing needed sponsorships, he aligned Miss America with the Children's Miracle Network to give the organization a national platform, and he got the pageant back on network television with ABC in 2010.[91] While he heralded these changes, others resented them.

Miss America 1998, Kate Shindle (herself an Ivy+ graduate, a Broadway performer, and as of 2015 the elected president of Actor's Equity, the union for professional stage actors and stage managers), took on Haskell in her 2014 book, *Being Miss America: Behind the Rhinestone Curtain.* She argued that his propensity to fire staff—especially Art Mc-Master, then CEO, a position Haskell took over—was a power grab.[92] She viewed the deal with Children's Miracle Network as a pay-to-play scheme that benefitted the Miss America Organization's office most of all.[93] And, she saw the ABC deal as a bad one for Miss America, since it was a time buy, targeted at advertisers and sponsors, as opposed to ABC paying for rights to televise the pageant, as they had in the past.[94] The fact that Haskell was paid $500,000 in consulting fees in 2012 for his roles did not sit well with most anybody, especially on the heels of the bankruptcy revelation.[95]

One Haskell success that no one took issue with was the pageant's return to Atlantic City from Las Vegas in 2014. While that was a huge win, attributable almost entirely to Haskell's connections and negotiations, soon former Miss Americas like Shindle and loyal volunteers grew concerned that Miss America was becoming the Sam Haskell show. In 2015 after another staff departure, Haskell was named executive chairman of the Miss America Organization, which essentially made him chairman of the board of directors, CEO, and president.[96] In 2016 pageant faithful were shocked and upset when Haskell led the charge to say that any Miss America local title holder who wanted to keep her title would not be allowed to compete in the National Sweetheart Pageant. It seemed an especially mean-spirited power grab against a single, rural Jaycees chapter in a time of growing division in the country.[97]

During the summer of 2016, in the midst of the Trump-Clinton presidential election, Gretchen Carlson filed a sexual harassment lawsuit against the chairman and CEO of Fox News, Roger Ailes. Carlson had worked at Fox since 2006, first as a cohost of the morning show *Fox & Friends* and later as the host of her own show, *The Real Story with Gretchen Carlson.* In her July 6, 2016, court complaint she is described as "a graduate of Stanford University, a former Miss America (1989), an accomplished violinist, an award-winning journalist and a Trustee of the March of Dimes."[98] Carlson, clearly a gifted woman, alleged her show was canceled because she refused Ailes's sexual advances. After she went public, several other women came forward with similar claims about Ailes. As a consequence of mounting pressure Ailes stepped down on

July 21, 2016, and in September of that year Carlson received a reported settlement of $20 million.

When the infamous Trump "grab them by the pussy" tape was leaked a month later, in October 2016, many women were particularly primed, based in part on the Carlson-Ailes case, to speak out and take action against men in power sexually harassing women. In the wake of the 2017 Women's March, anger continued to grow over the course of the next year, especially as the Trump administration promoted policies aimed at restricting women's rights.

That anger found a new focus in October 2017 when news stories broke about the serial sexual assault and harassment by now-convicted abuser Harvey Weinstein, a top Hollywood film producer. Alyssa Milano, an actress and activist, posted on Twitter, "If you've been sexually harassed or assaulted write 'me too' as a reply to this tweet." Milano later said that the hashtag idea was "suggested by a friend" who thought that getting people to chime in might give a sense of the magnitude of the problem. This was a technique started by organizer Tarana Burke, the woman who first used "Me Too" about a decade earlier, which she found especially useful in her work with young women of color.[99]

Carlson was already considered one of the most successful Miss Americas, but her new advocacy addressing sexual harassment in the workplace made her even more publicly respected, especially in pageant circles. That is part of the reason why, when the Haskell emails were leaked two months after #MeToo started, people were particularly upset about what he had written about Carlson, including the desire to drive her "INFUCKINGSANE."[100] Not that it ever was acceptable to refer to a group of women as "cunts," as former Miss Americas were referred to in Haskell's email exchanges (though not by him), but it was beyond unacceptable in the #MeToo era. The world had shifted, and language like that in Haskell's emails simply could not stand in an organization purporting to be about promoting women's success.

When the December 2017 *Huffington Post* story about the Haskell emails was published, the initial response of the Miss America board of directors was to suspend him. But a day later, Haskell resigned.[101] Within a few weeks, nearly the entire Miss America board of directors followed suit.

As 2018 began, the Miss America Organization was leaderless. It quickly became clear that the best person to step in was a woman, preferably a former contestant. Given Gretchen Carlson's life experiences—in the media, with the Miss America board of directors (which she served on with Sam Haskell, and the source of his ire toward her), and unfortunately with sexual harassment—she was the clear choice.[102] Carlson was publicly emerging as a leader who identified herself as a feminist.[103]

Carlson was not afraid to shake things up in Atlantic City, something she had been doing since her year as Miss America. (When she competed, Carlson's stated professional goal was attending Harvard Law School, but after being Miss America she switched to television journalism, a profession that increasing numbers of pageant queens are pursuing.)[104] In June 2018 Carlson announced two major changes to Miss America. The first was regarding language—contestants were now *candidates*, a platform was now a *social impact statement*, and Miss America was no longer a pageant but a *competition*. The second was saying bye-bye to the bikini.

Of these changes, it was the elimination of swimsuit that led to the most internal strife. While Miss America did start as a bathing beauty contest, it had been a problematic element since the 1930s, when Lenora Slaughter took over. Slaughter was always concerned that expecting women to parade around publicly in swimsuits did not always attract the "right" type of contestants. Recall from chapter 2 that Slaughter made efforts to minimize the bathing suit portion by changing its name, by no longer crowning a winner in swimsuit, and by not having Miss Americas do appearances in swimsuits—all decisions that ultimately gave birth to Miss USA/Miss Universe. During Second Wave feminism the swimsuit competition was a particular source of opprobrium; many reasonably asked what walking in a swimsuit had to do with scholarship money. In the 1990s bikinis came back, and there was a public vote over whether to keep that part of the competition. That was a lopsided and positive victory, which made it clear that keeping swimsuit as part of Miss America guaranteed a thin winner, even after body measurements were no longer reported in the official program books.

Former Miss Americas often expressed different opinions on whether the swimsuit competition should be included in the Miss America Pageant. Carlson had long been outspoken against it, so her decision should not have surprised people. In a 2004 interview about Miss America she said, "I'm adamantly opposed to swimsuits. . . . Women will never be taken seriously in a swimsuit."[105] Whatever individual contestants' opinions, nearly all agreed that after walking on national television in front of millions in a bathing suit (and often heels), they could do anything, whether that meant run for office, perform surgery, or regularly appear on the news. Whatever their sacrifices were—often eating less food than their bodies actually required, spending countless hours in the gym, and possibly even more damaging practices to reduce their weight to Barbie proportions—in the calculus of their lives, the sacrifices seemed worth it to most contestants.

While there were mixed feelings over the years, on the whole, swimsuit was embraced, which is part of the reason Gretchen Carlson's June 5, 2018, *Good Morning America* announcement did not exactly sit well with pageant faithful.[106] What irked many, including Shindle, who was again critical of pageant leadership, was that this decision seemed to be made at the top. It appeared Carlson made the call, with little consultation at the state or local level (which was very trying for state and local volunteers, many of whom had already selected state winners to compete at Miss America that year). This is why it is true, in a roundabout way, that #MeToo killed the swimsuit competition at Miss America.

By August 2018, concerns about Carlson's leadership mounted when the current Miss America, Cara Mund, wrote a letter saying that Carlson and other pageant leaders had "silenced me, reduced me, marginalized me, and essentially erased me in my role as Miss America in subtle and not-so-subtle ways on a daily basis."[107] Mund was upset that Carlson made appearances, especially on television, that Mund felt she should have done as the reigning Miss America. In reaction to that letter, a petition calling for Carlson's resignation was started. Seemingly in retaliation, several state directors were stripped of their licenses to run state pageants. The press, sometimes tongue-in-cheek, dubbed all the internal arguing the "Miss America Civil War."[108]

About eight months later Carlson did resign, explaining, "When I was asked to take this volunteer position over a year ago, I dedicated myself to helping the organization build on its history while working to secure its future, and am extremely proud of the work we have collectively done. With a promising network partnership, the time is ideal to give new leadership the opportunity to move forward with what has been accomplished."[109] The week before Carlson's resignation Miss America had announced that the Miss America 2020 pageant would be broadcast on NBC—though it would come with a venue and date change. Instead of the tradition of Atlantic City in September, Miss America took the show on the road to Mohegan Sun in Connecticut the week before Christmas 2019.

In the months leading up to the 2019 competition, another big change for Miss America, now dubbed "Miss America 2.0," was announced. This time it was the elimination of the evening gown category and the addition of a new one, a TED-like talk of no longer than ninety seconds to showcase a candidate's social impact initiative.

Around the same time, Miss America sent out an email announcing a new scholarship called the Equity and Justice Scholarship. The $3,000 award would go to the candidate who best exemplified inclusion in her social impact initiative. In explaining the impetus for the donation, the Miss America Organization wrote,

> While the scholarship will be awarded through a family trust, the donor chooses to remain anonymous. In reaching out to the Miss America Organization, the donor made clear the important reason for the generous gift. As a young woman who wanted to compete in a local Miss America competition in the 1980's, she was discouraged by her parents because they believed "Miss America does not look like us, and an educated woman does not parade around in a swimsuit."[110]

This paragraph sparked more strife among former Miss America contestants, most of whom were deeply offended by the implication that because they had competed in swimsuit, they were not educated. Miss Virginia 2005, Kristi Glakas Ingram, who was third runner-up at Miss America 2006, wrote a social media post that was emblematic of the hundreds that went up over the next twenty-four hours: "My two bachelor's degrees from the University of Virginia and my doctorate from U.Mass Amherst are laughing all the way to the beach. Where I'll parade around in any damn thing I please. Dear #MissAmerica, Peddle your anti-feminist misogyny to the 1940s where it belongs. Sincerely, Kristin Ingram, DNP, RN, BSN, RNC-OB, EFM-C."[111]

The response by Ingram and other Miss America contestants showed how Third Wave feminism was shaping beauty pageants. Contestants had no problem calling out those whom they felt were not seeing the full complexity of women and their achievements. A little over twenty-four hours later Miss America had to issue a statement apologizing to past and present participants who were offended by the suggestion that educated women should not "parade" in swimsuits onstage. It read, in part, "It is by no means the opinion of the MAO, its leadership, nor of the donor of the Equity and Justice Scholarship that educated women should not wear swimsuits, onstage or otherwise."

This was not a good start for the new, all-female leadership team at Miss America. The Miss America Organization was entirely led by women, surely fulfilling a dream of Lenora Slaughter's, though she would have been disappointed by all the controversy surrounding the organization. In 2018 Regina Hopper, Miss Arkansas 1983, was named president and CEO of the Miss America Organization, and in 2019 Shantel Swedlund Krebs (Miss South Dakota 1997, the year Kate Shindle won Miss America) was announced as the new board chairwoman, replacing Gretchen Carlson. Not surprisingly, by the end of January 2020, Hopper was no longer with the Miss America Organization, as Krebs took on all leadership roles, as Haskell had done.[112]

When Krebs competed at Miss America she said she wanted to be a corporate attorney, but instead she entered electoral politics, like many of her fellow state pageant queens. Krebs was first elected to the South Dakota House of Representatives in 2005 as a Republican. She rose to the position of Majority Whip there, and later in the state senate as well. In 2015 she was elected South Dakota's secretary of state. Krebs lost the Republican primary for the at-large US congressional seat representing South Dakota in 2018, which made her available to lead the Miss America Organization to its one hundredth anniversary in 2020, the same year that marks the one hundredth anniversary of the passage of the Nineteenth Amendment.

THIRD WAVE PAGEANTRY

In her 2016 book *Broad Influence: How Women Are Changing the Way America Works*, journalist Jay Newton-Small wrote, "It's amazing how far we've come in just a generation. . . . Fifteen years ago, [women] were still excluded from many caucuses, clubs, and meetings. Ten years ago, Senate women were often mistaken for wives and staffers."[113] Change has come quickly for American women, and some institutions, like the US Senate and Miss America, have been slower to catch up. As at other times in American history, beauty pageants during Third Wave feminism continue to provide a canvas on which feminist issues play out directly.

Pageants are still fighting to get women into the public sphere, just as they did in the nineteenth century. When the first former Miss America or Miss USA is elected to public office, that will be a milestone. A win by a national pageant winner would be more consequential than a win by a state queen because—without taking anything away from their victories—optics matter. Miss America is the (self-appointed but generally accepted) feminine ideal. As the face of American femininity, an electoral victory would show that women can win in politics and also be considered glamorous. Miss America or Miss USA being a successful politician would help change wider prejudice, showing that a pageant winner can be a politician and that smart *and* beautiful *and* successful women win pageants.

Though Donald Trump no longer owns the Miss Universe Organization, when he did, he reinforced some pernicious stereotypes, such as women can be reduced to only their looks, disregarding other accomplishments. After Hillary Clinton called out his previous treatment of Alicia Machado during the first presidential debate—behavior that not only belittled her as a woman but also as a Latina—instead of apologizing, Trump doubled down. The morning after the debate he called into *Fox & Friends*, the show Gretchen Carlson had previously cohosted. Trump said,

That person was a Miss Universe person, and she was the worst we ever had. The worst, the absolute worst. She was impossible, and she was a Miss Universe contestant and ultimately a winner who they had a tremendously difficult time with as Miss Universe. She was the winner, and, you know, she gained a massive amount of weight, and it was a real problem. We had a real problem. Not only that, her attitude, and we had a real problem with her, so Hillary [Clinton] went back into the years and she found this girl. This was many years ago, and found the girl and talked about her like she was Mother Teresa and it wasn't quite that way, but that's okay. Hillary has to do what she has to do.[114]

The tenets of Third Wave feminism include body positivity and no victim-shaming or slut-shaming. Just because a woman chooses to do a pageant should not leave her open to being harassed or abused in any way. Ultimately pageants can give women like Machado and Carlson skills to fight back against harassers like Donald Trump. They learn they have a voice and that they can celebrate their bodies. Women have many choices today, and pageants are one way among many to build a public platform to advocate for issues and promote one's own education. Whether in a swimsuit, or not.

The Future Reign of Beauty Pageants

A SECTION OF THE PROGRAM BOOK for the 2020 Miss America competition succinctly summarizes the tumultuous recent history of the pageant:

> [In 2018] the organization faces crises, both internal and external. In the 1980s, more than 80,000 young women pursued the dream of becoming Miss America. By 2018, less than 4,000 did. The organization had lost its relevance. The bathing suit had gone from a symbol of liberation to objectification. Women didn't need to wear bikinis to win scholarships or be great leaders. Getting rid of the swimsuit competition was the radical act now. Vicious backlash ensued including protests, hate mail and death threats.[1]

Despite dropping swimsuit—and other traditional parts of the competition, like evening gown—and adding new speaking portions, the 2020 Miss America "pageant" did not turn the tide of relevancy. In spite of being on a major network, the NBC broadcast hit an all-time low; the program averaged only 3.61 million viewers.[2] To put this number in perspective, other annual one-off events, like the Super Bowl and Academy Awards, had 98.2 million and 29.6 million viewers respectively in 2019.[3]

Part of the continued decline in interest in 2019 was the competition's move from Atlantic City, New Jersey, to the Mohegan Sun Casino and Resort in Uncasville, Connecticut. On top of that, the date also changed from September, after Labor Day, to the week before Christmas. But more than the date and location shifts, efforts to rebrand Miss America as something other than a beauty pageant angered longtime fans and confused contestants and their supporters.

The first page of the 2020 competition magazine reveals Miss America's new mission: "Prepare great women for the world. Prepare the world for great women." Below that statement is the new vision statement: "There she is . . . Miss Neurosurgeon, Miss Social Activist, Miss Jet Pilot, Miss Investigative Journalist, Miss Expert Coder, Miss CEO . . . Miss Whatever-She-Wants-to-Be . . . There she is. Miss America. No wonder she has a crown—she rules."

The problem is that no recent Miss America winners have done any of those things professionally. Moreover, many professions—like neurosurgeon, jet pilot, expert coder, CEO—have *never* been careers of any former Miss America. These specific jobs are named presumably because they are not considered traditionally female paths. But this brings into stark relief the reality that it is unclear how Miss America is preparing the world for great women.

I do believe that Miss America can play and has played a part in preparing great women for the world. Women like Miss America 1998, Kate Shindle, who has originated roles on Broadway and been elected president of Actors' Equity Association, or Miss America 2005, Deidre Downs, who is a reproductive endocrinologist helping those struggling with infertility. Other former Miss Americas have earned a JD or PhD. But none have yet held elected public office or led a major business as CEO. Those are two arenas in which women still lag behind men in America; so, former Miss Americas are not outliers. Yet, those vacancies reinforce that the Miss America Organization is not quite doing more than others to prepare the world for great women.

Miss America has changed its identity and competition as the roles of women have changed in the United States. The way the competition looks today is very different from how it looked when it began one hundred years ago. While this makes it harder to describe Miss America's purpose, it does accurately represent the muddled expectations regarding American femininity over time.

Miss USA, on the other hand, has never been confused about who it is and what it celebrates. The winner is supposed to be the most beautiful with the best swimsuit body. This is reflected in their mission statement:

"We celebrate beauty, all forms of it, and provide the tools that help women to feel their most beautiful: 'Confidently Beautiful.'"[4] While Miss USA still certainly has its detractors, the criticisms of it have not changed much since it began in 1952.

One hundred years is a long time for any American cultural institution to exist. Compared to other annual national events, like the Super Bowl and the Academy Awards, Miss America is the elder stateswoman (the Oscars' birthdate is close, in 1929, but the Super Bowl is much younger, born in 1967). It is a heavy lift for a cultural event to stay relevant for one hundred years.

While I don't see Miss America going away completely in the next decade, I would be surprised if it remains on television—especially network TV—for that long. Participating in Miss America has great value to many of the individual women who compete, but that doesn't mean the competition belongs on prime time. Few would question the significance of winning a Rhodes Scholarship, but those interviews aren't televised because, to most, they don't constitute entertainment.

Even if Miss America fades from our television screens (which unfortunately would likely affect the size of the scholarships awarded), that does not mean beauty pageant culture is not represented on that medium. Take *The Bachelor*. The January 6, 2020, premiere of the twenty-fourth season averaged 6.3 million viewers—nearly double Miss America 2020's ratings.[5] In that three-hour episode, five pageant participants appeared as contestants.[6] Four of them made the cut, so *The Bachelor*'s viewing audience got to see the reigning Miss Louisiana and Miss Texas USA, a former Miss Iowa USA, and a finalist at Miss Tennessee USA beyond a single two- or three-hour special.

Series like *The Bachelor* thrive on drama to keep people watching. This has actually negatively affected how viewers consume a pageant, where little internal conflict let alone serial arguments are on display. But having competed in a pageant seems to help women on *The Bachelor*, because they know how to do their own hair and makeup, compete with other women, and be interviewed about sometimes difficult topics. And, of course, they are used to being on camera in bikinis and evening gowns.

Since the emergence of Donald J. Trump the politician, beauty pageant culture has been very much in the cultural zeitgeist, taking various fictional forms. In 2018, for example, the best-selling novel *Dumplin'*,[7] about plus-size girls breaking stereotypes by competing in their town's beauty pageant, was made into a popular Netflix movie.[8] *Dumplin'* isn't alone; in 2018 Netflix also released the fictional series *Insatiable*, about teen pageants, and Facebook Watch did its own fictional series, *Queen America*, about a pageant coach.

Trump has also brought pageant culture to the White House, an example of how he perfected his ability to elevate appearance over substance. When he started interviewing potential cabinet members in late 2016, journalists likened the process to a beauty pageant where the "winners" would have "the look" of secretary of state or defense.[9] Susan Chira, then the gender correspondent and editor at the *New York Times*, wrote, "Call it cabinet selection as beauty pageant. As President-elect Donald J. Trump assembles his cabinet and prepares to govern, he is drawing on an underestimated asset: showmanship honed over years of television pageantry."[10]

Trump's behavior promotes a notion that has been peddled since at least the days of P. T. Barnum: life is easier when you are attractive. Ironically, neither Trump nor Barnum is considered conventionally handsome, but neither seemed to have had any problem prioritizing beauty in women. Both men promoted beauty contests, and they did so while simultaneously changing mass popular culture and ending their careers in elected office (Barnum served in the Connecticut legislature and then as the mayor of Bridgeport, Connecticut).

Despite the long history of beauty contests in America, many feminists still wonder why beauty pageants continue to exist. Feminism itself helps provide an answer. As I hope I've shown, since the nineteenth century, pageantry has played a role in getting women into the public sphere. The First Wave of feminism fought to bring women out of the sphere of private, domestic life, culminating in women's suffrage. Baby contests in which women carried their children onstage made it acceptable for women's bodies to appear, and be judged, in public. Later this took the form of bathing beauty contests and pageants like Miss America, Miss USA, and America's Junior Miss. Pageants drew inspiration from the sashes feminists wore at suffrage events, but transformed them into tools to identify the home regions of beauty pageant contestants who were competing against one another. During the second part of First Wave feminism, pageants played a part in helping women move into the public sphere, especially through the growing mass media. Lenora Slaughter reinvented Miss America as a pathway for women to pursue higher education through the creation of scholarships for winners—but due to racism, ableism, and likely anti-Semitism, she also excluded many women from accessing the monies.

Miss America was so effective at helping some individual women expand their opportunities that its popularity became the springboard for Second Wave feminism to share its message that all educational and professional opportunities needed to be accessible. Second Wave bra burners successfully fought for access to sports, reproductive freedom, and all types of higher education opportunities and career options. The next half of Second Wave feminism, characterized by intersectionality and identity politics, fought so that those realms were open to *all* women—not just white, heterosexual, able-bodied women.

If Second Wave feminism was about options, Third Wave feminism is about making sure that whatever choice a woman makes, she is safe there. Beauty pageants are one choice women can make off an ever-growing menu of options. To be safe there and in other realms means embracing body positivity, not slut-shaming, and fighting for policies—like quality and affordable childcare, paid family leave, and menstrual equity—that will help women succeed anywhere in the public sphere.

One of the messages young girls are taught in this era of Third Wave feminism is that they can be anything and like anything. Unabashed feminist Jerramy Fine sums up this idea in her 2016 book, *In Defense of the Princess*, in which she argues that femininity does not equal weakness, pink is not inferior, and girly-ness is compatible with ambition.[11] In other words, girls and women should not feel like they need a crown to be happy, but it is not wrong if a crown is one of the things that might make someone happy.

Still, some feminists would disagree with this sentiment. They argue that pageants remain harmful to women and girls because they continue to promote a potentially unattainable, and thus harmful, body type, along with an overemphasis on fashion and appearance that can have financial ramifications. Not to mention a continued societal preference for heterosexuality. (As I write this I can hear Lindy West in my head saying a line from her 2017 book *Shrill*: "In a certain light, feminism is just the long, slow realization that the stuff you love hates you.")[12]

It is undeniable that the beauty ideal associated with the "all-American face and form" has significantly expanded since the one Bernie Wayne's 1954 song, "There She Is, Miss America" immortalized. This is especially true when it comes to women of color. However, this is less true when it comes to body type, despite efforts toward more body positivity. In fact, as the average American woman has gotten larger, fashion models like Victoria's Secret's "angels" have gotten smaller. The same appears to be true for beauty pageant contestants.[13]

With increased social media platforms, especially image-based ones like Instagram, women of all ages are regularly bombarded with images of "perfect" bodies. Expectations about appearance have increased rather than decreased. Despite women being told that they are more than how they look, clothing worn by girls in school and women in the workplace are both formally and informally regulated in ways that simply do not exist for their male counterparts.

I am a Third Wave feminist, so this book is very much a product of Third Wave feminism. I have shown how pageants have been both feminist and flippant, and how that balance has changed over time as women's roles in the public sphere have shifted. The sash alone shows how women have used the symbolism of pageants in different ways at different points. Suffragists borrowed the sash from the military to secure the right to vote. Miss America organizers borrowed the sash from the suffragists to help identify and signify the ways in which women could publicly compete with one another, though mainly based on their looks. Today the sash has transformed into a common accessory at birthdays and bachelorette parties, available to all women to wear. Feminism and beauty culture are not only intertwined but deeply embedded in American life.

If reading this book has helped you make connections you had not made before, likely challenging your worldview as you see how pageantry is deeply woven into the social, cultural, and political history of this country, then I have succeeded. In writing it, I have drawn upon well-researched sources and deliberately limited secondhand anecdotes.

Honestly, beauty pageants are full of backstage drama, so there is a real temptation to engage in insider snark and innuendo. Because so many dismiss pageants as frothy, I have purposely presented beauty pageants as a serious subject worthy of our attention and not as a silly subculture to be portrayed with a gossipy tone (though pageants are undeniable fun for many participants and fans).

Pageants have been an enduring part of American society for over 160 years, and beauty culture has been around much longer than that. As American women continue to evolve, so too will beauty pageants. While much progress has been made for women in the public sphere, much remains to be done. Equality, not to mention equity, remains elusive. Today's girls are still growing up in a patriarchal society. Women, whether beauty queens or not, belong everywhere decisions are made. More women in more prominent and public positions will help everyone not only accept differences, physical or otherwise, but also celebrate them.

And I know someday a woman will be sitting behind a certain desk in the Oval Office.

Whether she has ever worn a crown or not.

ACKNOWLEDGMENTS

L AST SUMMER, my then five-year-old son, Quenton, started asking me daily, "Are you still working on your story, Mommy?" My older son, Carston, one day wondered exasperatedly, "How long have you been working on that book?!"

So, that's a hard question to answer. On some level, I've been working on this my whole life, and I officially began some of the research for this book as a sophomore in college. When you work on a project for so long, your list of people to thank is . . . extensive.

Let's start with the people who are actually responsible for getting this book into your hands, and that's the amazing team at Beacon Press. My editor, Helene Atwan, pushed me to go deeper—and gave me the space to do so. I'm so appreciative of her attention to detail, along with that of assistant editor Haley Lynch. Huge thanks also to the "pod" of Alyssa Hassan and Caitlin Meyer, along with Sanj Kharbanda. And kudos to those who really pay attention to details in production—Beth Collins, Susan Lumenello, and Andrea Lee—I am "very" grateful (trust me, they saved you from reading the word *very* too many times, along with an excessive use of quotation marks).

Major thanks go to my agent, Ellen Geiger of Frances Goldin Literary Agency, who found me in the slush pile and sent me the best initial email I could have imagined. She gave me the confidence to go, go, go.

Several people set me on this research path back in 1999, though at the time I had absolutely no idea where it would end. This work began in a required sociology class taught by Kenneth (Andy) Andrews, assisted by Shyon Baumann. They told me I could apply for research money (I could even use my work-study funds!) through the Harvard College Research Program. It's not an exaggeration to say that winning that first award changed the course of my life. Special shout-out to Christy McKellips for being supportive then, and now. Thanks also to Peter Marsden, who advised my senior thesis; he may not have known much about child beauty pageants, but he knows a lot about sociology.

Then, I became a professor myself. In fall 2015, the first class I taught at Brown University was Beauty Pageants in American Society, and did I luck out, because this was an enormously special group. Little did I know that in that seminar room was a future Miss Rhode Island (and doctor, Allie Coppa) and a future Miss America (Cara Mund, future lawyer, along with being an inspiration and forever friend). I must thank students Delaney, Sophie, Maria, LeTia, Elise, Michelle, Rachel, Karla, Emma, and Jaclyn (other class members who helped with research are mentioned below). Special shout-out to Madison Jones for always being on top of all things pop culture and to Tian-Mei Lee for being a great travel buddy and appreciating all facets of American culture. The second time I taught this class I found my student drag and TV expert in Adam Malkin, and my debutante and Mrs. Pageant expert in Alli Gordon. The third and final time I taught the course, those twenty-two young women gave me useful feedback on draft chapters.

I've been lucky to have able research assistants, especially those who coded and helped track down data. That list includes Fionna Chan, Tatyana Donaldson, Sara Erkal, Gabe Fagans, Joey Gutfleish, Ashleigh McEvoy, Laila Mirza, Jaclyn Parris, Yelena Salvador, Liv Simmons, Payton Smith, Zena Tadmoury, Avantika Tibrewala, and Allie Tsuchiya. Two RAs deserve a rock-star mention for cleaning and analyzing so much at the end: Jardelle Johnson and Ananya Poddar.

The list of those who sent me the pageant program books for some of my RAs to code is a long one, as that was no easy task (some states sadly didn't make it into the final product because of incomplete data, no matter how hard I tried). They include Wanda Aaberg (of South Dakota's Pioneer Museum), Michelle Burkhart (of Indiana's Michigan City Public Library), McNeil Chestnut, David Clegg, Valerie Clemens (forever Miss Maine), James Davis (of the State Historical Society of North Dakota), Earl Edris, Warren Egebo, Tricia Freeland (of the Hoopeston Public Library, along with her archivist Tom Sweeney), Donna Gutierrez, Bill Haggerty, Rob Hancock, LeeAnn Hibert, Gene Hill (aka Idaho's Bert Parks, of course), Rachel Hollis (of Idaho's State Archives), Kat Howland,

Stefanie Hunker (of the Browne Popular Culture Library at Bowling Green State University), Terry Iden, Eve Marie Lynch, Tina Marie Mares, Nancy Marston, Bo Miller, Renee Belanger Mills, Jan Mitchell, Pam Patterson, Heather Perez (of the Atlantic City Free Public Library), Randy Pruett, Steve Robinson, Dolly Ruffing, Aren Straiger, Brandon Werts (of the Historical Society of Long Beach), Agnes White, Lori Williamson (of Minnesota's Historical Society), and Christina Wolf (of Oklahoma City University's Special Collections).

Others who helped with the research process include, but are not limited to, Debbye Turner Bell (Miss America 1990), Chanel Bonheyo, Karen Bouchard (Brown University's amazing librarian who specializes in images), Christina Couto (a supporter from the very start), Michelle Crabtree (and the whole Sweetheart family!), Allie Curtis, Annette Dorey, Lori Ewing, Carole Gist (the first black Miss USA, representing my home state of Michigan), Erika Harold (Miss America 2003), Talia Hastie, Heather French Henry (Miss America 2000), Larry Hoffer, Sally Johnston, Donna Klamkin, Lauren Kuhn, Carrie Lakey (of Pageant Junkies), Laura Lawless, Rob Loy, Jackie Mayer (Miss America 1963), Blaire Pancake, BrYan Parker, Dolores "Buffy" Rabuffo, Allison Rogers, Rick Rose, Daryl Schabinger, Christopher Schram (of Crowned), and Lois Wims.

I am truly grateful to all I interviewed for this book; I know how precious time is. Not everyone could be named in these pages (some due to rules around research subject confidentiality), but know that I think every pageant politician, Ivy+ winner, and fellow members of the Miss America Daughter's Club are queens.

Two people I met through this pageants research deserve special mention. Sarahjayne Howland is a connector, a giver, a sharer, a cheerleader, and so much more. Freeman Stamper is the pageant and cultural historian we all need, and he does it with generosity and flair. They embody the best of "pageant people" and are now friends for life.

And then there are my writing/editing friends who transcend state boundaries! Some in groups (Varanya Chaubey, Julia Chuang, Andre Davis, Marc Dunkelman, Jennifer Jones, Susan Moffitt, Marty Rojas, Katherine Rooks, Rebecca Sullivan, Margaret Weir, and Joanna Weiss) and some individually (Abigail Altabef, Nina Badzin, Sarah Carter, Daisy Florin, Debbie Gordon, Michelle Kuo, Natalia Petrzela, Jane Teixiera, and Judi Zimmer) have read a collection of words or ideas that ended up here. Please know every single one of your comments helped, though of course all imperfections are mine. Friends from my Princeton days who remain fixtures in my crazy orbit today—Rebecca Casciano and Margarita Mooney—not only read but also listened to the angst. And, of course, thanks to Viviana Zelizer, who remains a dear and trusted mentor and advisor.

Grateful to so many Rhody political friends for being supportive as I wrote this book. Some of my Rhode Island ladies deserve named recognition for putting up with me, reading last-minute drafts, and trying to "get" how pageants and feminism mix. These wonder women include Kristine Frech, Peggy Mello, Emily Oster, and Christa Thompson. They show me that some people really can do it all. I'm lucky to know you in this life—and perhaps others.

My in-laws—Ben, Barbara, and Jeff—always provided wise counsel as well as company at get-togethers when I'd been in my office for too long. My father, Jules, tried to give me the space I needed to work. And, of course, turn back to the front to see the dedication to get a sense of the innumerable ways Mom has contributed to this book basically since I was born (I think it's finally done!).

A ginormous thanks to the best things I will ever create, my boys Carston and Quenton. In this case, the good looks did skip a generation. They were patient with their sometimes distracted and stressed mother (is it socially acceptable to also thank Apple for inventing the iPad?). Love you, love you.

My biggest and never-ending debt of gratitude is to my husband, John Friedman. John does everything 1000 percent. He inspires me to work harder every day. I hope I didn't let you down.

NOTES

PREFACE

1. Frank Deford, *There She Is: The Life and Times of Miss America* (New York: Viking, 1971), 198.

2. Alec D. B. McCabe, "Bert 'There She Is' Parks Back on Miss America," UPI Archives, August 15, 1990.

3. Vicki Smith, "Bert's Blunders Don't Bother Horn," *Press of Atlantic City,* September 10, 1990.

4. Julie Tamaki, "Ex-Miss America Host Bert Parks Dies," *Los Angeles Times,* February 3, 1992.

INTRODUCTION

1. While some feminist scholars resist the notion of *waves* on the grounds that the women's movement has never been monolithic and fully united (Linda Nicholson, "Feminism in 'Waves': Useful Metaphor or Not?," *New Politics* 11, no. 4 [2010]: 48), the evocative term has dominated popular discourse since it first appeared in the *New York Times* in March 1968. See Martha Weinman Lear, "What Do These Women *Want?* The Second Feminist Wave," *New York Times Magazine,* March 10, 1968.

2. During the child-bearing and rearing years, this translates into more affordable childcare, paid family leave, menstrual equity, and high-quality, affordable options when it comes to early childhood education.

3. Daniel S. Hamermesh, *Beauty Pays: Why Attractive People Are More Successful* (Princeton, NJ: Princeton University Press, 2011). See especially chapter 3.

4. John J. Gunnell and Stephen J. Ceci, "When Emotionality Trumps Reason: A Study of Individual Style and Juror Bias," *Behavioral Sciences & the Law* 28, no. 6 (November 2010): 850–77.

5. Elaine Hatfield and Susan Sprecher, *Mirror, Mirror: The Importance of Looks in Everyday Life* (Albany, NY: SUNY Press, 1986), 47.

6. Penny Howell Jolly and Gerald M. Erchak, *Hair: Untangling a Social History* (Saratoga Springs, NY: Frances Young Tang Teaching Museum and Art Gallery at Skidmore College, 2004), 47.

7. Nancy Etcoff, *Survival of the Prettiest: The Science of Beauty* (New York: Doubleday, 1999). See especially chapter 4.

8. Autumn Whitefield-Madrano, *Face Value: The Hidden Ways Beauty Shapes Women's Lives* (New York: Simon & Schuster, 2016). See especially chapter 3.

9. Joan Jacobs Brumberg, *The Body Project: An Intimate History of American Girls* (New York: Vintage Books, 1997), 61.

10. Brumberg, *The Body Project,* chapter 3.

11. Hatfield and Sprecher, *Mirror, Mirror,* 43.

12. Amanda M. Czerniawski, *Fashioning Fat: Inside Plus-Size Modeling* (New York: New York University Press, 2015), 16.

13. Peter N. Stearns, *Fat History: Bodies and Beauty in the Modern West* (New York: New York University Press, 2002), xviii.

14. Rebecca M. Herzig, *Plucked: A History of Hair Removal* (New York: New York University Press, 2015).

15. Naomi Wolf, *The Beauty Myth: How Images of Beauty Are Used against Women* (New York: Harper Perennial, 2002), 3.

16. Deford, *There She Is*, 195.

CHAPTER 1: AMERICA'S HANDSOMEST SUFFRAGISTS

1. Sally G. McMillen, *Seneca Falls and the Origins of the Women's Rights Movement* (New York: Oxford University Press, 2009), 90.

2. McMillen, *Seneca Falls and the Origins of the Women's Rights Movement*, 12.

3. Philip B. Kunhardt Jr., Philip B. Kunhardt III, and Peter W. Kunhardt, *P. T. Barnum: America's Greatest Showman* (New York: Knopf, 1995), 114.

4. Annette K. Vance Dorey, *Better Baby Contests: The Scientific Quest for Perfect Childhood Health* (Jefferson, NC: McFarland, 1999), 77.

5. "The Baby Show—Hurrah for Vienna, the Premium Baby Town!," *Lily*, November 1854.

6. Blain Roberts, *Pageants, Parlors, and Pretty Women* (Chapel Hill: University of North Carolina Press, 2014), 112.

7. Eleanor Flexnor, *Century of Struggle: The Woman's Rights Movement in the United States* (Cambridge, MA: Belknap Press, 1996), 83.

8. Ellen Carol DuBois, *Feminism and Suffrage: The Emergence of an Independent Women's Movement in America, 1848–1869* (Ithaca, NY: Cornell University Press, 1999), 46.

9. Kunhardt, Kunhardt, and Kunhardt, *P. T. Barnum*, 114.

10. Charles River Editors, *American Legends: The Life of P. T. Barnum* (Scotts Valley, CA: CreateSpace Independent Publishing, 2014).

11. Lois Banner, *American Beauty* (New York: Alfred A. Knopf, 1983), 256, quoting translation of (Paris: Pagnerre, 1857), 32–33.

12. Banner, *American Beauty*, 255.

13. Kunhardt, Kunhardt, and Kunhardt, *P. T. Barnum*, vii.

14. Richard Rudisill, *Mirror Image: The Influence of the Daguerreotype on American Society* (Albuquerque: University of New Mexico Press, 1971), 156.

15. *New York Tribune*, July 23, 1855.

16. S. L. Walker, *Poughkeepsie Journal*, August 11, 1855, 3.

17. *Humphrey's Journal* 7, no. 6 (July 15, 1855): 11.

18. Rudisill, *Mirror Image*, 156.

19. Kunhardt, Kunhardt, and Kunhardt, *P. T. Barnum*, 114.

20. "Barnum Forever—Attention, Ladies," *New York Times*, July 11, 1855.

21. Rudisill, *Mirror Image*, 157.

22. Banner, *American Beauty*, 256.

23. Bluford Adams, *E Pluribus Barnum: The Great Showman and the Making of U.S. Popular Culture* (Minneapolis: University of Minnesota Press, 1997), xii.

24. Rory Dicker, *A History of U.S. Feminisms* (Berkeley, CA: Seal Press, 2016), 38.

25. During this time is when the "myth" of Seneca Falls developed. This story is persuasively told in Lisa Tetrault, *The Myth of Seneca Falls: Memory and the Women's Suffrage Movement, 1848–1898* (Chapel Hill: University of North Carolina Press, 2014). Tetrault explains that while the meeting of Seneca Falls has never been in doubt, its seminal contribution is a construct of the late 1860s and early 1870s in order to solidify the leadership of Elizabeth Cady Stanton and Susan B. Anthony (who did not even attend Seneca Falls). Note that on the fortieth anniversary of Seneca Falls, in 1898, a lot of money was spent to celebrate "A Pageant for the Pioneers," though in this case "pageantry" is meant in the sense of exaggerated ritual. Tetrault, *The Myth of Seneca Falls*, 146.

26. Roberts, *Pageants, Parlors, and Pretty Women*, 108.

27. Banner, *American Beauty*, 259.

28. Roberts, *Pageants, Parlors, and Pretty Women*, 113.

29. Deford, *There She Is*, 109.

30. I include the word *reportedly* as there is no evidence Thomas Edison was nearby at the time, but this is what Deford reports. Local historians have taken issue with the naming of other judges, like Delaware Supreme Court judge Samuel Harrington, who was dead at the time of the contest. Michael Morgan, "Myths of 'Miss America' in Rehoboth," DelmarvaNow .com, March 16, 2014, https://www.delmarvanow.com/story/news/2014/03/16/michael -morgan-myths-of-miss-america-in-rehoboth/6509289.

31. Susan J. Pearson, "'Infantile Specimens': Showing Babies in Nineteenth-Century America," *Journal of Social History* (2008): 341.

32. Pearson, "Infantile Specimens," 350.

33. Pearson, "Infantile Specimens," 352.

34. Adams, *E Pluribus Barnum*, 99.

35. Pearson, "Infantile Specimens," 343.

36. Adams, *E Pluribus Barnum*, 100.

37. "Barnum's Baby Show vs. the Ten Governors," *New York Daily Times*, June 11, 1855.

38. Throughout the book, all calculations transforming older monetary amounts into today's values were made using the CPI inflation calculator at officialdata.org.

39. Adams, *E Pluribus Barnum*, 100.

40. Adams, *E Pluribus Barnum*, 111.

41. Pearson, "Infantile Specimens," 343.

42. Keith Lovegrove, *Pageant: The Beauty Contest* (New York: TeNeues, 2002), 16.

43. Banner, *American Beauty*, 250.

44. Roberts, *Pageants, Parlors, and Pretty Women*, 108.

45. Banner, *American Beauty*, 255.

46. Candace Savage, *Beauty Queens: A Playful History* (New York: Abbeville Press, 1998), 21–22.

47. *New York Times*, July 22, 1890.

48. *New York Times*, August 11, 1895.

49. Charles Musser, "Movies and the Beginnings of Cinema," in *American Cinema 1890–1909: Themes and Variations*, ed. Andre Gaudreault (New Brunswick, NJ: Rutgers University Press, 2009), 45–65.

50. *New York Times*, September 1, 1904.

51. Pearson, "Infantile Specimens," 343.

52. Steven Selden, "Transforming Better Babies into Fitter Families: Archival Resources and the History of the American Eugenics Movement, 1908–1930," in *Proceedings of the American Philosophical Society* 14, no. 2 (June 2005): 206.

53. Dorey, *Better Baby Contests*, 31.

54. Dorey, *Better Baby Contests*, 21, 43.

55. Dorey, *Better Baby Contests*, 5.

56. Dorey, *Better Baby Contests*, 80.

57. Pearson, "Infantile Specimens," 355.

58. Dicker, *History of U.S. Feminisms*, 45.

59. Karen W. Tice, *Queens of Academe: Beauty Pageantry, Student Bodies, and College Life* (New York: Oxford University Press, 2012), 28; Michaele Thurgood Haynes, *Dressing Up Debutantes: Pageantry and Glitz in Texas* (New York: Berg, 1998), 2.

60. Kathy Peiss, *Hope in a Jar: The Making of America's Beauty Culture* (New York: Owl Books, 1998), 97.

61. Banner, *American Beauty*, 211.

62. Banner, *American Beauty*, 216.

63. Banner, *American Beauty*, 216.

64. Geoffrey Jones, *Beauty Imagined: A History of the Global Beauty Industry* (New York: Oxford University Press, 2010), 88.

65. Brumberg, *The Body Project*, 61.

66. Herzig, *Plucked*, 11–12.

67. Stearns, *Fat History*, 10.

68. Stearns, *Fat History*, 54.

69. Peiss, *Hope in a Jar*, 122.

70. Wolf, *The Beauty Myth*, 62.

71. Jones, *Beauty Imagined*, 66.

72. Robert C. Allen, *Horrible Prettiness: Burlesque and American Culture* (Chapel Hill: University of North Carolina Press, 1991).

73. Janet M. Davis, *The Circus Age: Culture and Society Under the American Big Top* (Chapel Hill: University of North Carolina Press, 2002).

74. Davis, *The Circus Age*, 107.

75. Lily Rothman, "The Surprising Role of Circus Performers in the Fight for Women's Suffrage," *Time*, October 8, 2018.

76. Davis, *The Circus Age*, 89.

77. Karal Ann Marling, *Debutante: Rites and Regalia of American Debdom* (Lawrence: University of Kansas Press, 2004), 5.

78. Beverly Gordon, *Bazaars and Fair Ladies: The History of the American Fundraising Fair* (Knoxville: University of Tennessee Press, 1998).

79. David Glassberg, *American Historical Pageantry: The Uses of Tradition in the Early Twentieth Century* (Chapel Hill: University of North Carolina Press, 1990), 109.

80. Johanna Neuman, *Gilded Suffragists: The New York Socialites Who Fought for Women's Right to Vote* (New York: New York University Press, 2017).

81. Neuman, *Gilded Suffragists*, 62.

82. Note that Edith Bailey, a wealthy suffragist, had her twins appear in a 1911 suffrage pageant as well. Neuman, *Gilded Suffragists*, 79.

83. Neuman, *Gilded Suffragists*, 91.

84. Neuman, *Gilded Suffragists*, 111.

85. Madeleine Marsh, *Compacts and Cosmetics: Beauty from Victorian Times to the Present Day* (South Yorkshire, UK: Pen & Sword Books, 2009), loc. 634 of 2969 on Kindle.

86. Neuman, *Gilded Suffragists*, 2.

87. Banner, *American Beauty*, 206.

88. Anne Firor Scott, *The Southern Lady: From Pedestal to Politics, 1830–1930* (Charlottesville: University Press of Virginia, 1995), 181.

89. Diana B. Turk, *Bound by a Mighty Vow: Sisterhood and Women's Fraternities, 1870–1920* (New York: New York University Press, 2004), 14–15.

90. Margaret A. Lowe, *Looking Good: College Women and Body Image, 1875–1930* (Baltimore: Johns Hopkins University Press, 2003), 1.

91. Turk, *Bound by a Mighty Vow*, 43.

CHAPTER 2: SASHES AND SUFFRAGE

1. Elaine Weiss, *The Woman's Hour: The Great Fight to Win the Vote* (New York: Viking, 2018), 102.

2. "Women Displeased by Harding's Stand," *New York Times*, July 23, 1920.

3. Weiss, *The Woman's Hour*, 107.

4. "Tactics and Techniques of the National Womans [*sic*] Party Suffrage Campaign," Library of Congress, American Memory, https://www.loc.gov/collections/women-of-protest /articles-and-essays/tactics-and-techniques-of-the-national-womans-party-suffrage -campaign, accessed March 18, 2019.

5. Over-one-shoulder sashes were also sometimes worn by young girls in Civil War monument dedication ceremonies. While not staged as civic pageants, there were surely elements of ritual and civic pride in these ceremonies. The young girls would wear state names representing Confederate states, for example, as depicted on page 110 of Roberts's *Pageants, Parlors, and Pretty Women*.

6. Nancy Cott, *The Grounding of Modern Feminism* (New Haven, CT: Yale University Press, 1987), 3.

7. Cott, *The Grounding of Modern Feminism*, 13.

8. Weiss, *The Woman's Hour*, 3.

9. Weiss, *The Woman's Hour*, 325.

10. Bryant Simon, *Boardwalk of Dreams: Atlantic City and the Fate of Urban America* (New York: Oxford University Press, 2004), 19.

11. A. R. Riverol, *Live from Atlantic City: A History of the Miss America Pageant* (Bowling Green, OH: Bowling Green State University Popular Press, 1992), 12.

12. Angela Saulino Osborne, *Miss America: The Dream Lives On; a 75-Year Celebration* (Dallas: Taylor, 1995), 12.

13. Osborne, *Miss America*, 54.

14. Deford, *There She Is*, 111.

15. Deford, *There She Is*, 301.

16. Riverol, *Live from Atlantic City*, 12.

17. Osborne, *Miss America*, 54.

18. Deford, *There She Is*, 112.

19. Riverol, *Live from Atlantic City*, 14.

20. Her obituary by Robert McG. Thomas Jr. in the *New York Times*, October 5, 1995, lists her as "5 feet 1 inch and 108 pounds . . . with a 30–25–32 figure."

21. The Bathers Revue portion had four other competitive categories: comic, men, organizations, and, of course, cutest children. Riverol, *Live from Atlantic City*, 17.

22. Simon, *Boardwalk of Dreams*, 38.

23. "Bather Goes to Jail; Keeps Her Knees Bare," *New York Times*, September 4, 1921.

24. "Bather Goes to Jail."

25. Angela J. Latham, "Packaging Woman: The Concurrent Rise of Beauty Pageants, Public Bathing, and Other Performances of Female 'Nudity,'" *Journal of Popular Culture* 29, no. 3 (Winter 1995): 151.

26. Riverol, *Live from Atlantic City*, 22.

27. Deford, *There She Is*, 116.

28. Sarah Banet-Weiser, *The Most Beautiful Girl in the World: Beauty Pageants and National Identity* (Berkeley: University of California Press, 1999), 36.

29. "King Neptune Opens Seashore Pageant," *New York Times*, September 7, 1922.

30. "King Neptune Opens Seashore Pageant."

31. Deford, *There She Is*, 116.

32. "Two Beauties Call Upon Mayor Hylan," *New York Times*, January 21, 1923.

33. A September 10, 1922, article, written after her win, reports that she "will be the 'Miss America' of the 1923 pageant," but not that she herself has the title. "New Beauty Queen Ideal, Say Artists," *New York Times*.

34. Deford, *There She Is*, 118.

35. Osborne, *Miss America*, 72.

36. "Miss America: A History," https://missamerica.org/organization/history, accessed March 25, 2019.

37. "Atlantic City Set for Great Pageant," *New York Times*, September 6, 1927.

38. Osborne, *Miss America*, 75.

39. Glassberg, *American Historical Pageantry*, 238.

40. Glassberg, *American Historical Pageantry*, 284.

41. Banner, *American Beauty*, 16.

42. Riverol, *Live from Atlantic City*, 23.

43. Osborne, *Miss America*, 76.

44. Osborne, *Miss America*, 77.

45. "Miss America: A History."

46. Linda J. Lumsden, *Rampant Women: Suffragists and the Right of Assembly* (Knoxville: University of Tennessee Press, 1997). Photo inserts at back of book.

47. *Boardwalk Illustrated News*, September 7, 1925, 27, 29.

48. "400 Babies Parade at Coney Island," *New York Times*, May 18, 1923.

49. "12 Babies at Coney Win Parade Prizes," *New York Times*, September 16, 1928.

50. "Incubator Twins Win Coney Island Prize," *New York Times*, September 15, 1929.

51. "Asbury Park Picks Baby Miss America," *New York Times*, September 1, 1927.

52. "Baby Parades Hit as 'Exploitation,'" *New York Times*, September 22, 1932.

53. "Baby Awards End Joy at Mardi Gras," *New York Times*, September 20, 1936.

54. "Asbury Park Mayor Replies to Criticism on 'Unwholesome Reactions,'" *New York Times*, August 31, 1930.

55. Dorey, *Better Baby Contests*, 211.

56. Alexandra Minna Stern, "Making Better Babies: Public Health and Race Betterment in Indiana, 1920–1935," *American Journal of Public Health* 92, no. 5 (2002): 742–52.

57. Adolf Hitler's racially based social policies to promote the "best" genetic material (meaning white) meant that Jews, homosexuals, Gypsies, and others were subjected to horrible medical testing and death.

58. "200,000 See Baby Parade," *New York Times*, August 2, 1949.

59. "Babies on Parade at the Shore Today," *New York Times*, August 26, 1973.

60. Dorey, *Better Baby Contests*, 215.

61. Pearson, "Infantile Specimens," 359.

62. Cott, *The Grounding of Modern Feminism*, 87.

63. Susan A. Miller, *Growing Girls: The Natural Origins of Girls' Organizations in America* (New Brunswick, NJ: Rutgers University Press, 2007), 108.

64. Amanda Hawkins, "The Stylish History of Girls Scouts Uniforms," *Good Housekeeping*, March 4, 2015, https://www.goodhousekeeping.com/clothing/g801/girl-scout-uniforms/?slide=7.

65. Tice, *Queens of Academe*, 20.

66. Roberts, *Pageants, Parlors, and Pretty Women*, 130, 131.

67. "Preserving the Maid of Cotton Collection," National Museum of American History, November 29, 2010, https://americanhistory.si.edu/blog/2010/11/preserving-the-maid-of-cotton-collection.html.

68. "New Miss America Named," *New York Times*, June 24, 1930.

69. "New Orleans Girl Is 'Miss America,'" *New York Times*, August 5, 1930.

70. "Named as 'Miss America': Dorothy Hann of Camden, N.J. Wins Beauty Contest at Wildwood," *New York Times*, September 4, 1932.

71. Riverol, *Live from Atlantic City*, 26, 27.

72. Osborne, *Miss America*, 85.

73. Morton Sontheimer, "They've Got More Than Beauty," *Redbook*, September 1946, 46.

74. From the personal papers of Lenora Slaughter, collection 1227, National Museum of American History Archives Center.

75. "Saint Petersburg Festival of States," submitted by C. W. Bill Young to the American Folklife Center, Local Legacies: Celebrating Community Roots, Library of Congress, http://memory.loc.gov/diglib/legacies/loc.afc.afc-legacies.200002838, accessed April 4, 2019.

76. This story is according to a speech in Lenora Slaughter's private papers, housed in the National Museum of American History Archives Center at the Smithsonian Institution.

77. Riverol, *Live from Atlantic City*, 31.

78. "A Fond Farewell," editorial page, *Press of Atlantic City*, October 1, 1967.

79. Riverol, *Live from Atlantic City*, 32.

80. Riverol, *Live from Atlantic City*, 32.

81. Susan Dworkin, *Miss America, 1945: Bess Myerson's Own Story* (New York: Newmarket Press, 1987), 90.

82. Riverol, *Live from Atlantic City*, 33.

83. Banet-Weiser, *The Most Beautiful Girl in the World*, 41.

84. Ruth Malcomson, "How I Became Miss America," *Liberty Magazine* 19 (September 12, 1925): 19–21.

85. Dworkin, *Miss America, 1945*, 96.

86. Vicki Gold Levi and Lee Eisenberg, *Atlantic City: 125 Years of Ocean Madness* (Berkeley, CA: Ten Speed Press, 1979), 135, 174.

87. Dworkin, *Miss America, 1945*, 97.

88. Banet-Weiser, *The Most Beautiful Girl in the World*, 41.

89. Personal papers of Lenora Slaughter.

90. "Miss America," *American Experience*, dir. Lisa Ades (Arlington, VA: PBS, 2002).

91. In 1949 Miss America declared that contestants could only represent states. They made exceptions for (1) the "key" cities of New York, Chicago, Philadelphia, and Washington, DC; (2) Canada; and (3) any territories of the United States. It was not until 1959 that every state in the United States was represented. Key cities were not fully eliminated until 1964 (although Miss Memphis, Barbara Jo Walker, in 1947, was the last "city" contestant crowned Miss America). Riverol, *Live from Atlantic City*, 33.

92. "Miss America," *American Experience*.

93. Deford, *There She Is*, 157.

94. Keith Thrusby, "Jean Bartel Dies at 87; Miss America 1943 Pushed Pageant to Give Scholarships," *Los Angeles Times*, March 9, 2011.

95. Dworkin, *Miss America, 1945*, 98.

96. Dworkin, *Miss America, 1945*, 98.

97. Deford, *There She Is*, 159.

98. Sontheimer, "They've Got More Than Beauty," 46.

99. Sontheimer, "They've Got More Than Beauty," 111.

100. Lovegrove, *Pageant*, 20.

101. "The Story," Catalina Swimwear, http://www.catalinaswim.com/the-story, accessed April 13, 2019.

102. Deford, *There She Is*, 64.

103. Riverol, *Live from Atlantic City*, 40.

104. Thomas A. DiPrete and Claudia Buchmann, *The Rise of Women: The Growing Gender Gap in Education and What It Means for American Schools* (New York: Russell Sage, 2013), 222.

105. "Wedding Bells Ring Out for Beauty Pageant Directress," *Atlantic City Press*, August 13, 1948.

106. Kate Shindle, *Being Miss America: Behind the Rhinestone Curtain* (Austin: University of Texas Press, 2014), 32.

107. Adam Bernstein, "Yolande Betbeze Fox, a Miss America Who Rebelled, Dies at 87," *Washington Post*, February 25, 2016.

108. Bernstein, "Yolande Betbeze Fox."

109. Deford, *There She Is*, 180.

110. "Peril to Contest Seen," *New York Times*, July 19, 1959. This applied not just to Miss America contestants but also to Miss USA contestants. For some examples, see Bob Wells, "Miss New Mexico Attends Church," *Independent Press Telegram*, July 20, 1959, and "Miss Omaha of '59 Passes Crown to Another in Deference to Church," *Independent Press Telegram*, July 19, 1959.

111. Deford, *There She Is*, 181.

112. Deford, *There She Is*, 181.

113. Claudine Burnett, "Miss Universe and International Beauty Contests," *Long Beach's Past*, August 7, 2015, http://historiclongbeach.blogspot.com/2015/08/miss-universe-international-beauty.html.

114. Steve Harvey, "Swimwear Helped Bring the Universe," *Los Angeles Times*, March 14, 2010.

115. Larry L. Meyer and Patricia Larson Kalayjian, *Long Beach: Fortune's Harbor* (Tulsa, OK: Continental Heritage Press, 1983), 87.

116. L. A. C. Jr., "What Is Miss Universe?," *Long Beach Independent*, October 20, 1951.

117. "Miss Universe Beauty Pageant," program book, 1952, Long Beach Public Library.

118. This was not the first international beauty pageant held in the United States. That prize goes to the mouthful "International Pageant of Pulchritude," which was held in Galveston, Texas, in the 1920s until the start of the Depression. Savage, *Beauty Queens*.

119. It took only two years for a Miss USA to also capture the Miss Universe crown—twenty-one-year-old Miss South Carolina, Miriam Stevenson.

120. Spencer Crump, "Million Hail World Lovelies in Sunny L.B. Parade," *Long Beach Independent*, July 13, 1953.

121. Terry Huntingdon Tydings, *California Girl: Miss USA 1959* (Denver: Outskirts Press), 2013.

122. Don Short, *Miss World: The Naked Truth* (London: Everest Books, 1976).

123. 1955 Miss Universe program book, Long Beach Historical Society.

124. Internal document, Miss Universe Papers, Long Beach Public Library.

125. Riverol, *Live from Atlantic City*, 49.

126. Osborne, *Miss America*, 106.

127. Riverol, *Live from Atlantic City*, 49.

128. This number does appear to be lower than the 1953 pageant, which Riverol reports as at capacity at twenty-five thousand, though some seats may have been lost to television production, that number could not have totaled the seven thousand difference (*Live from Atlantic City*, 46, 54).

129. Deford, *There She Is*, 193.

130. Riverol, *Live from Atlantic City*, 56.

131. Susan Duff, *The Miss Universe Beauty Book: You Can Be a Pageant Winner—or Look Like One* (New York: Coward-McCann, 1983), 30.

132. Elissa Stein, *Here She Comes . . . Beauty Queen* (San Francisco: Chronicle Books, 2006), 45.

133. Peter B. Flint, "Albert A. Marks Jr. Is Dead at 76; Ex-Chief of Miss America Pageant," *New York Times*, September 25, 1989.

134. Deford, *There She Is*, 208.

135. Gene Lassers, "Long Beach Story: Miss Universe Pageant," *Long Beach Review*, February 1988, 18.

136. Meyer and Kalayjian, *Long Beach*, 148.

137. Meyer and Kalayjian, *Long Beach*, 148.

138. For more on the Japanese history of Miss International, see Miss International Beauty Pageant, https://www.miss-international.org/en/history, accessed May 21, 2019.

139. An abbreviated history of the National Sweetheart Pageant appears on the Hoopeston Jaycees website and within the program book from the seventy-fifth National Sweetcorn Festival in September 2018, http://www.hoopestonjaycees.org/pageant/about, accessed May 21, 2019.

140. "Our Story," Mobile Azalea Trail Maids website, http://mobileazaleatrailmaids.com /our-story, accessed May 22, 2019.

141. 1969 America's Junior Miss official program book.

142. 1958 America's Junior Miss Souvenir Program.

143. Patrice Gaunder Heeran, "You Gotta Be You!," in *Full Bloom: Cultivating Success*, ed. Amy E. Goodman, Anne Hagerman Wilcox, and Amy Osmond Cook (San Clemente, CA: Sourced Media Books, 2011), 82.

144. Amy Zimmer, *Meet Miss Subways: New York's Beauty Queens 1941–1976* (Kittery, ME: Smith/Kerr Associates, 2012), 24.

145. Zimmer, *Meet Miss Subways*, 24.

146. Zimmer, *Meet Miss Subways*, 4.

147. Haynes, *Dressing Up Debutantes*, 44.

148. Tice, *Queens of Academe*, 20–21.

149. Peiss, *Hope in a Jar*, 191.

150. Deford, *There She Is*, 308.

151. Lydia Reeder, *Dust Bowl Girls: The Inspiring Story of the Team That Barnstormed Its Way to Basketball Glory* (Chapel Hill, NC: Algonquin Books, 2017), 221, 223.

152. Peiss, *Hope in a Jar*, 238.

153. Peiss, *Hope in a Jar*, 256.

CHAPTER 3: BURNING VERSUS PADDING BRAS

1. Amanda Minton, "Our Very Own Miss America, Debra Dene Barnes," *Morning Sun*, October 18, 2018.

2. "Judi Ford 'Miss America,' *Rockford Register Star*, September 8, 1968.

3. Carol Hanisch, "What Can Be Learned: A Critique of the Miss America Protest," November 27, 1968, Robin Morgan papers, David M. Rubenstein Rare Book and Manuscript Library, Duke University.

4. Marcia Cohen, *The Sisterhood: The Inside Story of the Women's Movement and the Leaders Who Made It Happen* (Santa Fe, NM: Sunstone Press, 2009), 150.

5. Robin Morgan, "No More Miss America Press Release and Open Letter," August 22, 1968, Robin Morgan papers.

6. Robin Morgan, *Going Too Far: The Personal Chronicle of a Feminist* (New York: Random House, 1977), 62.

7. Robin Morgan, "Letter from Robin Morgan to Richard S. Jackson, Mayor of Atlantic City," August 29, 1968, Robin Morgan papers.

8. Richard S. Jackson, "Letter from Richard S. Jackson, Mayor of Atlantic City, to Robin Morgan," September 4, 1968, Robin Morgan papers.

9. Charlotte Curtis, "Miss America Pageant Is Picketed by 100 Women," *New York Times*, September 8, 1968.

10. Robin Morgan, "Women's Liberation: No More Miss America!," flyer inviting women to protest the Miss America Pageant, September 1968, Robin Morgan papers.

11. Cohen, *Sisterhood*, 150.

12. Morgan, "Women's Liberation:" No More Miss America!," Robin Morgan papers.

13. Robin Morgan, "Annotated Planning Notes for the Miss America Protest," September 1968, Robin Morgan papers.

14. Art Buchwald, "Uptight Dissenters Go Too Far in Burning Their Brassieres," *Washington Post*, September 12, 1968.

15. Morgan, "No More Miss America Press Release and Open Letter."

16. Morgan, "Annotated Planning Notes for the Miss America Protest."

17. Cohen, *Sisterhood*, 149–50.

18. Deford, *There She Is*, 309.

19. Gail Collins, *When Everything Changed: The Amazing Journey of the American Woman from 1960 to the Present* (New York: Back Bay Books, 2010), 179.

20. Denton E. Morrison and Carlin Paige Holden, "The Burning Bra: The American Breast Fetish and Women's Liberation," in *Sociology for Pleasure*, ed. Marcello Truzzi (Englewood Cliffs, NJ: Prentice-Hall, 1974), 358.

21. Morgan, *Going Too Far*, 62.

22. Maren Lockwood Carden, *The New Feminist Movement* (New York: Russell Sage, 1974), 19.

23. Susan Ware, *American Women's History: A Very Short Introduction* (New York: Oxford University Press, 2015), 104.

24. Robin Morgan, "Open Letter Inviting Women to Participate in 1969 Miss America Protest, by the Ad-Hoc Committee for the Miss America Demonstration, 1969," August 28, 1969, Robin Morgan papers.

25. Robin Morgan, "Miss America Demonstration Press Release, Aug. 28, 1969," Robin Morgan papers.

26. A. J. Cafiero, "The Miss America Pageant Restraining Order against Protesters, Filed Sept. 4, 1969," Robin Morgan papers.

27. "Pepsi Leaves Miss America," *Washington Post*, October 23, 1968.

28. Pat Ryan, "There She Is, Miss America," *Sports Illustrated*, October 6, 1969.

29. Ryan, "There She Is, Miss America."

30. Marjorie Ford, *Sharing the Crown* (Litchfield, IL: Publication Investments, 1971), 67–68.

31. Dicker, *History of U.S. Feminisms*, 72.

32. Riverol, *Live from Atlantic City*, 90.

33. National Organization for Women, "Statement of Purpose," https://now.org/about /history/statement-of-purpose, accessed February 24, 2020.

34. Dicker, *History of U.S. Feminisms*, 59.

35. Cohen, *Sisterhood*, 141.

36. Mom had two memorable experiences in Vietnam: (1) a tent collapsing during the performance, which led to an evacuation, and (2) another evacuation when the "enemy forces were getting so close that [the US military] wanted to get us out of there. As they evacuated us in tanks, I kept thinking about the poor guys who had to go back to it." Ann-Marie Bivans, *The Miss America Cookbook* (Nashville: Rutledge Press, 1995), 174.

37. While I have found no evidence of actual bra burners on the Boardwalk in Atlantic City in September 1970, George's point that her time as Miss America was surrounded by questions on these issues is fair, and her thoughts are still relevant. I suspect George was referring to a compilation of the historical record and not a specific incident. Phyllis George, *Never Say Never: 10 Lessons to Turn "You Can't" into "Yes I Can"* (New York: McGraw-Hill, 2003), 18.

38. Patricia Hill Burnett, *True Colors: An Artist's Journey from Beauty Queen to Feminist* (Troy, MI: Momentum Books, 1995).

39. "Miss America," *American Experience*.

40. "Miss America," *American Experience*.

41. K. S. McNutt, "Jane Jayroe: Oklahoma Native Reflects on Her Miss America Win," *Oklahoman*, September 11, 2016.

42. Jane Jayroe (with Bob Burke), *More Grace Than Glamour: My Life as Miss America and Beyond* (Oklahoma City: Oklahoma Heritage Association, 2006), citations in this section from pages 138, 145, 146, 150, and 157.

43. "Miss America," *American Experience*.

44. "Miss America," *American Experience*.

45. Judy Klemesrud, "Can Feminists Upstage Miss America?," *New York Times*, September 8, 1974.

46. Carlo M. Sardella, "'Miss America' Faces Ms.," *New York Times*, September 1, 1974.

47. Taylor Marsh, *The Sexual Education of a Beauty Queen: Relationship Secrets from the Trenches* (New York: Open Road Integrated Media, 2014), 14.

48. This does not include any local or state scholarships earned, which in some states were and are substantial. It also does not take into account any out-of-pocket expenses contestants had, like extra wardrobe or hair and makeup costs.

49. Ware, *American Women's History*, 195.

50. Deford, *There She Is*, 313.

51. Deford, *There She Is*, 316.

52. Carol Byrd-Bredbenner, Jessica Murray, and Yvette R. Schlussel, "Temporal Changes in Anthropometric Measurements of Idealised Females and Young Women in General," *Women and Health* 41, no. 2 (2005): 19.

53. "Miss America Concedes; No More Measurements," UPI, September 8, 1986.

54. Nancie S. Martin, *Miss America through the Looking Glass: The Story behind the Scenes* (New York: Little Simon, 1985), 33.

55. Joan Jacobs Brumberg, *Fasting Girls: The History of Anorexia Nervosa* (New York: Vintage, 2000), 11.

56. Two with red hair and four with black hair won, in case you wondered what the remaining 13 percent were.

57. I mainly refer to this pageant as America's Junior Miss (AJM) because that is what it was predominantly known as for over fifty years. In 2010 it was renamed Distinguished Young

Woman, in an effort to distinguish it from other pageants (the winner does not receive a crown but rather a medal).

58. Because I could not locate a complete collection of programs, I use programs in approximately five-year intervals for AJM. The programs included are from 1960, 1964, 1970, 1975, 1980, 1985, 1990, 1994, 2000, 2005, 2011, and 2015.

59. I do not have information for 1982.

60. This also may be due to the same format being used each year.

61. The years collected include 1975, 1980, 1985, 1990, 1995, 2000, 2005, 2010, and 2015.

62. The years included 1980, 1985, 1990, 1995, 2000, and 2015.

63. For Idaho I could not locate a 2000 program book so used 1999 instead.

64. Mandy McMichael, *Miss America's God: Faith and Identity in America's Oldest Pageant* (Waco, TX: Baylor University Press, 2019).

65. Personal emails from October and November 2019.

66. Robin Morgan, "Early Career," https://www.robinmorgan.net/early-career, accessed June 29, 2019.

67. Jack Gould, "'The Little Miss America' Contest," *New York Times*, September 5, 1968, TV section.

68. "Babies on Parade at the Shore Today," *New York Times*, August 26, 1973.

69. "Cinderella History," http://cinderellapageant.com, accessed June 30, 2019.

70. "About Us," https://sunburstbeauty.com/about-us, accessed June 30, 2019.

71. Zimmer, *Meet Miss Subways*, 214.

72. "Pageant History," Miss Gay America, http://www.missgayamerica.com/pageant -history.html, accessed June 30, 2019.

73. "About Us," Senior America, http://senioramerica.org/aboutus.asp, accessed June 30, 2019.

74. "About," Ms. Wheelchair America, http://www.mswheelchairamerica.org/about, accessed June 30, 2019.

75. "NAD History," National Association of the Deaf, https://www.nad.org/about-us/nad -history, accessed July 7, 2019.

76. "Legacy," Mrs. America, https://mrsamerica.com/2019/01/21/legacy, accessed June 30, 2019.

77. Manisha Aggarwal-Schifellite, "The Long, Strange Life of the Mrs. America Pageant," *Jezebel*, January 5, 2016, https://pictorial.jezebel.com/the-long-strange-life-of-the-mrs -america-pageant-1750888725.

78. Tony Kornheiser, "After 25 Years, It's Bye-Bye Bertie," *Washington Post*, January 4, 1980.

79. "There He Goes . . . ," *New York Times*, January 6, 1980.

80. Jane Rieker, "There He Was—After 25 Years, the Miss America Pageant Tells Bert Parks to Take a Walk," *People*, January 21, 1980.

81. W. Joseph Campbell, *Getting It Wrong: Debunking the Greatest Myths in American Journalism* (Berkeley: University of California Press, 2016), 116–29.

82. Dorothy Sue Cobble, Linda Gordon, and Astrid Henry, *Feminism Unfinished: A Short, Surprising History of American Women's Movements* (New York: Liveright, 2014), 69.

83. Bonnie J. Dow, "Feminism, Miss America, and Media Mythology," *Rhetoric and Public Affairs* 6, no. 1 (2003): 143.

84. "About," Lindsy Van Gelder, https://lindsyvangelder.com/about, accessed June 30, 2019.

85. M. G. Lord, *Forever Barbie: The Unauthorized Biography of a Real Doll* (New York: Walker & Company, 2004), 90.

CHAPTER 4: PENTHOUSE AND PLATFORMS

1. Vanessa Williams and Helen Williams with Irene Zutell, *You Have No Idea: A Famous Daughter, Her No-Nonsense Mother, and How They Survived Pageants, Hollywood, Love, Loss (and Each Other)* (New York: Gotham Books, 2012), 39.

2. Williams and Williams, *You Have No Idea*, 37.

3. These statistics are accurate at least through 2019.

4. Maxin Leeds Craig, *Ain't I a Beauty Queen? Black Women, Beauty, and the Politics of Race* (New York: Oxford University Press, 2002), 66.

5. Craig, *Ain't I a Beauty Queen?*, 47.

6. Craig, *Ain't I a Beauty Queen?*, 53.

7. Roberts, *Pageants, Parlors, and Pretty Women*, 197.

8. Elwood Watson and Darcy Martin, eds., *"There She Is, Miss America:" The Politics of Sex, Beauty, and Race in America's Most Famous Pageant* (New York: Palgrave MacMillan, 2004), 5.

9. Angela Perez Baraquio, *Amazing Win, Amazing Loss: Miss America Living Happily, EVEN After* (Anaheim, CA: APB, 2014), 98.

10. Lillian Ross, "Symbol of All We Possess," *New Yorker*, October 15, 1949.

11. Jennifer Preston, *Queen Bess: An Unauthorized Biography of Bess Myerson* (Chicago: Contemporary Books, 1990), 24.

12. Preston, *Queen Bess*, 25.

13. Craig, *Ain't I a Beauty Queen?*, 70.

14. Roberts, *Pageants, Parlors, and Pretty Women*, 261.

15. Craig, *Ain't I a Beauty Queen?*, 4.

16. Gabrielle Emanuel, "Protesting Miss America, But Not in Two-Part Harmony," WGBH, September 7, 2018.

17. "Negroes Plan Show to Rival Contest for Miss America," *New York Times*, August 28, 1968.

18. Note that Ford reportedly weighed in at the same amount as Williams but was three inches taller.

19. Judy Klemesrud, "There's Now Miss Black America," *New York Times*, September 9, 1968.

20. Ann-Marie Bivans, *Miss America: In Pursuit of the Crown* (New York: MasterMedia Ltd., 1991), 27.

21. "Miss America: A History," Miss America, https://www.missamerica.org/organization /history/#1970s, accessed July 5, 2019.

22. *Miss Black America Pageant 1967–1977*, produced by Frances Presley Rice and Bayer Mack (Black Starz Music Television, 2016).

23. Turner's first runner-up was Asian, which was notable because, up to that point, no Asian American Miss America had been crowned.

24. Gist, interview with the author, October 27, 2019.

25. Before her year was up, and after placing as first runner-up at Miss Universe, Gist sued Miss USA for labor practices. She said she was not treated well (for example, she was forced to wear high heels even when she had painful and bleeding bunions), and she did not receive all her announced prizes. Gist is the only national pageant winner to sue a pageant. She does not believe this was racially motivated. In fact, a group lawsuit was brought by several white winners. All the cases were settled, and positive changes were soon made for future Miss USA winners. For more, see Roxanne Roberts, "Beauty and the Beef," *Washington Post*, February 22, 1991.

26. "Black Leaders Praise Choice of First Black Miss America," *New York Times*, September 19, 1983.

27. Susan Chira, "To First Black Miss America, Victory Is a Means to an End," *New York Times*, September 19, 1983.

28. Chira, "To First Black Miss America."

29. Banet-Weiser, *The Most Beautiful Girl in the World*, 135.

30. Williams and Williams, *You Have No Idea*, 45.

31. K. Sue Jewell, *From Mammy to Miss America and Beyond: Cultural Images and the Shaping of US Social Policy* (New York: Routledge, 1993), 52.

32. Williams and Williams, *You Have No Idea*, 46–47.

33. Susan Chira, "First Black Miss America Finds Unforeseen Issues," *New York Times*, April 3, 1984.

34. Williams and Williams, *You Have No Idea*, 9.

35. Williams and Williams, *You Have No Idea*, 39.

36. Williams and Williams, *You Have No Idea*, 40.

37. Williams and Williams, *You Have No Idea*, 41.

38. Peter Kerr, "Penthouse Says Nude Photos Are Those of Miss America," *New York Times*, July 20, 1984.

39. Peter B. Flint, "Albert A. Marks, Jr. Is Dead at 76; Ex-Chief of Miss America Pageant," *New York Times*, September 25, 1989.

40. Kerr, "Penthouse Says Nude Photos Are Those of Miss America."

41. Williams and Williams, *You Have No Idea*, 43.

42. Donald Janson, "Miss America Asked to Quit Over Photos Showing Her Nude," *New York Times*, July 21, 1984.

43. Williams and Williams, *You Have No Idea*, 41.

44. Georgia Dullea, "Essence Marks 15 Years of Serving Black Women," *New York Times*, April 5, 1985.

45. Howard J. Wiarda, *Political Culture, Political Science, and Identity Politics: An Uneasy Alliance* (New York: Routledge, 2014), 150.

46. Kimberlé Crenshaw, "Demarginalizing the Intersection of Race and Sex: A Black Feminist Critique of Antidiscrimination Doctrine, Feminist Theory and Antiracist Politics," in *University of Chicago Legal Forum* (1989), article 8.

47. Kimberlé Crenshaw, "Mapping the Margins: Intersectionality, Identity Politics, and Violence against Women of Color," *Stanford Law Review* 43, no. 6 (1991): 1241–99.

48. "Home Early: A Miss America Ponders an Unsettled Future," *New York Times*, September 1, 1984.

49. Ellen Willis, "Lust Horizons: Is the Women's Movement Pro-Sex?," *Village Voice*, June 1981.

50. Organizations like NOW were still stumbling through their response to the Lavender Menace, a group of lesbian radical feminists who publicly sparred with Betty Friedan and other NOW leaders. NOW wanted to distance itself from the image of "man-hating, lesbian" feminists.

51. Lindsey Gruson, "Miss America Back in 'Festive Mood,'" *New York Times*, September 11, 1984.

52. Sheri L. Dew, *Sharlene Wells, Miss America* (Salt Lake City: Deseret Book, 1985), xii.

53. Dew, *Sharlene Wells, Miss America*, 4.

54. Dew, *Sharlene Wells, Miss America*, 110.

55. Dicker, *History of U.S. Feminisms*, 118.

56. Shindle, *Being Miss America*, 89.

57. Shindle, *Being Miss America*, 91, 90.

58. Gretchen Carlson, *Getting Real* (New York: Viking, 2015), 76.

59. William Goldman, *Hype and Glory* (New York: Villard Books, 1990), 207, 20.

60. Carlson, *Getting Real*, 3.

61. Shindle, *Being Miss America*, 92.

62. Melinda Beck, "A Controversial 'Spectator Sport,'" *Newsweek*, September 17, 1984, 56–60.

63. Beck, "A Controversial 'Spectator Sport,'" 60.

64. Tice, *Queens of Academe*, 20.

65. Roberts, *Pageants, Parlors, and Pretty Women*, 190.

66. Roberts, *Pageants, Parlors, and Pretty Women*, 175.

67. Craig, *Ain't I a Beauty Queen?*, 57.

68. Roberts, *Pageants, Parlors, and Pretty Women*, 152.

69. Craig, *Ain't I a Beauty Queen?*, 61.

70. Oprah Winfrey, "How Winning This Contest Changed My Life," February 29, 2016, https://www.linkedin.com/pulse/how-winning-contest-changed-my-life-oprah-winfrey; Ann-Marie Bivans, *101 Secrets to Winning Beauty Pageants* (New York: Citadel Press, 1995), 3.

71. Nan Robertson, "A Beauty Winner with 'Positivity,'" *New York Times*, July 19, 1981.

72. Erica Thompson, "Miss Black America at 50: A Look Back at the Pageant's History of Protest and Pride," Mic.com, August 17, 2018, https://www.mic.com/articles/190777/miss-black-america-50th-anniversary-a-look-back-at-the-pageants-history-of-protest-and-pride#.3iYyJyqQe.

73. Evan West, "The Decision: Mike Tyson's Rape Trial, 25 Years Later," *Indianapolis Monthly*, January 20, 2017.

74. Mitch Gelman, "Shattered," *Los Angeles Times*, March 31, 1995.

75. "Miss Black USA—The Pageant Celebrating Black Beauty," *Newsweek*, https://www.youtube.com/watch?v=LDZwa1miHcY, accessed July 9, 2019.

76. "About," Miss Black USA Talented Teen, http://www.missblackusatalentedteen.org, accessed July 9, 2019.

77. "About the Pageant," Miss Africa USA Pageant, https://missafricausa.org/about-3/about, accessed July 9, 2019.

78. Shelby Fleig, "Miss Black America Pageant Reclaims Activist Roots in 'Rebirth' at 50," *USA Today*, August 17, 2018.

79. Robin Givhan, "'You Can Be Unapologetically Black': How Miss Black America Has Endured 50 Years," *Washington Post*, August 28, 2018.

80. Mihir Zaveri, "Miss America, Miss Teen USA and Miss USA Are All Black Women for the First Time," *New York Times*, May 5, 2019.

81. Christine Reiko Yano, *Crowning the Nice Girl: Gender, Ethnicity, and Culture in Hawaii's Cherry Blossom Festival* (Honolulu: University of Hawai'i Press, 2006), 60.

82. Rebecca Chiyoko King-O'Riaian, *Pure Beauty: Judging Race in Japanese American Beauty Pageants* (Minneapolis: University of Minnesota Press, 2006, 10.

83. King-O'Riaian, *Pure Beauty*, 8.

84. King-O'Riaian, *Pure Beauty*, 13.

85. King-O'Riaian, *Pure Beauty*, 12.

86. Yano, *Crowning the Nice Girl*, 184.

87. "Origins," Chinese New Year Festival and Parade, https://chineseparade.com/origins, accessed July 7, 2019.

88. *Miss Chinatown U.S.A.*, dir. Kathy Huang (2006).

89. Susan Supernaw, *Muscogee Daughter: My Sojourn to the Miss America Pageant* (Lincoln: University of Nebraska Press, 2010).

90. Note that the title Miss Oklahoma refers to a title holder in the Miss America system. A qualification of the pageant system is needed, here "USA," if it is not Miss America, which illustrates both the age of Miss America and the supremacy of the Miss America system in pageant hierarchy.

91. Gregory Nickerson, "All-American Indian Days and the Miss Indian American Pageant," *Montana: The Magazine of Western History* (Summer 2017): 4.

92. Nickerson, "All-American Indian Days," 16.

93. Wendy Kozol, "Miss Indian America: Regulatory Gazes and the Politics of Affiliation," *Feminist Studies* 31, no. 1 (Spring 2005): 75.

94. "History," Gathering of Nations, https://www.gatheringofnations.com/history.aspx, accessed July 7, 2019.

95. Kozol, "Miss Indian America," 75.

96. *Miss Navajo*, dir. Billy Luther (2006).

97. Jennifer Nez Denetdale, "Chairmen, Presidents, and Princesses: The Navajo Nation, Gender, and the Politics of Tradition," *Wicazo Sa Review* 21, no. 1 (Spring 2006): 18.

98. Hilda Llorens, "Latina Bodies in the Era of Elective Aesthetic Surgery," *Latino Studies* 11, no. 4 (2013): 547–69.

99. Sarah Grainger, "Inside a Venezuelan School for Child Beauty Queens," BBC News, September 3, 2012.

100. Thatiana Diaz, "Miss America Has a Latina Problem," Refinery29, September 12, 2018.

101. "Home," Miss U.S. Latina, http://www.missuslatina.com/, accessed July 7, 2019.

102. Miss Latina USA, "Hall of Fame," https://www.misslatina.com/hall-of-fame.html, accessed July 7, 2019.

103. "About Us," Miss Mundo Latina USA, http://missmundolatina.com/us/, accessed July 7, 2019.

104. Julia Alvarez, *Once Upon a Quinceañera: Coming of Age in the USA* (New York: Viking, 2007).

105. Noel Ignatiev, *How the Irish Became White* (New York: Routledge, 1995).

106. Rose of Tralee International Festival, "Boston Rose," http://bostonnerose.weebly.com/boston-rose.html, accessed July 7, 2019.

107. "About Us," Arizona Colleen, https://www.azcolleen.org, accessed July 7, 2019.

108. "About," South Carolina Rose Center, http://www.southcarolinarose.com/south-carolina-center, accessed July 7, 2019.

109. Amy O'Connor, "How to Explain the Rose of Tralee to Your Non-Irish Friends," *Daily Edge*, August 21, 2017.

110. "Home," Miss US Italia Pageant, http://missusitalia.com, accessed August 2, 2018.

111. Megan Finnerty, "Americans More Multiethnic, yet Heritage Pageants Abide," *Republic/AZCentral*, March 13, 2014.

112. Whitestone has since had cochlear implants.

113. Heather Whitestone, *Listening with My Heart* (New York: Galilee, 1998).

114. Daphne Gray, with Gregg Lewis, *Yes, You Can, Heather! The Story of Heather Whitestone, Miss America 1995* (Grand Rapids, MI: Zondervan, 1995), 171.

115. "Frequently Asked Questions," National Association of the Deaf, accessed July 7, 2019.

116. "History," Miss & Mister Deaf International, http://missmisterdeafinternational.org/history, accessed July 7, 2019.

117. "Miss Black Deaf America," National Black Deaf Advocates, https://www.nbda.org/content/mbda, accessed July 7, 2019.

118. Nicole Johnson, *Living with Diabetes: Nicole Johnson, Miss America 1999* (Washington, DC: LifeLine Press, 2001).

119. Abbey Curran with Elizabeth Kaye, *The Courage to Compete: Living with Cerebral Palsy and Following My Dreams* (New York: Harper, 2015), 135.

120. Curran, *The Courage to Compete*, 2.

121. Curran, *The Courage to Compete*, 51.

122. Curran, *The Courage to Compete*, 131.

123. Curran, *The Courage to Compete*, 186.

124. "Our Story," Ms. Wheelchair USA, https://www.mswheelchairusa.org/page4.html, accessed July 7, 2019.

125. "Ms. Full-Figured Pageant USA (29th Annual)," https://www.youtube.com/watch?v=03JHLNScvJk, accessed July 7, 2019.

126. Not many Christian-only pageants exist, though some pageants, including Miss America, have a well-deserved reputation for being very Christian and even evangelical at times. One pageant system, Virtue International Pageants, which began in 2000 (Tice, *Queens of Academe*, 184), is an exception; but as of 2008 they only have online, not in-person, competitions. https://www.teenagerpageants.com/pageants/virtue_international_pageant.htm, accessed July 8, 2019.

127. Miss Plus America, https://missplusamerica.com, accessed July 7, 2019.

128. *There She Is*, dir. Veena Rao and Emily Sheskin (2013).

129. David L. Chapman and Patricia Vertinsky, *Venus with Biceps: A Pictorial History of Muscular Women* (Vancouver, BC: Arsenal Pulp Press, 2010), 278.

130. Chapman and Vertinsky, *Venus with Biceps*, 294.

131. Chapman and Vertinsky, *Venus with Biceps*, 11.

132. Abby Ellin, "Pageant Glamour for Those Who Have Reached the Age of Elegance," *New York Times*, December 2, 2016.

133. "Senior Pageants Group," Ms. Senior USA, https://www.msseniorusa.org, accessed July 7, 2019.

134. "Beauty Queens Vie for Nursing Home Crown," Associated Press, August 26, 2009.

135. Jane Evershed, *Don't Assume I Don't Cook! Recipes for Women's Lives* (Washington, DC: National Organization for Women, 1998), 78.

136. Janice Crompton, "Dorothy 'Cindy Gams' Judd Hill," obituary, *Pittsburgh Post-Gazette*, March 13, 2019.

137. Bivans, *101 Secrets to Winning Beauty Pageants*, 15.

138. Martin, *Miss America through the Looking Glass*, 29.

139. *Drop Dead Gorgeous*, dir. Michael Patrick Jann (1999).

140. Margaret Raitt and David F. Lancy, "Rhinestone Cowgirl: The Education of a Rodeo Queen," *Play and Culture* 1 (1988): 269.

141. National Outdoor Show, https://nationaloutdoorshow.org, accessed July 7, 2019. *Muskrat Lovely*, dir. Amy Nicholson (2005).

142. David Farenthold, "Fur Flies at Beauty Pageant (But It's Not What You Think)," *Washington Post*, March 1, 2008.

143. *The Bituminous Coal Queens of Pennsylvania*, dir. David Hunt and Jody Eldred (2005).

144. Emily Atkin, "'Coal Princesses': Inside the World of Coal-Themed Beauty Pageants," Think Progress, June 12, 2014.

145. Brenda West, "Mobley, Mary Ann," in *Encyclopedia of Southern Culture*, vol. 4, ed. Charles Reagan Wilson and William Ferris (1989), 535.

146. Blain Roberts, "The Ugly Side of the Southern Belle," *New York Times*, January 15, 2013.

147. Don Wycliff, "There She Is, Miss Different," *New York Times*, Editorial Notebook, September 19, 1989.

148. *Miss . . . Or Myth?*, dir. Geoffrey Dunn and Mark Schwartz (1987).

149. Gene Yasuda, "Pageant Protestor Hits Contest 'Indignities,'" *Los Angeles Times*, June 15, 1988.

150. "Miss California Crowned with Slurs by Angry Loser," Associated Press, June 14, 1998.

151. Michelle Anderson went on to Yale Law School and is now the president of Brooklyn College. Joe Patrice, "The Law Dean Who Became an Undercover Beauty Queen," Above the Law, May 16, 2016, https://abovethelaw.com/2016/05/the-law-dean-who-became-an-under over-beauty-queen/?rf=1. Marlise (Ricardos) Boland is a film producer.

152. Dicker, *History of U.S. Feminisms*, 117.

153. Shindle, *Being Miss America*, 121.

154. Shindle, *Being Miss America*, 122.

CHAPTER 5: TABLOIDS AND TIARAS

1. John Ramsey and Patsy Ramsey, *The Death of Innocence: JonBenét's Parents Tell Their Story* (New York: Onyx, 2001), 57.

2. Ramsey and Ramsey, *The Death of Innocence*, 55.

3. Deford later said of Patsy Paugh Ramsey that she was "too programmed" for his taste. Carlton Smith, *Death of a Little Princess: The Tragic Story of the Murder of JonBenet Ramsey* (New York: St. Martin's Press, 1997), 22.

4. Steve Thomas and Don Davis, *JonBenét: Inside the Ramsey Murder Investigation* (New York: St. Martin's Press, 2000), 5.

5. Ramsey and Ramsey, *The Death of Innocence*, 55.

6. Ramsey and Ramsey, *The Death of Innocence*, 56.

7. Ramsey and Ramsey, *The Death of Innocence*, 57–58.

8. John Ramsey with Marie Chapian, *The Other Side of Suffering: The Father of JonBenét Ramsey Tells the Story of His Journey from Grief to Grace* (New York: FaithWords, 2012).

9. Paula Woodward, *We Have Your Daughter: The Unsolved Murder of JonBenét Ramsey Twenty Years Later* (Westport, CT: Prospecta Press, 2016), 220.

10. While some boys do participate in child beauty pageants, they are a distinct minority, and I focus only on girls.

11. The "college scholarships" were mostly savings bonds that were advertised as scholarships but in reality could be cashed in and used for anything at any time.

12. "Our History," Our Little Miss, http://www.ourlittlemiss.com/story-of-olm.html, accessed July 13, 2019.

13. Anna Stanley, *Producing Beauty Pageants: A Director's Guide* (San Diego: Box of Ideas, 1989), 265.

14. Jim Gallagher, "Pageants: Little Misses, Big Dreams (for Their Mommies)," *Chicago Tribune*, July 28, 1977.

15. A box within the *Newsweek* spread featured the aftermath of the Vanessa Williams scandal discussed in chapter 4.

16. Jerry Adler, Pamela Abramson, and John McCormick, "Babes in Pageantland," *Newsweek*, September 17, 1984, 58.

17. Pat Jordan, "The Curious Childhood of an 11-Year-Old Beauty Queen," *Life*, April 1994, 56.

18. *Painted Babies*, dir. Jane Treays (1996).

19. All quotes in the following three paragraphs are from *Painted Babies*.

20. Jeannie Ralston, "The High Cost of Beauty," *Parenting*, November 2001, 132–38.

21. *Living Dolls: The Making of a Child Beauty Queen*, dir. Shari Cookson (2001).

22. Eleanor Von Duyke with Dwight Wallington, *A Little Girl's Dream? A JonBenét Ramsey Story* (Austin, TX: Windsor House, 1998), 25.

23. Madisyn Verst was featured as the cover story in the September 26, 2011, issue of *People* magazine. *People* also featured articles on *Toddlers & Tiaras* child pageant contestants in the November 10, 2010, and August 24, 2016, issues.

24. "*Toddlers & Tiaras* Celebrity Edition," *People*, October 10, 2011, 52–53.

25. The *natural* category is pretty much what it sounds like. No makeup is allowed, and dresses are purchased in a store ("off-the-rack"). Overall, pageant fees are relatively low. For the 2020 American Royal Beauties pageant, a state contest, it cost $150 for a child age six or under to enter. In general, "hobby glitz" participants live in the geographic region where the pageant is being held. At a hobby glitz pageant, the dresses are often pageant-style "cupcake" dresses, with details like lace, rhinestones, or bustles. The term *cupcake dress* comes from the skirt's shape, which is like an upside-down cupcake. At this level the custom dresses are often purchased via the internet (message board, Facebook groups, or eBay) and range from $100 to $500. A hair and makeup artist who is attending the pageant will, for a fee typically ranging from $100 to $300, do the hair and makeup for contestants. While winners receive monetary awards, they are usually not larger than a $500 savings bond, so the amounts awarded are not big enough to cover travel fees, hotel rooms, clothes, and hair and makeup at the pageant. New competition categories appear at *nationals*, such as Western wear or a 1950s theme. This means costs are higher, but the prizes are also larger. There is usually a minimum of $550 in fees, which does not include the hotel bill (or cover travel costs). National-level pageants most often take place in the South and typically last at least three days. Because these events tend to be held in warm locales with tourist attractions nearby, mothers see this as a way to get away with the family and have fun at the hotel, swimming and eating with pageant friends. However, this also means participation can be very costly financially and may mean time away from other children and family members. At the national level, coaches are consulted regularly, either in person or via the internet, which is another cost. The time and money invested at all the other levels combined cannot match what goes on at a *circuit* pageant, a "high glitz" event. On the circuit, girls can earn in one summer prizes worth $40,000, and, of course, they

can also spend that much money, with used dresses alone costing upward of $1,000 for the six-and-under set. The natural is not celebrated here: there are flippers to make teeth appear white and perfectly even, hair extensions or falls or dye, tanning cream or artificial spray tans for skin, fake eyelashes, and retouched photos. With money, cars, and cruises on the line, mothers take no chances as they compete to win. Since the events are so stressful, directors try to have parties every night and organize activities for the parents so that they can relax. Despite these efforts and because of the expense, the number of contestants is not as high as at national pageants—but the competition is much fiercer and more political (it matters which vendors you work with for coaching, clothes, and hair and makeup, for example).

26. Charlotte Triggs, "*Toddlers & Tiaras* Controversy: Are They Growing Up Too Fast?," *People*, September 14, 2011, 164.

27. Susan Anderson, *High Glitz: The Extravagant World of Child Beauty Pageants* (Brooklyn: powerHouse Books, 2009), 135.

28. Peggy Orenstein, *Cinderella Ate My Daughter: Dispatches from the Front Lines of the New Girlie-Girl Culture* (New York: Harper, 2012), 77.

29. Orenstein, *Cinderella Ate My Daughter*, 77.

30. Richard Goldstein, "The Girl in the Fun Bubble: The Mystery of JonBenét," *Village Voice*, June 10, 1997.

31. Interestingly, some pageant moms have pointed out similarities between child beauty pageants and animal shows. A few of them did horse shows growing up, and they see pageants with their young daughters as comparable experiences. Like pageants, animal shows have to do with appearance, self-presentation, and competition, especially when it comes to grooming an "other"—in one case a horse and in another a child. The mockumentary *Best in Show* illustrates the similarities between dog shows and child beauty pageants as well.

32. In defining social class, I use the definition of Tiffany Chin and Meredith Phillips ("Social Reproduction and Child-Rearing Practices: Social Class, Children's Agency, and the Summer Activity Gap," *Sociology of Education* 77 [2004]: 188), which says that a middle-class family has at least one parent who has, at minimum, a four-year college degree or is in a professional or managerial occupation. A working-class family is composed of parent(s) who lack a four-year college degree or a professional or managerial occupation but who draw an income above the poverty line.

33. Per Institutional Review Board approvals from three different institutions, the names of mothers and daughters used in this chapter are pseudonyms. It is the only occasion in *Here She Is* when I use pseudonyms or conceal identity in any way.

34. Heather Ryan, *Unleashing a Momster: A Peek Behind the Curtain at the Tragic Life of America's Most Successful Child Pageant Star* (Amazon Digital Services, 2013), 25.

35. Margarethe Kusenbach, "Salvaging Decency: Mobile Home Residents' Strategies of Managing the Stigma of 'Trailer' Living," *Qualitative Sociology* 32 (2009): 399–428.

36. Beulah Amsterdam, "Mirror Self-Image Reactions before Age Two," *Developmental Psychobiology* 5, no. 4 (1972): 297–305.

37. Stacy Malkan, "Not So Pretty in Pink: Marketing Toxic Makeup to Young Girls," *Utne Reader* (January–February 2009).

38. Andrea Darvi, *Pretty Babies: An Insider's Look at the World of the Hollywood Child Star* (New York: McGraw-Hill, 1983), 101.

39. *Painted Babies at 17*, dir. Jane Treays (2008).

40. A reminder that pseudonyms are used here for former pageant contestants.

41. Anna L. Wonderlich, Diann M. Ackard, and Judith B. Henderson, "Childhood Beauty Pageant Contestants: Associations with Adult Disordered Eating and Mental Health," *Eating Disorders: Journal of Treatment and Prevention* 13 (2005): 291.

42. Personal communication with author, July 23, 2019.

43. Susan Murray and Laurie Ouellette, *Reality TV: Remaking Television Culture* (New York: NYU Press, 2009), 4.

44. Jennifer L. Pozner, *Reality Bites Back: The Troubling Truth about Guilty Pleasure TV* (Berkeley, CA: Seal Press, 2010), 9.

45. Julie Klam, *The Stars in Our Eyes: The Famous, the Infamous, and Why We Care Way Too Much about Them* (New York: Riverhead, 2017), 141.

46. Amy Kaufman, *Bachelor Nation: Inside the World of America's Guilty Pleasure* (New York: Dutton, 2018), 20.

47. Kaufman, *Bachelor Nation*, 21.

48. Ashley Mears, *Pricing Beauty: The Making of a Fashion Model* (Berkeley: University of California Press, 2011), 172.

49. Katherine Sender, *The Makeover: Reality Television and Reflexive Audiences* (New York: New York University Press, 2012).

50. Brenda R. Weber, *Makeover TV: Selfhood, Citizenship, and Celebrity* (Durham, NC: Duke University Press, 2009).

51. Sarah Banet-Weiser and Laura Portwood-Stacer, "'I Just Want to Be Me Again!' Beauty Pageants, Reality Television and Post-Feminism," *Feminist Theory* 7, no. 2 (2006): 255–72.

52. The choice of Vegas really rankled old-school Miss America fans because it was so strongly associated with gambling. Gambling did not come to Atlantic City until 1978 and provoked a crisis for the Miss America organization. For years they would not allow Miss Americas to appear in casinos.

53. Owen Edwards, "The Object at Hand: American Idol," *Smithsonian Magazine*, January 2006.

54. Iver Peterson, "'Fear Factor' Era Poses a Challenge for Miss America," *New York Times*, April 9, 2005.

55. From 2003 to 2005, Miss USA and *Fear Factor* did crossover episodes featuring state contestants.

56. One exception was the rise of the *Victoria's Secret Fashion Show*, a one-off special that started airing in 2001.

57. Miss America 2004, Ericka Dunlap, competed during season 15 of *The Amazing Race*. Mallory Ervin, Miss Kentucky 2009, competed multiple times on the show. Other pageant winners, like Miss South Carolina Teen USA 2007, Caitlin Upton (of the final answer blunder "the Iraq, such as . . . For our children"), competed multiple times on *The Amazing Race*. Miss Rhode Island USA 2008, Amy Diaz, won season 23 of *The Amazing Race*.

58. Frank DeCaro, *Drag: Combing through the Big Wigs of Show Business* (New York: Rizzoli, 2019), 218.

59. Mike Miksche, "The Meaning of Miss Gay America in the Age of 'RuPaul's Drag Race,'" NewNowNext, October 4, 2017.

60. In 2017, a trans teenager competed in a preliminary for the Miss New Hampshire's Outstanding Teen Program.

61. Lee Bailey, "Queen of Tots: Gay Men Are the Unsung Heroes of the Child Beauty Pageant Circuit," Radar Online, August 6, 2008.

62. Molly Rose Pike, "Gypsy Pageant Queen Rips Off Her Skirt in Risqué Routine," *Daily Mail*, September 8, 2017.

63. Frank Hall, *Competitive Irish Dance: Art, Sport, Duty* (Madison, WI: Macater Press, 2008), 62–63.

64. *Jig*, dir. Sue Bourne (2011).

65. Hilary Levey, "Reality TV Kids Need the Law on Their Side," *USA Today*, June 25, 2010.

66. Dick Moore, *Twinkle, Twinkle Little Star (but Don't Have Sex or Take the Car)* (New York: Harper & Row, 1984), 198.

67. Lindsay Lieberman, "Protecting Pageant Princesses: A Call for Statutory Regulation of Child Beauty Pageants," *Journal of Law and Policy* 18, no. 2 (2010): 739–74.

68. Hilary Levey Friedman, "Balloon Boy *plus Ei8ht*? Children and Reality Television," *Contexts* 9, no. 2 (Spring 2010): 72–75.

69. *Little Miss Sunshine*, dir. Valerie Faris and Jonathan Dayton (2006).

70. Diane E. Levin and Jean Kilbourne, *So Sexy, So Soon: The New Sexualized Childhood and What Parents Can Do to Protect Their Kids* (New York: Ballantine, 2009).

71. American Psychological Association, Task Force on the Sexualization of Girls, *Report of the APA Task Force on the Sexualization of Girls* (2007), 1, http://www.apa.org/pi/women/programs/girls/report-full.pdf.

72. M. Gigi Durham, *The Lolita Effect: The Media Sexualization of Young Girls and What We Can Do about It* (New York: Overlook Press, 2008), 126.

73. Jessica Valenti, "SlutWalks and the Future of Feminism," *Washington Post*, June 3, 2011.

74. Shout-out to Kate Hoey, Brown University, '18.

CHAPTER 6: THE PAGEANTRY OF POLITICS

1. Abby Phillip, "Miss Universe Winner Criticized as 'Fat' Featured in New Clinton Video," *Washington Post*, September 27, 2016.

2. For example, the woman whom my mother crowned Miss America 1971, Phyllis George, went on to be the First Lady of Kentucky. She married John Young Brown Jr., who served as the fifty-fifth governor of Kentucky from 1979 to 1983 (that marriage ended in divorce in 1998). George was not the first Miss America to marry a politician. Donna Axum, Miss America 1964, married Gus Mutscher, a Texas state representative who became Speaker of the House in Austin. Mutscher had to resign as Speaker in 1971 after being convicted of bribery; in 1972 Axum divorced him.

3. Another Miss Arkansas, Lencola Sullivan, Miss Arkansas 1980, was also rumored to have had an affair with Clinton. You may recall from chapter 4 that Sullivan was the first black contestant to make the Top Five at Miss America and to win a preliminary talent award.

4. David Plotz, "All the President's Women," *Slate*, January 29, 1998.

5. Associated Press, "Beauty Queen Apologizes for Tryst," *Gainesville Sun*, April 26, 1998.

6. Howard Kurtz, "Marla 'I Love Him,'" *Washington Post*, April 20, 1990.

7. Jeremy Gerard, "Marla Maples Talks on TV but Says Little of Trump," *New York Times*, April 20, 1990.

8. Nina Burleigh, *Golden Handcuffs: The Secret History of Trump's Women* (New York: Gallery Books, 2018), 99.

9. Art Harris, "The Hometown of the Killer Blondes," *Washington Post*, February 19, 1990.

10. Elizabeth Sporkin, "Ohh-La-La Marla!," *People*, March 5, 1990.

11. Charlotte Triggs, "Marla Maples Opens Up about Surprisingly Modest Lifestyle after Her Split from Donald Trump," *People*, May 2, 2016.

12. Burleigh, *Golden Handcuffs*, 101.

13. Trump considered buying the Miss America pageant in the 1980s but ultimately did not pursue it because of the organization's nonprofit status, though he judged Miss America 1990, the year Debbye Turner won, and she stayed in one of his Atlantic City hotels.

14. Burleigh, *Golden Handcuffs*, 154.

15. Donald J. Trump, *How to Get Rich* (New York: Random House, 2004), loc. 1257 of 2373 on Kindle.

16. "Ain't That a Beauty: Marla to Co-Host 'Miss Universe,'" *New York Daily News*, April 1, 1997.

17. "Dogged by Weight Issue, Miss Universe Re-emerges in Public," CNN, August 22, 1996.

18. Jeanne Moos, "Expanding Miss Universe Works to Shed Pounds," CNN, January 29, 1997.

19. Andrew Metz, "Mar-a-Lago Club to Be Beauty Queen's Fat Farm," *Palm Beach Post*, February 6, 1997.

20. "I'm Not Married, Says Dethroned Miss Universe," *Sydney Morning Herald*, September 25, 2002.

21. Trump, *How to Get Rich*, loc. 1284 of 2373 on Kindle.

22. Tice, *Queens of Academe*, 175.

23. Trump, *How to Get Rich*, loc. 1284 of 2373 on Kindle.

24. Jo Piazza, "Queen Is Way Out of Line," *New York Daily News*, December 16, 2008.

25. Christine Hauser, "Miss USA Agrees to Rehab to Preserve Reign," *New York Times*, December 19, 2006.

26. Karen Thomas, "That Wasn't Miss South Carolina's Final Answer," *USA Today*, August 29, 2007.

27. Meghan Daum, "Carrie Prejean vs. Perez Hilton," *Los Angeles Times*, September 16, 2014.

28. Carrie Prejean, *Still Standing: The Untold Story of My Fight against Gossip, Hate, and Political Attacks* (New York: Perseus, 2009), 4.

29. Another pageant story in the news in 2009 was the arrest and imprisonment of Roxana Saberi, Miss North Dakota 1997, in Iran. She was charged with espionage, though she was released after 101 days. She wrote about the experience in her 2010 book *Between Two Worlds: My Life and Captivity in Iran* (New York: HarperCollins).

30. Dalton has gone on to write two faith-based books; for example, *The Sparkle Effect: Step into the Radiance of Your True Identity* (New York: FaithWords, 2018). Interestingly, Miss America 2009, Katie Stam Irk, has also published a devotional book, *Merely Moving Shadows: Psalms 39:4-7; a 10-Week Devotional Guide to Living God's Purpose through His Plan* (Carol Stream, IL: Esther Press, 2018).

31. Prejean, *Still Standing*, 68.

32. Prejean, *Still Standing*, 69.

33. Kendall Taggart, Jessica Garrison, and Jessica Testa, "Teen Beauty Queens Say Trump Walked In on Them Changing," BuzzFeed, October 13, 2016.

34. Fred Barbash, "Former Miss Arizona: Trump 'Just Came Strolling Right In' on Naked Contestants," *Washington Post*, October 12, 2016.

35. Samantha Holvey, "Thanks to Donald Trump, I Know What It Feels Like to Be Eyed Like a Piece of Meat," NBC News, December 19, 2017.

36. Andrew Kaczynski, Chris Massie, and Nate McDermott, "Donald Trump to Howard Stern: It's Okay to Call My Daughter a 'Piece of Ass,'" CNN, October 9, 2016.

37. "Donald Trump Announces a Presidential Bid," *Washington Post*, June 16, 2015.

38. Brian Stelter, "Donald Trump Settles with Univision over Miss USA Pageant," CNN, February 11, 2016.

39. Jeremy Alford and John Koblin, "Miss USA Pageant Finds a Televised Venue," *New York Times*, July 2, 2015.

40. Ellen Killoran, "Donald Trump Sells Miss Universe, Miss USA Pageants to WME/IMG—but They Still Need a Network," *Forbes*, September 14, 2015.

41. Burleigh, *Golden Handcuffs*, 157.

42. Jeffrey Toobin, "Trump's Miss Universe Gambit," *New Yorker*, February 19, 2018.

43. Toobin, "Trump's Miss Universe Gambit."

44. Erica Chenoweth and Jeremy Pressman, "This Is What We Learned by Counting the Women's Marches," *Washington Post*, February 7, 2017.

45. Ari Shapiro, "Women's March Organizer: 'We Are Committed' to Fighting for Change," *All Things Considered*, NPR, January 23, 2017.

46. The two other Miss Americas were Venus Ramey and Erika Harold. Ramey, Miss America 1944, was the first to run for office, and she ran not once but twice. At age twenty-six she ran as a Democrat for the Kentucky legislature, the first-ever female political candidate in the history of Lincoln County, Kentucky. Almost four decades later, in 1979, she ran for the Cincinnati City Council as an independent. Harold, Miss America 2003, ran for a US congressional seat out of Illinois in both 2012 and 2014, though she failed to secure the Republican nomination.

47. Miss Hawaii 2011, Lauren Cheape Matsumoto, is another state queen who was serving in elected office in her home state in 2019. Matsumoto has been a member of Hawaii's House of Representatives since 2013 as a Republican (she also performed one of my favorite Miss America talents of all time, an intense jump-rope routine in which she bounces on her derriere).

48. Leila Fadel, "A First: Women Take the Majority in Nevada Legislature and Colorado House," NPR, February 4, 2019.

49. Katie Couric, "Palin Opens Up on Controversial Issues," CBS News, September 30, 2019.

50. Though her seat on the city council is nonpartisan, Blackburn previously ran for a seat in the Georgia House of Representatives in 2010 as a Democrat.

51. "24-Year-Old Taking Seat in Washington State House," *Columbian*, November 8, 2014.

52. George Golding, "I Feel Terrific . . . Wow," *San Mateo Times*, June 25, 1977.

53. Golding, "I Feel Terrific . . . Wow."

54. This quote originally appeared in a November 14, 2012, article I wrote for *The Hill*, "Rep.-Elect Lauren Cheape's Path to Victory."

55. Beth Anne Rankin, Miss Arkansas 1994, who ran in 2012 to represent Arkansas's fourth congressional district, was even more specific. According to Rankin she developed an in-depth knowledge of her home state, traveling to all seventy-five counties as Miss Arkansas. She would often visit six cities in a single day and have to "roll out of the car after a five-hour drive and give a speech and roll back in the car and get to another"—a skill she highlighted as coming in handy during her intense campaigns. This quote originally appeared in an October 3, 2012, article I wrote for *The Hill*, "From Reigning to Campaigning: Beauty Queen Political Candidates."

56. Personal interview with author, June 26, 2019.

57. Jennifer L. Lawless, *Becoming a Candidate: Political Ambition and the Decision to Run for Office* (New York: Cambridge University Press, 2012), 117.

58. Parts of this section appeared in a June 26, 2012, article I wrote for *Slate*, "Here She Comes, Miss (Elected) America."

59. Personal interview with author, June 5, 2012.

60. Portions of this appeared in a September 18, 2017, article I wrote for the *Washington Post*, "Running for Miss America Now Looks a Lot Like Running for Office."

61. Al Franken, the Emmy Award–winning comedian, was elected to the US Senate in 2008, representing Minnesota. Another Minnesota politician, Jesse Ventura, who was governor of the state from 1998 to 2002, began his career as a professional actor-wrestler.

62. *Pumping Iron*, dir. George Butler (1977).

63. Philip Drake and Michael Higgins, "'I'm a Celebrity, Get Me into Politics': The Political Celebrity and the Celebrity Politician," in *Framing Celebrity: New Directions in Celebrity Culture*, ed. Su Holmes and Sean Redmond (New York: Routledge, 2006), 87–100.

64. Nancy Cohen, *Breakthrough: The Making of America's First Woman President* (Berkeley, CA: Counterpoint Press, 2016), 94.

65. Lowden was also Miss District of Columbia USA 1971 (and a Top Twelve finalist at Miss USA) when she went by Susan Pluskowski.

66. Quoted from a personal interview with the author for my 2012 *Slate* article.

67. Women around the world have used their experiences in the Miss World and Miss Universe pageants to springboard their political careers. Irene Sáez, Miss Universe 1981, used her celebrity to (unsuccessfully) run for president of her native Venezuela in 1998. She has served as both a mayor and a governor in Venezuela. Miss World 1993, Lisa Hanna of Jamaica, also leveraged her pageant success to help her win election to the Jamaican Parliament in 2007. Others, like Anke Van dermeersch, who represented Belgium at Miss World 1991 and Miss Universe 1992, and who is now a Belgian senator, use their pageant experience as part of their political toolkit of skills to secure an election victory. One of Van dermeersch's Miss World 1991 competitors, Inese Šlesere, represented Latvia, where she has also served in Parliament. Asian countries also have beauty-queen politicians, like Rosy Senanayake, now mayor of Colombo, Sri Lanka, and who represented her country at Miss World 1980. Many of these women are discussed in Magda Hinojosa and Jill Carle, "From Miss World to World Leader: Beauty Queens, Paths to Power, and Political Representations," *Journal of Women, Politics and Policy* 37, no. 1 (2016): 24–46.

68. Baraquio, *Amazing Win, Amazing Loss*, 4–5.

69. Note that three of the Ivies have never sent a student to compete at Miss America (Columbia, Dartmouth, and Yale), and one of the Ivy League + schools has not (Caltech, not surprisingly, given that their student body, even in 2015, was only 31 percent female).

70. Miss America 1954, Evelyn Ay, graduated in 1955 from University of Pennsylvania's College for Women, which existed from 1933 to 1974.

71. Personal interview with author, July 15, 2016. Tiu is now a successful, working actress in Hollywood.

72. Personal interview with author, August 3, 2016. Martin is now an elementary school teacher, with a focus on arts education.

73. Personal interview with author, July 28, 2016. Lee is now an entrepreneur in the technology sector.

74. Personal interview with author, July 20, 2016.

75. Penny Pearlman, *Pretty Smart: Lessons from Our Miss Americas* (Bloomington, IN: AuthorHouse, 2009), 45.

76. "Facts and Figures 2005–2006," University of Alabama at Birmingham, 52, https://www.uab.edu/institutionaleffectiveness/images/factbook/ff0506.pdf, accessed November 9, 2019.

77. Personal interview with author, September 14, 2016.

78. "Miss America Pageant: Last Week Tonight with John Oliver," September 21, 2014, on YouTube, https://www.youtube.com/watch?v=oDPCmmZifE8.

79. Amy Kuperinsky, "Following John Oliver Critique, Miss America Organization Shares Review of Scholarship Program," NJ.com, September 4, 2015.

80. Note that two Miss Americas have also been Coca-Cola Scholars: Miss America 2004, Ericka Dunlap, and Miss America 2018, Cara Mund.

81. Cara McCollum, "All That Glitters: The Pretty, the Plastic, and the Problematic of the Miss America Pageant," senior thesis, Princeton University, April 7, 2015, 81.

82. McCollum, "All That Glitters," 59.

83. McCollum, "All That Glitters," 24.

84. Portions of my discussion of Cara McCollum previously appeared in an obituary I wrote, "Cara McCollum '15: With Smarts and Beauty, She Wanted to Be Relevant," *PAW* (*Princeton Alumni Weekly*), February 8, 2017.

85. Emily Yayr, "Miss North Dakota Wins the Miss America Pageant for the First Time in History," *Washington Post*, September 11, 2017.

86. Yashar Ali, "The Miss America Emails: How the Pageant's CEO Really Talks about the Winners," *Huffington Post*, December 21, 2017.

87. Sam Haskell, *Promises I Made My Mother* (New York: Ballantine, 2009), 47–48.

88. Haskell, *Promises I Made My Mother*, 126–27.

89. Haskell, *Promises I Made My Mother*, 127.

90. Haskell, *Promises I Made My Mother*, 127–28.

91. Haskell, *Promises I Made My Mother*, 128–29.

92. Shindle, *Being Miss America*, 203–4.

93. Shindle, *Being Miss America*, 197.

94. Shindle, *Being Miss America*, 195–96.

95. Jennifer Bogdan, "Miss America's Finances Fluctuate, Records Show," *Press of Atlantic City*, February 8, 2014.

96. "New Leadership at Miss America Organization," *Press of Atlantic City*, February 27, 2015.

97. Jeff Bossert, "Miss America Ban Could Mean End to Hoopeston Pageant," Illinois Public Media, March 1, 2016.

98. Gretchen Carlson v. Roger Ailes, Superior Court of New Jersey, civil suit filed July 6, 2016, https://www.documentcloud.org/documents/2941030-Carlson-Complaint-Filed.html.

99. Christie D'Zurilla, "In Saying #MeToo, Alyssa Milano Pushes Awareness Campaign about Sexual Assault and Harassment," *Los Angeles Times*, October 16, 2017.

100. Ali, "The Miss America Emails."

101. Billy Perrigo, "Who Is Sam Haskell? Miss America CEO Resigns over Emails Criticizing Contestants," *Time*, December 22, 2017.

102. Some of the ideas about Carlson's tenure as chair of Miss America were previously expressed in a piece I wrote for *USA Today*, "Good Riddance to the Miss America Swimsuit Contest, But Did We Have to Lose Fitness, Too?," June 6, 2018.

103. Gretchen Carlson, "Growing into Feminism," *InStyle*, November 2017, 208.

104. Dana Rosengard, "Now That's Entertaining," *Pageantry*, Winter 2013.

105. Kate Kitchen, *The Strength of Grace* (Greensboro, NC: Eastman Press, 2004), 209.

106. Katie Kindelan, "'Bye Bye Bikini': What the New Miss America Will Be without the Swimsuit Competition," *Good Morning America*, June 5, 2018.

107. Carly Mallenbaum, "Gretchen Carlson: I 'Never Bullied' Miss America Cara Mund, Her Letter Cost Org $75,000," *USA Today*, August 17, 2018.

108. Harron Walker, "Miss America: Civil War," *Jezebel*, October 9, 2018, https://jezebel.com/miss-america-civil-war-1829626519.

109. "Gretchen Carlson Resigns from Miss America Chairwoman Post," Associated Press, June 5, 2019.

110. Miss America, "Miss America Announces NEW Equity and Justice Scholarship," email sent September 23, 2019.

111. Kristi Glakas Ingram, Facebook post, September 24, 2019.

112. Mark Melhorn, "Miss America President and CEO Regina Hopper No Longer with Organization," *Press of Atlantic City*, January 28, 2020.

113. Jay Newton-Small, *Broad Influence: How Women Are Changing the Way America Works* (New York: Liberty Street, 2016), 9.

114. Yousef Saba, "Former Miss Universe Calls Trump's Attacks on Her Weight 'a Really Bad Dream,'" *Politico*, September 27, 2016.

CONCLUSION

1. Mary Jane Clark, "Dreamers and Disruptors," in *Miss America 2.0 2020* (Little Rock, AR: SquareOne Graphics, 2019), 35.

2. Rick Porter, "TV Ratings: Miss America Hits Low for 2nd Straight Year," *Hollywood Reporter*, December 20, 2019.

3. Anthony Crupi, "NFL Games Account for Nearly Three-Quarters of the Year's Top Broadcasts," *AdAge*, January 8, 2020.

4. "About," Miss USA, https://www.missuniverse.com/missusa/about#our-mission, accessed January 9, 2020.

5. Rick Porter, "TV Ratings: 'The Bachelor' Opens Strong, 'AGT: Champions' Returns Lower," *Hollywood Reporter*, January 7, 2020.

6. Jessica Vacco-Bolanos, "5 Contestants on Peter Weber's Season of 'The Bachelor' Are Former Pageant Queens: Meet the Ladies!," *Us Weekly*, September 19, 2019.

7. Julie Murphy, *Dumplin'* (New York: Balzer + Bray, 2015).

8. *Dumplin'*, dir. Anne Fletcher (2018).

9. Philip Rucker and Karen Tumulty, "Donald Trump Is Holding a Government Casting Call. He's Seeking 'the Look,'" *Washington Post*, December 22, 2016.

10. Susan Chira, "There He Is, Mr. Cabinet Secretary," *New York Times*, December 14, 2016.

11. Jerramy Fine, *In Defense of the Princess: How Plastic Tiaras and Fairytale Dreams Can Inspire Smart, Strong Women* (Philadelphia: Running Press, 2016).

12. Lindy West, *Shrill: Notes from a Loud Woman* (New York: Hachette, 2017), 19–20.

13. Kay Lazar, "As Women Have Grown Larger, Victoria's Secret Models Have Shrunk," *Boston Globe*, January 2, 2020.

IMAGE CREDITS

1. Asbury Park baby parade: Library of Congress: Prints and Photographs Division
2. 1913 suffrage parade: Maryland State Archives
3. 1921 Miss America contestants: Miss America Organization Archive
4. Miss Pittsburgh in rolling chair: Library of Congress: George Grantham Bain Collection
5. Lenora Slaughter: Abbeville Press
6. Bess Myerson: Charles Freeman Stamper
7. Jackie Loughery: Historical Society of Long Beach, CA
8. 1968 Miss America protest: Shutterstock
9. Miss Black America: Uncredited/AP/Shutterstock
10. Author's mother: Author's Collection
11. Vanessa Williams and Suzette Charles: Anonymous/AP/Shutterstock
12. Alicia Machado and Marla Maples: Eric Draper/AP/Shutterstock
13. Patsy's Magazine cover: Author's Collection
14. Miss Navajo Nation: Photo by Donovan Shortey
15. Trump and Culpo: Kabik/MediaPunch/Shutterstock

INDEX

ABC, 57–58, 206, 207
ableism, 6, 108
abortion rights, 83, 87, 118
Access Hollywood (television show), 184
activists *vs.* advocates, 82–83
addiction and child beauty pageants, 160–61
Ad-Hoc Committee for the Miss America Demonstration, 77–78
advocates *vs.* activists, 82–83
African American. *See specific entries for black people*
Agalarov, Emin, 190
agricultural fairs, 14, 20
Ailes, Roger, 207–8
AJM pageant. *See* America's Junior Miss (AJM) pageant
All-America Baby and Juvenile Review, 43
Amateur Athletic Union, 63
The Amazing Race (television show), 176, 244n57
"American Babies," 24
American Ballet Theater, 76
American Beauties Plus, 133
An American Family (television show), 172
American Gallery of Female Beauty, 14, 15–18, 20
American Girl stores, 180
American Idol (television show), 173, 175
American Museum (Barnum's), 16, 17, 20
American Pageant Association, 27

American Royal Beauties pageant, 242n25
American Woman Suffrage Association, 18, 82
America's Junior Miss (AJM) pageant: deaf contestant at, 131; Ivy League competitors at, 199–200; and Jaycees, 60–61; mockumentary based on, 135–36; program book of, 89, 90, 96–97; and protests, 81–82; racial diversity at, 112; renaming of, xv, 235–36n57; Southern contestants in, 137–38
America's Next Top Model (television show), 173
Anderson, Aleta, 125
Anderson, J. Morris, 110–11, 112
Anderson, Michelle, 138, 241n151
animal shows and child beauty pageants, 243n31
anorexia, 92, 138–39
Anthony, Susan B., 15, 82, 227n25
Anti-Defamation League, 109
anti-Semitism, 109–10
The Appeal (newspaper), 107
appearance, impact of, 7–10
Apple Princess, 135
The Apprentice (television show), 175, 187, 190, 195
Arden, Elizabeth, 28
Asbury Park baby parade, 22–23, 40, 41, 102–3
Asian American contestants, 107, 127, 137, 237n23